The TRUCK, VAN AND 4X4 Book

1995 Edition

The Definitive Guide to Buying a Truck

by Jack Gillis

with

Karen Fierst
and
Jay Einhorn

HarperPerennial

A Division of HarperCollinsPublishers

Publisher's Note

Every attempt has been made to ensure that the ratings, statistics, and other data found in this book were current and accurate when this book went to press. Because of occasional changes by automobile manufacturers in their vehicles' design and performance, however, some of this data may change. During the year, new information released by the government, manufacturers or private sources may affect the data in the book.

About the Author

Jack Gillis spent three years as a marketing analyst with the U.S. Department of Transportation's National Highway Traffic Safety Administration. While at NHTSA, he prepared the first edition of *The Car Book* in 1980, and in 1981 he began developing the guide independently. Since its introduction, nearly 3 million consumers have received copies of his *Car Books*.

Gillis recently joined NBC as consumer correspondent for "The Today Show." He is a Contributing Editor at *Good Housekeeping* and has appeared on all three network evening news programs as well as local and national talk shows, including "Donahue," "Nightline," "The Oprah Winfrey Show," "Good Morning America," and "The Larry King Show." He is frequently quoted in *The Wall Street Journal*, *The New York Times*, *Business Week*, *Money* magazine, *The Washington Post*, and *USA Today*.

Gillis was cited by the National Press Club as one of the best in consumer journalism. Two of his books were among *Money* magazine's "10 Best Personal Finance Books of 1988," and *Sylvia Porter's Personal Finance Magazine* selected him as one of America's personal finance heroes. He is Director of Public Affairs for the Consumer Federation of America, the nation's largest consumer advocacy organization, and Executive Director of the Certified Automotive Parts Association—a non-profit, quality standards organization.

He received his MBA from The George Washington University and BA from the University of Notre Dame. Gillis is married to Marilyn Mohrman–Gillis, and they have four children, Katie, John, Brian, and Brennan.

Also by Jack Gillis

The Used Car Book
The Truck, Van and 4x4 Book
The Car Repair Book
The Social Security Book for Women
The Childwise Catalog (coauthor)
How to Make Your Car Last Almost Forever
The Armchair Mechanic (coauthor)
How to Fly (coauthor)
The Bank Book (editor)
The Product Safety Book (editor)
Money in the Bank (editor)

THE TRUCK, VAN AND 4x4 BOOK *(1995 edition)*. Copyright © 1994, 1993, 1992, 1991, 1990 by Jack Gillis. All rights reserved. Printed in the United States of America. No part of this book may be used or reproduced in any manner whatsoever without written permission except in the case of brief quotations embodied in critical articles and reviews. For information, address HarperCollins Publishers, Inc., 10 East 53rd Street, New York, NY 10022.

HarperCollins books may be purchased for educational, business, or sales promotional use. For information, please write: Special Markets Department, HarperCollins Publishers, Inc., 10 East 53rd Street, New York, NY 10022.

ISSN: 1062-2578

ISBN 0-06-273284-6

95 96 97 CW 5 4 3 2

Cover design by © Gilllis and Associates
Photo credits: American Isuzu Motors, Inc.
Ford Motor Co.
General Motors Corp.
Mitsubishi Motors Sales

Contents

Acknowledgements

As is the case each year, many talented individuals have contributed to this *fifth* edition of *The Truck, Van and 4x4 Book*. Once again, thanks to the incredibly talented Jay Einhorn, we were able to bring together thousands of pieces of data on the 1995 models. Under his direction, the staff collected, analyzed and tabulated many thousands of bits of information about today's new vehicles. In addition to his project management skills, his keen analytical ability enabled us to develop ways to present complex test results in a meaningful and easy-to-understand way. Jay was able to accomplish great feats due, in particular, to the tremendous assistance of David Lewkowict, who arrived in the nick of time, and ace researcher Scott Beatty. The steady hand and valuable experience of 10 year *Car Book* veteran Karen Fierst was was a key element in making this book a reality.

There are two key components of *The Truck, Van and 4x4 Book*—the data and the presentation. This year, Amy Burch stepped in to take charge of one of the more complex *Truck, Van and 4x4 Book* designs to date. Thanks to her rapidly acquired page-making skills, her hard work and her incredible calm under immense pressure, this was one of the smoothest years ever for the production of this graphically complex book. She was able to accomplish this amazing feat nearly singlehandedly, thanks to the excellent start given her by Alisa Feingold, who, once again, was there when we really needed her—both at the beginning and end.

This year's edition would not have been possible without essential contributions from many other talented individuals including: Clarence Ditlow and the staff of the Center for Auto Safety, including Anu Ashutosh and Debra Barclay; John Noettl, president of Vehicle Support Systems and his staff, Karen S. Noettl and David J. Noettl; Susan Cole, our very talented (and understanding!) graphic designer; Pat Donlon and Ray Weiss of Ten Point Type; legal expert Phil Nowicki; computer wizard Toufic Rahman; and, Jill Rosensweig, our newest staffer. Very special thanks go to my friend and great literary agent, Stuart Krichevsky.

As always, the most important factor in being able to bring this information to the American consumer for five years is the constant encouragement, support and love from my brilliant and beautiful wife, Marilyn Mohrman–Gillis.

–J.G.

As Always,

for Marilyn &
Katie, John, Brian and Brennan

Introduction

America's traditional love affair with the car is taking a back seat to our growing desire for trucks—not your standard commercial variety—but a whole new generation filled with luxury, comfort and power, but a little short on safety.

The fastest growing types of vehicles on the market continue to be minivans, 4x4s, and pickups. Many of the criteria that consumers evaluate to select passenger cars are also important for trucks and vans. However, because of their unique designs, trucks, vans, and 4x4s have other features that aren't available on passenger cars—hence, *The Truck, Van & 4x4 Book.*

Like our other annual consumer references, *The Car Book* and *The Used Car Book*, our goal with *The Truck, Van & 4x4 Book* is to guide you through the various criteria used in selecting the very best vehicle. This fifth edition of the book includes over twice the amount of data included in the first edition—all at your fingertips. This year we've continued our full page, easy-to-understand, vehicle rating pages which detail the information you need to make a smart and safe choice. We've also completely updated the "Buying Guide" which allows you to easily compare individual vehicles with others in their size class.

Minivans are popular because very few station wagons are large enough to hold growing families. Pickups are well-liked because many are priced in the $9,000 to $12,000 range. If you are interested in buying one of these vehicles, be warned: *They do not have to meet many of the same safety standards applied to passenger cars.*

While thousands of Americans buy these vehicles for family and non-commercial use, these vehicles are not required to adhere to the same safety standards as cars. For example, bumpers need not meet any strength requirements. Thanks to pressure from safety advocates and consumers, the government will be phasing-in requirements that trucks meet safety requirements similar to cars. The phase-in begins in 1995 and a percentage of trucks are required to meet car side-impact standards and have passive restraints. This phase-in will not be completed until the 1999 model year. A new standard on roof strength is also being adopted, however, it does not go far enough to effectively protect occupants in a rollover situation.

Recently, Americans have learned about incredible accidents from which drivers have simply walked away—all because a simple bag inflated to cushion the impact. But what about the buyers of trucks and sport utility vehicles? Tragically, too many companies have chosen not to offer such life-saving protection.

So how does today's consumer buy safety? Many people mistakenly believe that handling and performance are the key elements in a vehicles' safety. While an extremely unresponsive vehicle could cause an accident, most new vehicles meet basic handling requirements. In fact, many people actually feel uncomfortable driving high-performance vehicles because the responsive steering, acceleration, and suspension systems can be difficult to get used to. But the main reason handling is overrated as a safety measure is that automobile collisions are, by nature, accidents. Once they've begun, they are beyond human ca-

Typical Operating Costs

The table below shows the operating costs of some popular vehicles. For this comparison, these costs include operating expenses (fuel, oil, maintenance and tires) and ownership expenses (insurance, depreciation, financing, taxes and licensing) and were based on keeping the vehicle for three years and driving 20,000 miles per year.

	Annual Costs		
	Operating	Ownership	Total
Ford Club Wagon Custom	$2,750	$6,098	$8,848
Chevy S10 Blazer (Blazer)	$2,280	$6,261	$8,541
Dodge Caravan	$2,070	$6,118	$8,188
Chevy Lumina Minivan	$2,080	$6,095	$8,175
Jeep Cherokee	$2,470	$5,633	$8,103
Chevy Fleetside Pickup	$2,340	$5,205	$7,545
Ford Ranger	$2,140	$5,223	$7,363

Source: Runzheimer International, Rochester, Wisconsin.

pacity to prevent, no matter how well your vehicle handles. Since accidents are, unfortunately, statistically inevitable, the key to protecting yourself is to purchase a vehicle that offers good crash protection.

Consumer concern for safety has influenced auto makers attitudes, as have our demands for quality—U.S. vehicles are better built than ever. And because we're demanding that companies stand behind their products, we're seeing better warranties, too. Since we began providing comparative warranty information a few years ago, a number of auto makers have told us that they've been forced to offer better warranties now that consumers can tell the difference.

There is no question that buyers of pickups, minivans, and 4x4s need help, and that's what *The Truck, Van and 4x4 Book* is all about—information on a very important and expensive purchase. Consumers are learning that they can get better-performing and safer choices by buying vehicles with good safety records, low maintenance costs, long warranties, and insurance discounts. These and many other features are summarized in "The Buying Guide," which includes more information than ever before—all at your fingertips. Then you can read the individual chapters to learn more about each model.

"The Safety Chapter" presents crash test results, as well as lists of special features. Consumers can look for these features, such as anti-lock brakes and air bags, to compensate for the fact that these vehicles do not have to meet the same safety standards as passenger cars. We also discuss the serious problem of rollover and have calculated rollover ratings for many of the new vehicles. Finally, we include tips for safe towing and off-roading.

"The Fuel Economy Chapter," in addition to describing special gas-saving devices, provides fuel economy tips for truck and van owners, as well as the complete EPA mileage ratings for trucks, vans, and sport utility vehicles.

"The Maintenance Chapter" allows you to compare maintenance costs, offers advice on service contracts, and tips for dealing with a mechanic.

"The Warranty Chapter" offers a critical comparison of the new warranties and lets you know the best and worst before you get into trouble down the road. It will also tip you off to the secret warranties.

"The Insurance Chapter" will help you save money on an expense that is often forgotten in the showroom.

Because most of us can't tell one tire from another, we've included "The Tire Chapter" to help you select the best.

"The Complaint Chapter" provides a road map to resolving inevitable problems quickly and efficiently. We provide consumers with their only access to the hundreds of thousands of vehicle complaints on file with the U.S. Government. Thanks to the efforts of the Center for Auto Safety, we continue to include this otherwise unavailable information—and it's all-new and updated for 1995.

Review "The Showroom Strategy Chapter" for tips on getting the best price—for many of us one of the hardest and most distasteful aspects of car buying.

Finally, our all new "Ratings Chapter" provides a detailed review of each of the 1995 models. These pages provide, at a glance, an overview of all the criteria you need to make a good choice. Here you'll be able to quickly assess key features and see how the vehicle you're interested in stacks up against its competition so you can make sure your selection is the best vehicle for you. Prices have more than doubled since 1980, so we've also included the percent of *dealer* mark-up to help you negotiate the very best price.

The information in *The Truck, Van & 4x4 Book* is based on data collected and developed by our staff, private automobile engineering firms, the U.S. Department of Transportation, and the Center for Auto Safety. With all of this data in hand, you'll find some great choices for 1995. *The Truck, Van & 4x4 Book* will guide you through the trade-offs, claims, promises, facts, and myths to the vehicle that will best meet your needs.

—Jack Gillis

BUYING GUIDE

The Buying Guide provides an overall comparison of 1995 vehicles in terms of safety, fuel economy, maintenance, insurance costs, warranty, complaint ratings and other key items. Based on this comparison, this chapter also offers a list of the Best Bets—the 1995 minivans, sport utility vehicles and pickups that rated well in all of these categories.

Also included is summary information on towing, cargo space and average prices. You can find more detailed information on these categories throughout the book.

In general, there are five key steps to buying a vehicle.

First, you want to narrow your choice down to a particular class of vehicle—sport utility, pickup, minivan or van. These are general classifications and some vehicles may fit into more than one category. In most cases, *The Truck, Van & 4x4 Book* presents the vehicles by size class.

Second, you want to determine what features are really important to you. Most buyers consider safety on the top of their list, which is why "The Safety Chapter" is right up front in *The Truck, Van & 4x4 Book*. Air bags, power options, ABS, the number of doors and passengers, as well as "hidden" elements such as maintenance and insurance costs should be considered at this stage in your selection process.

Third, you want to find 3 or 4 vehicles that meet the needs you outlined above *and* your pocketbook. It's important not to narrow your choice down to one vehicle, because then you lose all your bargaining power in the showroom. In fact, because vehicles today are more similar than dissimilar, it's not hard to keep three or four choices in mind. On the rating pages in the back of the book, we suggest some competitive choices for your consideration. For example, if you are interested in the Jeep Cherokee, you should definitely consider the Ford Explorer.

Fourth, make sure you take a good long test drive. The biggest buying mistake most of us make is to overlook those nagging problems that seem to surface only after we've brought the vehicle home. Spend at least an hour driving the vehicle. This includes time on the highway, parking, taking it in and out of your driveway or garage, sitting in the back seat, and using the storage area and, whatever you do, *don't talk price until you're ready to buy!*

Fifth, comes the stage most of us dread, negotiating the price. While price negotiation is a buying tradition, a few car makers and dealers are trying to break tradition by offering so-called "no-haggle pricing". Because they're still in the minority and because it's almost impossible to establish true competition between dealers as individuals, we offer a new means to avoid negotiating altogether by using the non-profit CarBargains pricing service.

Now that you have a quick guide to the necessary steps in making a good choice—use the tables that follow to quickly review the new vehicles and the pages in the back for a detailed critique of each model. See "The Showroom Strategy Chapter" for more details on getting the best price.

The "Buying Guide" will allow you to quickly compare the 1995 models.

To fully understand these summary charts, it is important to read the appropriate section of the book. You will note that here and throughout the book, some of the charts contain empty boxes. This indicates that data were unavailable at the time of printing.

Here's how to understand what's included in "The Buying Guide."

Page Reference: The page in the back of the book where you'll find all the details for this vehicle.

Overall Rating: This is the "bottom line." This shows how well this vehicle stacks up on a scale of 1 to 10 when compared to all others on the market. The overall rating considers safety, maintenance, fuel economy, warranty, insurance costs and complaints. Due to the importance of crash tests, vehicles with no crash test results as of our publication date cannot be given an overall rating. More recent results may be available from the Auto Safety Hotline at 1-800-424-9393 (see page 73).

Crash Test Rating: This indicates how well the vehicle performed in the U.S. Government's 35-mph frontal crash test program. We have analyzed the 1995 models, compared them to all the government tests ever performed and given them a rating from *very good* to *very poor*. These ratings allow you to compare the test results of one vehicle with another relative to all of your choices.

Air Bags: Hidden in the steering wheel hub and, in some cases, the passenger side of the dashboard, air bags inflate instantly in frontal crashes to prevent the occupant from violently hitting the dashboard, windshield or steering wheel. An asterisk indicates that the feature is optional, whereas "driver" or "dual" (on both driver and passenger sides) indicates that air bags are standard.

Anti-lock Brake System (ABS): These keep your wheels from locking up by automatically "pumping" the brakes up to five times per second. ABS decreases braking distance, prevents skidding, and allows more control in a sudden stop. Although ABS is typically connected to all four wheels, in many sport utility vehicles it is connected to only the rear wheels. Two-wheel anti-lock

Best Bets for 1995

Based on information in the *Buying Guide*, this list shows the highest-rated vans, sport utility and pickup trucks in each of the size categories. Ratings are based on expected performance in six important categories (crash tests, fuel economy, repair costs, warranties, insurance costs, and complaints), with the heaviest emphasis on crash test performance. In some of the weight classes, not many vehicles (or none at all) were deemed worthy of selection as a "best bet."

Minivans
Dodge Caravan (10)
Ford Windstar (10)
Plymouth Voyager (10)
Pontiac Trans Sport (9)
Chrysler Town & Country (9)
Chevy Lumina (9)

Large Sport Utility
Ford Bronco (8)

Compact Pickups
Dodge Dakota (7)
Isuzu Pickup (6)*
Ford Ranger (6)

Standard Pickups
Toyota T100 (8)
GMC Sierra (7)
Chevy C/K-Series
Ford F-Series (6)

* No airbags available on this model.

brakes are not as effective as four-wheel.

Rollover: The higher the center of gravity and the narrower the track width, the more likely the vehicle is to rollover. *Very high, high, moderate,* and *low* ratings compare the potential likelihood of these vehicles to roll over.

Fuel Economy: This is the EPA-rated fuel economy for city and highway driving measured in miles per gallon. A single model may have a number of fuel economy ratings because of different engine and transmission options. We have included the figure for what is expected to be the most popular model.

Repair Rating: This rating is based on nine typical repairs after the warranty expires and the cost of following the manufacturer's preventive maintenance schedule during the warranty period.

Warranty Rating: This is an overall assessment of the vehicle's warranty when compared to all other warranties. The rating considers the important features of each warranty, with emphasis on the length of the basic and powertrain warranties.

Complaint Index: This rating is based on the number of complaints about that vehicle on file at the U.S. Department of Transportation. The complaint index will give you a general idea of experiences others have had with models which are essentially un-

changed for this model year. An empty box means that the vehicle is entirely new for 1995 or that we had insufficient data to calculate a rating.

Insurance Cost: Many automobile insurance companies use ratings based on the vehicle's accident and occupant injury history to determine whether or not the insurance premium of a vehicle should be a *discount* or a *surcharge*. (Your insurance company may or may not participate in a rating program.) If the vehicle is likely to receive neither, we label it *regular*.

Typical Price: This price range will give you a general idea of the "sticker," or asking price of a vehicle. It is based on the lowest to highest retail price of the various models, and it does not include options or the discount that you should be able to negotiate using a service such as CarBargains (see page 90).

Other Specifications: Most people buy a truck, van, or sport utility vehicle because they have some special needs—carrying lumber, towing, off-roading, or carpooling. In order to help you narrow down your choice to those vehicles which best meet your requirements, we've included a variety of key specifications on each page in *The Ratings* pages at the end of the book.

Trucks Are Hot!

The U.S. truck population has grown to over 60 million vehicles—over three times the number of trucks that were on the road 20 years ago. Twenty-eight percent of all trucks are 12 years old or over and 23 percent are under three years old. The average truck age is over eight years old.

Vehicle	See Pg.	Overall Rating■ Poor ↔ Good	Crash Test	Air Bags	Anti-Lock Brakes	Rollover	Fuel Economy
Minivans							
Chevrolet Astro	99		Very Poor	Driver	4-wheel	High	16/21
Chevrolet Lumina	102		Good	Driver	4-wheel	Moderate	19/23
Chrysler T & C	107		Good	Dual	4-wheel	Moderate	17/23
Dodge Caravan	108		Good	Dual	4-wheel*	Moderate	20/24
Ford Aerostar	112		Moderate	Driver	2-wheel	Very High	17/23
Ford Windstar	118		Very Good	Dual	4-wheel	Moderate	17/24
GMC Safari	99		Very Poor	Driver	4-wheel	High	16/21
Honda Odyssey	126		No Test	Dual	4-wheel	Moderate	19/23
Mazda MPV	140		No Test	Driver	2-wheel	High	16/22
Mercury Villager	141		Moderate	Driver	4-wheel	Moderate	17/23
Nissan Quest	146		Moderate	Driver	4-wheel*	Low	17/23
Olds Silhouette	147		Good	Driver	4-wheel	Moderate	17/25
Plymouth Voyager	148		Good	Dual	4-wheel*	Moderate	20/24
Pontiac Trans Sport	149		Good	Driver	4-wheel	Moderate	19/23
Toyota Previa	156		Moderate	Dual	4-wheel*	High	17/22
Full Size Vans							
Chevy Van/Sport Van	106		Poor	Driver*	4-wheel	High	14/16
Dodge Ram Vn/Wgn.	111		No Test	Driver	2-wheel**	Very High	15/17
Ford Econ./Clb Wgn.	114		Moderate	Driver	2-wheel		13/17
GMC Vandura/Rally	123		Poor	Driver*	2-wheel	High	14/16

■ Due to the importance of crash tests, vehicles with no crash test results as of publication date cannot be given an overall rating.

Warranty	Complaint Rating	Insurance Rating	Repair Rating	Typical Price $	Overall Rating ▪ Poor ↔ Good	See Pg	Vehicle
Minivans							
Very Poor	Good	Discount	Very Good	$18-21,500		99	Chevrolet Astro
Very Poor	Very Good	Regular	Very Good	$17-20,000		102	Chevrolet Lumina
Poor	Very Poor	Discount	Very Good	$28-30,000		107	Chrysler T & C
Poor	Poor	Discount	Very Good	$17-27,000		108	Dodge Caravan
Very Poor	Average	Discount	Good	$18-24,000		112	Ford Aerostar
Very Poor		Regular	Good	$18-24,000		118	Ford Windstar
Very Poor	Good	Discount	Very Good	$18-21,500		99	GMC Safari
Very Poor		Regular	Poor	$22-25,000		126	Honda Odyssey
Average	Poor	Regular	Poor	$21-28,000		140	Mazda MPV
Very Poor	Very Poor	Discount	Good	$19-25,000		141	Mercury Villager
Average	Poor	Discount	Good	$20-27,000		146	Nissan Quest
Very Poor	Average	Discount	Very Good	$21-23,000		147	Olds Silhouette
Poor	Poor	Discount	Very Good	$17-26,000		148	Plymouth Voyager
Very Poor	Good	Discount	Very Good	$18-20,000		149	Pontiac Trans Sport
Poor	Average	Discount	Poor	$23-32,000		156	Toyota Previa
Full Size Vans							
Very Poor	Very Good	Discount	Good	$20-23,500		106	Chevy Van/Sport Van
Poor	Very Good	Discount	Average	$15-21,000		111	Dodge Ram Vn/Wgn.
Very Poor	Good	Discount	Very Good	$17-25,000		114	Ford Econ./Clb Wgn.
Very Poor	Very Good	Discount	Good	$19-22,000		123	GMC Vandura/Rally

▪ Based on 1994 data; *Optional; **4-wheel optional

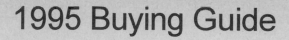
Vehicle	See Pg.	Overall Rating ■ Poor ↔ Good	Crash Test	Air Bags	Anti-Lock Brakes	Rollover	Fuel Economy
Small Sport Utility							
Geo Tracker	125		No Test	None	2-wheel	High	24/26
Isuzu Amigo	128		Poor	None	2-wheel	Very High	16/20
Jeep Wrangler	134		Poor	None	4-wheel*	Very High	19/20
Kia Sportage	135		No Test	None	2-wheel	High	20/24
Land Rover Def. 90	136		No Test	None	None	Very High	12/16
Suzuki Samurai	150		Moderate	None	None	Very High	28/29
Suzuki Sidekick	151		No Test	None	2-wheel*	High	23/26
Mid-Size Sport Utility							
Chevrolet Blazer	100		No Test	Driver	4-wheel	Very High	17/22
Ford Explorer	115		No Test	Dual	4-wheel	High	15/20•
GMC Jimmy	119		No Test	Driver	4-wheel	Very High	16/21
Isuzu Trooper	131		No Test	Dual	2-wheel**	Very High	15/18
Jeep Cherokee	132		No Test	Driver	4-wheel*	Moderate	17/19
Land Rvr. Discovery	137		No Test	Dual	4-wheel	Very High	13/16
Nissan Pathfinder	144		Poor	None	2-wheel*	High	15/18
Toyota 4Runner	152		No Test	None	2-wheel *	High	19/21
Large Sport Utility							
Chevrolet Suburban	104		Very Good	Driver	4-wheel	High	13/15
Chevrolet Tahoe	105		No Test	Driver	4-wheel	High	12/16
Ford Bronco	113		Very Good	Driver	4-wheel	High	14/19
GMC Suburban	122		Very Good	Driver	4-wheel	High	12/15
GMC Yukon	124		No Test	Driver	4-wheel	High	12/15
Honda Passport	127		Poor	None	2-wheel	High	16/19
Isuzu Rodeo	130		Poor	None	2-wheel	High	15/18
Jeep Gr. Cherokee	133		Moderate	Driver	4-wheel	High	15/20
Land Rover Rng. Rvr.	138		No Test	Dual	4-wheel	Very High	12/15
Mitsubishi Montero	143		Good	Driver	4-wheel*	Very High	15/18
Toyota Land Cruiser	153		No Test	None	4-wheel*	High	12/15

■ Due to the importance of crash tests, vehicles with no crash test results as of publication date cannot be given an overall rating.

Warranty	Complaint Rating	Insurance Rating	Repair Rating	Typical Price $	Overall Rating• Poor ↔ Good	See Pg	Vehicle
							Small Sport Utility
Very Poor	Very Good	Surcharge	Average	$12-15,000		125	Geo Tracker
Very Good	Good	Surcharge	Good	$15-19,000		128	Isuzu Amigo
Poor	Average	Regular	Good	$12-16,000		134	Jeep Wrangler
Poor		Regular	Good	$14-18,000		135	Kia Sportage
Average		Regular	Very Poor	$28-30,000•		136	Land Rover Def. 90
Very Poor	Very Good	Regular	Good	$10-12,000		150	Suzuki Samurai
Very Poor	Very Good	Regular	Average	$12-17,000		151	Suzuki Sidekick
							Mid-Size Sport Utility
Very Poor		Regular	Good	$19-22,500		100	Chevrolet Blazer
Very Poor		Regular	Very Good	$18-30,000		115	Ford Explorer
Very Poor		Surcharge	Good	$18-22,000		119	GMC Jimmy
Very Good	Very Good	Regular	Average	$24-33,500		131	Isuzu Trooper
Poor	Poor	Regular	Good	$14-21,000		132	Jeep Cherokee
Average		Regular	Very Poor	$28-30,000		137	Land Rvr. Discovery
Average	Very Good	Surcharge	Average	$21-30,000		144	Nissan Pathfinder
Poor	Good	Surcharge	Poor	$22-24,000		152	Toyota 4Runner
							Large Sport Utility
Very Poor	Very Poor	Discount	Good	$22-27,500		104	Chevrolet Suburban
Very Poor		Discount	Good	$22-26,000		105	Chevrolet Tahoe
Very Poor	Good	Discount	Good	$22-28,000		113	Ford Bronco
Very Poor	Very Poor	Discount	Good	$22-26,000		122	GMC Suburban
Very Poor	Very Poor	Regular	Good	$22-25,000		124	GMC Yukon
Very Poor		Regular	Good	$17-26,000		127	Honda Passport
Very Good	Average	Surcharge	Good	$16-27,000		130	Isuzu Rodeo
Poor	Very Poor	Regular	Good	$23-31,000		133	Jeep Gr. Cherokee
Average	Average	Surcharge	Very Poor	$53-54,000		138	Land Rover Rng Rvr.
Poor	Good	Surcharge	Poor	$28-37,000		143	Mitsubishi Montero
Poor	Poor	Surcharge	Poor	$37-39,000		153	Toyota Land Cruiser

• Based on 1994 data; *Optional; **4-wheel optional.

13

Vehicle	See Pg.	Overall Rating Poor ↔ Good	Crash Test	Air Bags	Anti-Lock Brakes	Rollover	Fuel Economy
Compact Pickups							
Chevrolet S-Series	103		No Test	Driver	2-wheel**	High	17/21
Dodge Dakota	109		Very Good	Driver	2-wheel**	High	15/19
Ford Ranger	117		Good	Driver	2-wheel**	Moderate	21/24
GMC Sonoma	121		No Test	Driver	2-wheel**	High	16/22
Isuzu Pickup	129		Moderate	None	2-wheel	Very High	17/20
Mazda B-Series	139		Good	Driver	2-wheel	High	16/21
Mitsu. Mighty Max	142		Moderate	None	None	Moderate	19/23
Nissan Pickup	145		Moderate	None	2-wheel	Very High	18/20
Toyota Pickup	154		Average	None	2-wheel*	High	19/22
Standard Pickups							
Chevrolet CK Series	101		Very Good	Driver*	4-wheel	High	15/18
Dodge Ram	110		No Test	Driver	2-wheel**	Moderate	12/16
Ford F-Series	116		Good	Driver*	2-wheel		15/19
GMC Sierra	120		Very Good	Driver*	4-wheel	High	15/19
Toyota T100	155		Very Good	Driver	4-wheel*	Moderate	17/19

■ Due to the importance of crash tests, vehicles with no crash test results as of publication date cannot be given an overall rating.

Warranty	Complaint Rating	Insurance Rating	Repair Rating	Typical Price $	Overall Rating Poor ↔ Good	See Pg	Vehicle
							Compact Pickups
Very Poor		Surcharge	Good	$11-17,500	▮▮▮▮▮▮▮▮▮	103	Chevrolet S-Series
Poor	Good	Regular	Good	$11-19,500	▮▮▮▮▮▮▮▮▮	109	Dodge Dakota
Very Poor	Good	Surcharge	Very Good	$10-15,000*	▮▮▮▮▮▮▮▮▮	117	Ford Ranger
Very Poor		Regular	Good	$12-17,000	▮▮▮▮▮▮▮▮▮	121	GMC Sonoma
Very Good	Very Good	Surcharge	Good	$10-15,500	▮▮▮▮▮▮▮▮▮	129	Isuzu Pickup
Average		Surcharge	Good	$10-18,000*	▮▮▮▮▮▮▮▮▮	139	Mazda B-Series
Poor	Very Good	Surcharge	Poor	$10-12,000	▮▮▮▮▮▮▮▮▮	142	Mitsu. Mighty Max
Average	Very Good	Surcharge	Good	$10-21,000	▮▮▮▮▮▮▮▮▮	145	Nissan Pickup
Poor	Very Good	Surcharge	Average	$11-20,500	▮▮▮▮▮▮▮▮▮	154	Toyota Pickup
							Standard Pickups
Very Poor	Very Good	Regular	Good	$16-24,000	▮▮▮▮▮▮▮▮▮	101	Chevrolet CK Series
Poor		Regular	Average	$14-21,000	▮▮▮▮▮▮▮▮▮	110	Dodge Ram
Very Poor	Very Good	Regular	Good	$13-20,000	▮▮▮▮▮▮▮▮▮	116	Ford F-Series
Very Poor	Very Good	Regular	Good	$15-23,000	▮▮▮▮▮▮▮▮▮	120	GMC Sierra
Poor	Very Good	Regular	Average	$14-21,500	▮▮▮▮▮▮▮▮▮	155	Toyota T100

• Based on 1994 data; *Optional; ** 4-wheel optional.

Corporate Twins

"Corporate twin" is a term for similar cars sold under different names. In many cases, the cars are virtually identical, such as the Chevrolet Lumina Minivan, the Oldsmobile Silhouette, and the Pontiac Trans Sport. Sometimes the difference is in body style and luxury options, as with the Chrysler Town and Country and the Dodge Grand Caravan. Generally, twins have the same mechanics, engine, drive train, size, weight, and internal workings. In the past, this was mainly an American phenomenon. Recently, U.S. manufacturers have been selling Asian imports marketed under a U.S. name. In most cases, the only difference is the name plate and the price, sometimes, you will find differences in style. We call these "Asian Cousins."

Twins

General Motors

Chevrolet Lumina Minivan
Oldsmobile Silhouette
Pontiac Trans Sport

Chevrolet Astro
GMC Safari

Chevrolet Van/Sport Van
GMC Vandura/Rally

Chevrolet Blazer
GMC Jimmy

Chevrolet Suburban
GMC Suburban

Chevrolet S-10 Pickup
GMC Sonoma

Chevrolet C/K Pickup
GMC Sierra

Chevrolet Tahoe
GMC Yukon

Chrysler

Chrysler Town & Country
Dodge Grand Caravan
Plymouth Grand Voyager

Dodge Caravan
Plymouth Voyager

Isuzu

Isuzu Rodeo
Honda Passport

Asian Cousins

Ford Ranger—*Mazda B-Series*
Geo Tracker—*Suzuki Sidekick*
Mercury Villager—*Nissan Quest*

SAFETY

For most of us, safety is one of the most important factors in choosing a new vehicle, yet it is also one of the most difficult items to evaluate. To give the greatest possible protection to its occupants, a vehicle should offer a wide variety of safety features including dual air bags and anti-lock brakes. While these features are becoming more widely available, they are not yet found on all models.

Another key factor in occupant protection is how well a vehicle performs in a crash test. In order for you to use the crash test information to evaluate your new vehicle choices, we have analyzed and presented the results of the U. S. Department of Transportation crash test program in this chapter. The crash tests measure how well each vehicle protects the driver and front-seat passenger in a frontal crash.

Also described in this chapter are current options and safety features available in this year's models. Additionally, we've included a state-by-state list of the safety belt laws and a detailed discussion of an important, and too often overlooked, safety feature—the child safety seat.

Crash Test Program: In 1979, the U.S. Department of Transportation began an experimental program to compare the occupant protection of one car to that of another. The crash test that was developed has shown significant differences in the abilities of various automobiles to protect belted occupants during frontal crashes.

In the test, an automobile is sent into a concrete barrier at 35-mph, causing an impact which is similar to that of two identical cars crashing head on at 35-mph. The test car contains electronically monitored dummies in the driver and passenger seats. These electronic data are analyzed to determine the impact of such a collision on a human being.

The government releases an incomplete and confusing array of numbers that are very difficult to understand and almost impossible to use in comparing cars.

We have analyzed the data and presented the results using our own *Crash Test Index*. This Index provides an overall means of comparing the results. The following tables allow you to compare the crash test performances of today's cars.

It is best to compare the results within weight class, such as compacts to compacts. Do not compare vehicles with differing weights. For example, a small sport utility that is rated *Good* may not be as safe as a full size van with the same rating.

The results evaluate performance in frontal crashes only, which account for about 50 percent of auto-related deaths and serious injuries. Even though the tested car may have airbags, the dummies are also belted.

We rate the crash test results of each vehicle relative to all of the vehicles ever crash tested. This method of rating the vehicles gives you a better idea of the true top performers among the '95 models and identifies those which have substantial room to improve their occupant protection. *The Truck, Van & 4x4 Book* wants to stimulate competition, and that's what this new rating program is intended to do. You, the buyer, now know which are the truly best performers. Those manufacturers who have chosen to build better performing vehicles will likely be rewarded with your decision to purchase their models.

Crash Tests: How the Vehicles are Rated

A vehicle's ability to protect you in a crash depends on its ability to absorb the force of impact rather than transfer it to you, the occupant. This is a function of the vehicle's size, weight, and, most importantly, design. The crash tests measure how much of the crash force is transferred to the head, chest, and thighs of the occupants in a 35-mph crash into a barrier.

The vehicles are listed here by weight class, then alphabetically by manufacturer. The first column provides our overall Crash Test Index. This Index is a number which describes all the forces measured by the test. Lower index numbers are better. The Index is best used to compare vehicles within the same size and weight class.

The second column provides an overall rating of *Very Good*, *Good*, *Average*, *Poor* or *Very Poor*. These results reflect the vehicle's performance in relation to all other models ever tested. This exclusive **Truck, Van & 4x4 Book Crash Test Rating** lets you compare, at a glance, the overall performance of the vehicles you'll find in the showroom this year.

The next two columns indicate the likelihood of each occupant sustaining a life-threatening injury, based on the dummies' head and chest scores. Lower percentages mean a lower likelihood of being seriously injured. This information is taken directly from government analysis of the crash test results.

The last two columns indicate how the dummies' legs fared. Legs labeled *Poor* did not meet the government's standards. Those that did meet the standards are rated *Average*, *Good* and *Very Good*, reflecting performance relative to all other vehicles ever tested. These leg injury ratings are not weighted as heavily as head and chest results in determining overall performance.

Results on the following pages indicate how this year's vehicles can be expected to perform in the tests. They are included here only when the design has not changed enough to dramatically alter results. Vehicles marked with footnote 2 were tested with less crash protection than is standard on the 1995 model. It is expected that, with more crash protection, the current model should produce similar or better results.

Crash test results may vary due to differences in the way vehicles are manufactured, in how models are equipped, and in test conditions. There is no absolute guarantee that a vehicle that passed the test will adequately protect you in an accident. "Corporate twins" that are structurally the same, such as the Dodge Caravan and Plymouth Voyager, can be expected to perform similarly. Keep in mind that some two-door models may not perform exactly like their four-door counterparts and pickups with different-sized cabs or beds may perform differently.

Crash Test Performance: The Best

Here is a list of the best crash test performers (among the 1995 vehicles for which crash test information is available). Lower Crash Test Index numbers indicate better performance. See the following tables for more results.

Minivans
Ford Windstar (1911)
Chrys. Town and Country (2648)
Dodge Caravan (2648)
Plymouth Voyager (2648)

Small Pickups
Dodge Dakota (2302)

Large Sport Utility
Ford Bronco 4 dr. 4x2 (1505)
Ford Bronco 2 dr. 4x4 (1834)
Chevy Suburban 4x4 (2388)
GMC Suburban 4x4 (2388)

Large Pickups
Ford F150 (w/air bag) (1590)
Chevy C1500 (2306)
GMC Sierra 1500 (2306)
Toyota T100 (2316)

Crash Test Performance	Injury Index	Truck Book Rating	Likelihood of Life Threatening Injury		Leg Injury Rating	
			Driver	Passngr	Driver	Passngr
Minivans						
Chevy Astro	7258	**Vry. Pr.**	31%	66%	Moderate	Good
Chevy Lumina (Tr. Sport)	3263	Good	10%	23%	Moderate	Moderate
Chrysler T & C (Caravan)	2648	Good	15%	11%	Good	Moderate
Dodge Caravan	2648	Good	15%	11%	Good	Moderate
Ford Aerostar	3544	Average	15%	23%	Moderate	Good
Ford Windstar	1911	*Vry. Gd.*	10%	8%	Good	Good
GMC Safari (Astro)	7258	**Vry. Pr.**	31%	66%	Moderate	Good
Mercury Villager (Quest)	3670	Average	19%	22%	Moderate	Moderate
Nissan Quest	3670	Average	19%	22%	Moderate	Moderate
Olds Silhouette (Tr. Sport)	3263	Good	10%	23%	Moderate	Moderate
Plymouth Voyager (Caravan)	2648	Good	15%	11%	Good	Moderate
Pontiac Trans Sport	3263	Good	10%	23%	Moderate	Moderate
Toyota Previa	3858	Average	20%	23%	Moderate	Good
Full-Size Vans						
Chevy Sport Van	5159	**Poor**	32%	29%	Poor	Vry. Gd.
Ford Econoline	4098	Average	19%	29%	Moderate	Vry. Gd.
GMC Rally (Sport Van)	5159	**Poor**	32%	29%	Poor	Vry. Gd.
Small Sport Utility						
Isuzu Amigo 4X4[1]	4782	**Poor**	31%	30%	Vry. Gd.	Vry. Gd.
Jeep Wrangler 4x4[1]	4890	**Poor**	42%	16%	Moderate	Vry. Gd.

HOW TO READ THE CHARTS:

| 1234 | **Injury Index**

The overall numerical injury rating for front seat occupants in a frontal crash. *Lower numbers mean better performance.*

| Very Good | **Truck Book Rating**

How the vehicle compares among all government test results to date. The range includes very good, good, average, poor and very poor.

| 00% | **Likelihood of Life Threatening Injury**

The chance of life threatening injury to the driver/passenger in a frontal 35 mph crash. *Lower percentages mean better performance.*

| Good | **Leg Injury Rating**

Injury rating for driver and passenger legs in a frontal crash, when compared to all government test results to date.

Crash Test Performance	Injury Index	Truck Book Rating	Likelihood of Life Threatening Injury		Leg Injury Rating	
			Driver	Passngr	Driver	Passngr
Suzuki Samurai 4X4[1]	3724	Average	25%	16%	Moderate	Good
Mid-Size Sport Utility						
Nissan Pathfinder 4X2[1]	6618	**Poor**	51%	29%	Moderate	Moderate
Large Sport Utility						
Chevrolet Suburban 4X4[2]	2388	*Vry. Gd.*	13%	11%	Good	Good
Ford Bronco 4 dr. 4X2[2]	1505	*Vry. Gd.*	9%	6%	Vry. Gd.	Vry. Gd.
Ford Bronco 2 dr. 4X4	1834	*Vry. Gd.*	12%	7%	Good	Vry. Gd.
GMC Suburb. (Ch. Sub.) 4X4[2]	2388	*Vry. Gd.*	13%	11%	Good	Good
Honda Passport (Rodeo) 4X4[1]	5214	**Poor**	35%	26%	Moderate	Good
Honda Passport (Rodeo) 4X2[1]	6895	**Poor**	56%	43%	Vry. Gd.	Vry. Gd.
Isuzu Rodeo 4X4[1]	5214	**Poor**	35%	26%	Moderate	Good
Isuzu Rodeo 4X2[1]	6895	**Poor**	56%	43%	Vry. Gd.	Vry. Gd.
Jeep Grand Cherokee 4X4	3827	Average	17%	25%	Moderate	Vry. Gd.
Mitsubishi Montero 4X4	3402	Good	25%	14%	Good	Vry. Gd.
Compact Pickups						
Dodge Dakota	2302	*Vry. Gd.*	7%	18%	Vry. Gd.	Vry. Gd.
Ford Ranger[2]	3288	Good	26%	10%	Good	Vry. Gd.
Isuzu Pickup[1]	4007	Average	29%	19%	Vry. Gd.	Vry. Gd.
Mazda B-Series (Ranger)[2]	3288	Good	26%	10%	Good	Vry. Gd.
Mitsubishi Mighty Max[1]	3912	Average	25%	21%	Good	Vry. Gd.
Nissan Pickup[1]	3865	Average	31%	13%	Good	Vry. Gd.
Toyota Pickup 4X2[1]	4098	Average	35%	11%	Good	Good
Toyota Pickup 4X4[1]	5601	**Poor**	48%	20%	Good	Good
Standard Pickups						
Chevrolet C1500[2]	2306	*Vry. Gd.*	15%	8%	Moderate	Good
Dodge Ram 1500	---	---	10%	---	Vry. Gd.	---
Ford F150 (driver air bag)	1590	*Vry. Gd.*	9%	6%	Good	Vry. Gd.
Ford F150 (manual belts)[2]	2828	Good	21%	10%	Good	Vry. Gd.
GMC Sierra (C1500)[2]	2306	*Vry. Gd.*	15%	8%	Moderate	Good
Toyota T100	2316	*Vry. Gd.*	14%	10%	Good	Vry. Gd.

Empty box means data unavailable. Parentheses indicate actual model tested. Vehicles are two-wheel drive, unless noted otherwise.
[1] No air bags are available on this vehicle.
[2] Vehicle tested with fewer air bags than now available. Similar or better results should occur with 1995 air bag offering.

Crash Protection

Even though thousands of Americans buy minivans, pickups, and 4x4s for family and non-commercial use, the National Highway Traffic Safety Administration has only recently taken steps to improve their safety, and it will take years to fully implement these rules.

As of 1992, trucks and vans must have head restraints in order to reduce the frequency and severity of head and neck injuries, and they are required to have rear-seat lap and shoulder belts in order to prevent injury to passengers in the back seat of a vehicle. There are also new testing rules for manual belt systems to ensure their strength and reliability, and new limitations on the rearward displacement of the steering column will lower the chances of chest, neck, or head injuries.

Missing Safety: While these are steps in the right direction, here are some key safety standards that will not be required until 1995:

1. Significant roof-crush resistance for rollover crash protection.

2. Automatic crash protection— requirement phase-in begins in 1995 with full implementation delayed until 1998.

Automatic Crash Protection: One safety feature that many trucks, vans, and 4x4s are missing is automatic crash protection. Over a decade ago, in cooperation with the federal government, the automobile industry developed two forms of automatic crash protection: air bags and automatic safety

belts. While these devices will not prevent all deaths, they will cut in half your chances of being killed or seriously injured in a car.

Federal law requires all new *passenger* cars to be equipped with automatic crash protection that will protect the driver and front-seat passenger in a 30-mph collision into a fixed barrier. But, this protection is not required in all pickups, vans, or 4x4s until 1998.

Unfortunately, because they are not required by the government, many of this year's light trucks do not have air bags. Here's what the buyer's of those vehicles are missing because the government dragged its feet on this lifesaving requirement.

Hidden in the steering wheel hub and the right side of the dashboard, air bags provide unobtrusive and effective protection in frontal crashes. By spreading crash forces over the head and chest, air bags protect the body from contact with hard surfaces.

Studies of the actual operation of the air bags in 10,000 test vehicles reported no cases of failure to deploy or malfunction of the

inflator. This reliability rate (99.995 percent) is far higher than that of such safety features as brakes, tires, steering, and lights, which show failure rates of up to 10 percent.

Here are some answers to typical questions asked about air bags.

Is the gas that inflates air bags dangerous? Nitrogen, which makes up 79.8 percent of the air we breathe, is the gas that inflates the bags. A solid chemical, sodium azide, generates this nitrogen gas. Sodium azide presents no hazard in normal driving, in crashes or in disposal.

Will air bags inflate by mistake? Air bags will inflate only in frontal impacts equivalent to hitting a solid wall at about 10-mph or higher. They will not inflate when you go over bumps or potholes or when you hit something at low speed.

In the unlikely event of an inadvertent air bag deployment, you would not lose control of the vehicle. Air bags are designed to deploy and then deflate in fractions of a second.

TIP — A Note for Pregnant Women:

The American College of Obstetricians and Gynecologists strongly urges pregnant women to always wear a safety belt, including on the ride to the hospital to deliver the baby! In a car crash, the most serious risk to an unborn baby is that the mother may be injured. Obstetricians recommend that the lap and shoulder belts be used, with the lap belt as low as possible on the hips, under the baby. And remember, when bring your baby home from the hospital, "Make the first ride a safe ride!"

Will air bag systems last very long? Air bags are reliable and require no maintenance. Because they have only one moving part, the device that senses impact, there is nothing to wear out. Although they work throughout the life of the vehicle, some manufacturers suggest inspections at anywhere from two to ten years.

Will air bags protect children? Studies of actual crashes indicate that children are protected by air bags. However, most vehicles do not offer air bags on the passenger side, where children often sit. In addition, rear-facing child safety seats should not be used in the front seat of a vehicle with a passenger air bag.

Will air bags protect occupants without seat belts? Air bags are designed to protect unbelted front-seat occupants in 30-mph frontal crashes into a wall. Equipping vehicles with air bags reduced the average injury severity in serious frontal crashes by 64-percent, even though over 80-percent of the occupants were unbelted. Air bags do not protect you in a side or rear crash. The best protection is provided by a combination of air bags and lap and shoulder safety belts. With air bags and seat belts, you'll be protected in the event of side impact and rollover crashes, as well as in frontal crashes.

The following list indicates which front seat passengers will be unprotected by air bags this year.

Who's NOT Offering Air Bags?

Vehicle	Which Front Occupant Unprotected
Minivan	
Chevrolet Astro/Lumina Minivan	Passenger Unprotected
Ford Aerostar	Passenger Unprotected
GMC Safari	Passenger Unprotected
Mazda MPV	Passenger Unprotected
Mercury Villager	Passenger Unprotected
Nissan Quest	Passenger Unprotected
Oldsmobile Silhouette	Passenger Unprotected
Pontiac Trans Sport	Passenger Unprotected
Volkswagen Eurovan	Both Unprotected
Full Size Van	
Chevrolet Sport Van	Both Unprotected*
Dodge Ram Wagon/Van	Passenger Unprotected
Ford Econoline	Passenger Unprotected
GMC Rally/Vandura	Both Unprotected*
Small Sport Utility	
Geo Tracker	Both Unprotected
Isuzu Amigo	Both Unprotected
Jeep Wrangler	Both Unprotected
Suzuki Samurai/Sidekick	Both Unprotected
Mid-Size/Large Sport Utility	
Chevrolet Blazer/Tahoe/Suburban	Passenger Unprotected
Ford Bronco	Passenger Unprotected
GMC Jimmy/Suburban/Yukon	Passenger Unprotected
Honda Passport	Both Unprotected
Isuzu Rodeo	Both Unprotected
Jeep Cherokee	Passenger Unprotected
Jeep Grand Cherokee	Passenger Unprotected
Land Rover Defender 90	Both Unprotected
Mitsubishi Montero	Passenger Unprotected
Nissan Pathfinder	Both Unprotected
Toyota 4Runner/Land Cruiser	Both Unprotected
Compact Pickup	
Chevrolet S-10	Passenger Unprotected
Dodge Dakota	Passenger Unprotected
Ford Ranger	Passenger Unprotected
GMC Sonoma	Passenger Unprotected
Isuzu Pickup	Both Unprotected
Mazda B-Series	Passenger Unprotected
Mitsubishi Mighty Max	Both Unprotected
Nissan Pickup	Both Unprotected
Toyota Pickup	Both Unprotected
Standard Pickup	
Chevrolet C/K Series	Both Unprotected*
Dodge Ram	Passenger Unprotected
Ford F-Series	Both Unprotected*
GMC Sierra	Both Unprotected*
Toyota T100	Passenger Unprotected

* Driver airbag optional

Anti-Lock Brakes

Almost all manufacturers are now offering anti-lock braking systems (ABS). ABS shortens stopping distance on dry, wet, even icy roads. It works by sensing the speed of each wheel. If a wheel begins to lock up or skid, it automatically releases the wheel's brakes, allowing the wheel to roll normally again and thus stopping the skid. When the wheel stops skidding, the brakes are instantly reapplied. This cycle can be repeated many times per second. Remember—don't pump your brakes in a skid, the ABS does it for you.

All truck, van and 4x4 manufacturers offer some form of ABS with the exceptions of the Suzuki Samurai, Mitsubishi Mighty Max and Land Rover Defender 90. The best systems work on all four wheels. Many truck manufacturers have chosen to only offer it on the rear wheels. Two-wheel ABS is not as effective as four-wheel. The following table indicates what the various manufacturers are offering.

Vehicle	ABS
Chevy Astro	4-wheel
Chevy Blazer	4-wheel
Chevy CK Pickup	4-wheel
Chevy Sport Van	4-wheel
Chevy Lumina Mnvn	4-wheel
Chevy S-Series	4-wheel*
Chevy Suburban	4-wheel
Chevy Tahoe	4-wheel
Chry. T & C	4-wheel
Dodge Caravan	4-wheel*
Dodge Dakota	4-wheel*
Dodge Ram Pickup	4-wheel*
Ddge Ram Van/Wgn.	4-wheel*
Ford Aerostar	2-wheel
Ford Bronco	4-wheel
Ford Econ/Club Wgn.	2-wheel
Ford Explorer	4-wheel
Ford F-Series	2-wheel
Ford Ranger	4-wheel*
Ford Windstar	4-wheel

Vehicle	ABS
GMC Jimmy	4-wheel
GMC Vandura/Rally	2-wheel
GMC Safari	4-wheel
GMC Sierra	4-wheel
GMC Sonoma	4-wheel*
GMC Suburban	4-wheel
GMC Yukon	4-wheel
Geo Tracker	2-wheel
Honda Passport	2-wheel
Isuzu Amigo	2-wheel
Isuzu Pickup	2-wheel
Isuzu Rodeo	2-wheel
Isuzu Trooper	4-wheel*
Jeep Cherokee	4-wheel*
Jeep Gr. Cherokee	4-wheel
Jeep Wrangler	4-wheel*
Kia Sportage	2-wheel
Lnd Rvr Defender 90	None
Lnd Rvr Discovery	4-wheel
Lnd Rvr Range Rvr	4-wheel

Vehicle	ABS
Mazda B-Series Pickup	2-wheel
Mazda MPV	2-wheel
Mercury Villager	4-wheel
Mits. Mighty Max	None
Mits. Montero	4-wheel*
Nissan Pathfinder	2-wheel*
Nissan Pickup	2-wheel
Nissan Quest	4-wheel*
Olds Silhouette	4-wheel
Plymouth Voyager	4-wheel*
Pontiac Trans Sport	4-wheel
Suzuki Samurai	None
Suzuki Sidekick	2-wheel*
Toyota 4Runner	2-wheel *
Toyota Land Cruiser	4-wheel*
Toyota Pickup	2-wheel
Toyota T100	4-wheel*
Toyota Previa	4-wheel*

* Optional

23

Rollover

The risk of rollover is a significant safety issue with sport utility vehicles. Because of their relatively high center of gravity, they don't hug the road like smaller, lower automobiles and trucks. As a result, they are much more likely to turn over on sharp turns or corners. Not only does a rollover increase the likelihood of injuries, but it also increases the risk of the occupant being thrown from the vehicle. In fact, the danger of rollover with these vehicles is so severe that manufacturers are now required to place a sticker, shown below, where it can be seen by the driver every time the vehicle is used.

To understand the concept behind these vehicles' propensity to roll over, consider this: Place a section of 2x4 lumber on its 2-inch side. It is easily tipped over by a force pushing against the side. But if you place it on its 4-inch side, the same force will cause it to slide rather than tip over. Similarly, in a moving vehicle, the forces generated by a turn can cause a narrow, tall vehicle to roll over.

Ironically, even though sport utility vehicles have a higher tendency to roll over than passenger cars, the government does not require these vehicles to have the same side impact or roof protection.

When the government itself looked into this problem, they reported that some sport utility vehicles were nearly 20 times more likely than a passenger car to experience a fatal rollover. One way to prevent the rollover problem is to widen the distance between the center of the tires (called the track). Thankfully, some manufacturers have begun to do just that. But can vehicles already in use be modified to reduce rollover risk? One possibility is the use of smaller-diameter tires, which would reduce the height of the vehicle and lower its center of gravity. Another alternative is to weld weights underneath the vehicle to make it more stable. Be careful, however—neither of these alternatives has been fully tested. You should not attempt any modifications without checking with the manufacturer. And, most importantly, don't increase your vehicle's probability of rollover by adding larger tires and wheels or a higher suspension system.

As the trend of buying light trucks, minivans, and sport utility vehicles for private passenger use grows, the Center for Auto Safety is fighting to require safety standards for vehicle stability. If you experience a problem with your sport utility vehicle, use the Vehicle Owner's Questionnaire at the back of the book to let the government know about your experience.

In order to alert consumers to the problem of rollover, the government requires the following warning on certain vehicles.

This is a multipurpose passenger vehicle which will handle and maneuver differently from an ordinary passenger car, in driving conditions which may occur on streets and highways and off road. As with other vehicles of this type, if you make sharp turns or abrupt maneuvers, the vehicle may roll over or may go out of control and crash. You should read driving guidelines and instructions in the Owner's Manual, and wear your seat belt at all times.

Rollover Rating

Rollover is, in fact, a serious problem with many of the vehicles in this book. In order to help you evaluate this danger, we have developed a *Rollover Index* to compare the potential likelihood of these vehicles to roll over.

The following tables provide the *Rollover Index* and *Rating*. Zero is our cut-off number. Numbers above 0 mean that the vehicle has a relatively high likelihood of rolling over. Numbers below 0 indicate that the vehicle is less likely to rollover. In short, higher numbers indicate a greater chance of rollover.

We have included a *Rollover Index* for many of the vehicles in *The Truck, Van & 4x4 Book*. The *Rollover Index* is based on the track width of the vehicle (the distance between the tires) and the vehicle's center of gravity. Basically, the higher the center of gravity and the narrower the track width, the more likely the vehicle is to roll over.

You will note that most of the vehicles in this book have a rating above zero. That's because these types of vehicles are more likely to rollover than regular passenger cars. To help you better understand the index, we have divided the rated vehicles into four categories. The higher numbers are rated *Very High* and the lowest numbers (those below zero) are rated *Low*. Those in between are rated *Moderate* or *High*. It is important to consider the Index as a *relative* means of comparing the vehicles.

Vehicle	Index	Rating
Minivans		
Chevrolet Astro	13	High
Chevy Lumina Minivan	5	Moderate
Chry. Town and Country	6	Moderate
Dodge Caravan	4	Moderate
Dodge Grand Caravan	6	Moderate
Ford Aerostar	16	Very High
Ford Aerostar Ext.	17	Very High
Ford Windstar	3	Moderate
GMC Safari	13	High
Honda Odyssey	3	Moderate
Mazda MPV 2WD	9	High
Mazda MPV 4WD	13	High
Mercury Villager	3	Moderate
Nissan Quest	-1	Low
Oldsmobile Silhouette	5	Moderate
Plymouth Voyager	4	Moderate
Plymouth Grand Voyager	6	Moderate
Pontiac Trans Sport	5	Moderate
Toyota Previa	8	High

Vehicle	Index	Rating
Full-Size Vans		
Chevy Van G30	16	Very High
Chevy Van G20	13	High
Dodge Ram Van/Wgn SWB	15	Very High
Dodge Ram Van/Wgn LWB	16	Very High
GMC Rally G2500/3500	13	High
GMC Rally G3500 Ext.	17	Very High
Small Sport Utilities		
Geo Tracker 2WD	13	High
Geo Tracker 4WD	14	High
Isuzu Amigo	17	Very High
Jeep Wrangler	16	Very High
Kia Sportage	11	High
Land Rover Defender 90	29	Very High
Suzuki Samurai	20	Very High
Suz. Sidekick 2-dr. 2WD	13	High
Suz. Sidekick 2-dr. 4WD	14	High
Suz. Sidekick 4-dr. 2WD	15	Very High
Suz. Sidekick 4-dr. 4WD	17	Very High

Vehicle	Index	Rating
Mid-Size Sport Utilities		
Chevrolet Blazer	15	Very High
GMC Jimmy	15	Very High
Isuzu Trooper	21	Very High
Jeep Cherokee	6	Moderate
Land Rover Discovery	26	Very High
Nissan Pathfinder	14	High
Toyota 4Runner	14	High
Large Sport Utilities		
Chevy Suburban C1500	8	High
Chevy Suburban C2500	10	High
Chevy Suburban K1500	9	High
Chevy Suburban K2500	5	Moderate
Chevrolet Tahoe	10	High
Ford Bronco	11	High
GMC Suburban C1500	8	High
GMC Suburban C2500	6	Moderate
GMC Suburban K1500	10	High
GMC Suburban K2500	5	Moderate
GMC Yukon	10	High
Honda Passport	12	High
Isuzu Rodeo	12	High
Jeep Grand Cherokee	8	High
Land Rover Range Rover	17	Very High
Mitsubishi Montero LS	26	Very High
Mitsubishi Montero SR	22	Very High
Toyota Land Cruiser	13	High
Compact Pickups		
Chevrolet S-Series Pickup	10	High
Dodge Dakota	8	High
Ford Ranger Reg. Cab	7	Moderate
Ford Ranger Super Cab	13	High
GMC Sonoma	10	High
Isuzu Pickup 2WD	10	High
Isuzu Pickup 4WD	16	Very High
Mazda B-Series 2WD	9	High

Vehicle	Index	Rating
Mazda B-Series 4WD	13	High
Mitsubishi Mighty Max	1	Moderate
Nissan Pickup 4x2	10	High
Nissan Pickup 4x4	14	High
Toyota Pickup 4x2	10	High
Toyota Pickup 4x4	15	Very High
Toyota Pickup XtraCab 4x2	9	High
Toyota Pickup XtraCab 4x4	16	Very High
Standard Pickups		
Chevy 1500 2WD	7	Moderate
Chevy 1500 4WD	12	High
Chevy 2500	12	High
Chevy 3500 2WD	14	High
Chevy 3500 4WD CrwCab	7	Moderate
Chevy 3500 4WD RegCab	10	High
Dodge Ram 1500 4WD	6	Moderate
Dodge Ram 1500 2WD	3	Moderate
Dodge Ram 2500 4WD Reg	6	Moderate
Dodge Ram 2500 2WD Clb	3	Moderate
Dodge Ram 3500 4WD	4	Moderate
Dodge Ram 3500 2WD	-2	Low
GMC Sierra 2WD	6	Moderate
GMC Sierra 2WD Crew	9	High
GMC Sierra 4WD	12	High
GMC Sierra 4WD Crew	4	Moderate
Toyota T100	3	Moderate
Toyota T100 1-ton 4x2	4	Moderate
Toyota T100 DX 4x4	7	Moderate
Typical Cars		
Dodge Neon	-11	Low
Chevy Camaro coupe	-28	Low
Geo Metro	-3	Low
Lincoln Town Car	-18	Low
Mercury Sable	-21	Low
Oldsmobile Achieva	-11	Low
Toyota MR2	-28	Low

Off-Road Driving

One reason to buy an off-road vehicle is the ability to take advantage of some of our country's more remote areas. But off-roading also presents some unique hazards. The best way to ensure your safety is to understand the dangers, and to be prepared.

Before going out, be sure your vehicle is in top shape. Fill up the tank, and check the spare tire and the fluid levels. Also, find out about the local laws that apply to off-roading through the law enforcement people in the area.

Loading up: It is important to load your vehicle carefully and safely. The heaviest items should be on the floor as far forward of the rear axle as possible. Be sure you secure the load, so that loose objects can't hit someone or fall out of the vehicle. And remember, heavy loads on the roof or piled high in the cargo area will raise the vehicle's center of gravity and increase your chances of rolling over.

Controlling your vehicle: On an unpaved surface, the best way to control your vehicle is to control your speed—at a higher speed, you have less time to look for and react to obstacles. Off the road, your vehicle will bounce more and your wheels may leave the ground, so keep a firm grip on the steering wheel. You'll also need more distance for braking.

Off-roading can take you over a wide variety of surfaces, including rocks, grass, sand, mud, snow, and ice. Each of these surfaces affects the control of your vehicle in different ways.

Driving in mud reduces your traction and increases your braking distance. It is best to use a low gear, and to keep your vehicle moving so that you don't get stuck. Driving on sand, snow, and ice severely reduces tire traction.

Before driving through water, make sure that it isn't too deep, or your vehicle may be damaged. If you decide to go ahead, drive slowly—otherwise water can splash your ignition system or tailpipe, causing you to stall. *Caution:* Rushing water is especially dangerous and should be avoided. It can sweep your vehicle away. Even at low speeds, it can wash away the ground from under your tires, and you could lose control.

Driving on hills: Off-road terrain often requires you to drive up, down, or across a hill, each of which presents its own safety hazards. There are some hills that can't be driven—they are simply too steep for any vehicle. If you have any doubt about the steepness, don't drive the hill. Here are some things to keep in mind as you approach a hill:
- Is there a constant incline, or does the hill get sharply steeper in places?
- Is there good traction on the hillside, or will the surface cause you to slip?
- Is there a straight path up or down the hill?
- Are there trees or rocks on the hill that block your path?
- What's beyond the hill? Walk it first if you don't know—it's the smart way to see if you'll find a cliff, a fence, or another steep hill.
- Is the hill simply too rough? Steep hills often have ruts, gullies, and exposed rocks because they are more susceptible to erosion.

Driving uphill: If you decide you can safely drive up a hill, use a low gear, and get a smooth start up the hill. Try to maintain your speed. If you use more power than you need, the wheels may start to spin or slide. Avoid twists and turns, if possible, and drive as straight a route as you can. Always slow down as you approach the top of the hill. If your vehicle stalls on the hill, quickly brake to prevent yourself from rolling backwards. Then restart your engine, shift into reverse, and slowly back down the hill. Never shift into neutral to "rev up" the engine and go forward. Your vehicle will roll backwards quickly, and you may

---

Environmental Concerns

Off-road vehicles can damage and erode soil, disturb wildlife and its habitat, pollute natural areas, and endanger other land users. The U.S. Forest Service has developed a code of conduct for off-roaders called "Tread Lightly." This program provides tips on how to enjoy off-roading responsibly, without damaging the environment.

For information about the "Tread Lightly" program, or if you have any questions about off-roading and the environment, write to the U.S. Department of Agriculture, U.S. Forest Service, P.O. Box 96090, 14th and Independence Ave, SW, Washington, D.C. 20090-6090, or call the U.S. Forest Service at 202-205-1706.

lose control. And never attempt to turn around. If the hill is steep enough to stall your vehicle, it is certainly steep enough to make you roll over.

Driving downhill: If you decide you can go down a hill safely, keep your vehicle headed straight down and use a low gear. The engine drag will help your brakes. Never drive downhill with your transmission in neutral, because your brakes will have to do all the work and could overheat and fade. Drive slowly, and avoid turns that take you across the hill. Avoid braking so hard that you lock the wheels or you won't be able to steer your vehicle. If your wheels lock up during downhill braking and the vehicle starts to slide, just ease off the brakes quickly and you should straighten out.

Driving across a hill: Even a hill that's not too steep to drive straight up or down can be a problem to drive across. Since your vehicle is not as wide as it is long, driving across a steep hill can cause your vehicle to roll over. Watch out for loose gravel and wet grass which can cause your tires to slip downhill. If the vehicle does slip sideways, it could hit something that will trip it and make it roll. If you feel your vehicle starting to slide sideways, turn downhill. This should help you straighten out and stop your slipping.

If your vehicle stalls when you're crossing a hill, be sure that you and your passengers get out on the uphill side, even though that door is harder to open. If you get out on the downhill side and the vehicle starts to roll over, you'll be right in its path.

Safe Towing

If you regularly tow a camper, boat, or other trailer, it is important that your vehicle be capable of safely towing the load. Towing a trailer puts considerable strain on a vehicle, making every system work harder. The tires, brakes, and engine all experience extra stress, with the most strain on the automatic transmission. Power from the engine is transmitted to the wheels through a fluid coupling (called a torque converter) that can become extremely hot when towing. If the fluid is burned from overheating, the transmission can be severely damaged.

If you do a great deal of towing over long distances, installing an *auxiliary transmission cooler* will reduce the operating temperature of the fluid and help prevent damage to your transmission. You can also prolong the life of your vehicle by towing in drive rather than overdrive, except on long stretches of road. Towing in drive provides more power, and it places less stress on the entire vehicle than does overdrive.

The vehicle rating pages in the back of the book include the weight rating that a vehicle can safely tow. Many of these vehicles can pull more; however, they will need special modification.

1. Never pull more than the maximum allowable trailer weight listed in your owner's manual.

2. Never attempt to tow if your engine is not running smoothly.

3. Check tire inflation regularly, and keep a spare trailer tire in your truck when towing.

4. Service your cooling system regularly.

5. Replace tires, brakes, and shock absorbers well before you normally would. They need to be kept in above average condition to tow safely.

6. Use overload shocks if the hitch weight requires it.

7. Be especially cautious when towing a boat, because tires can be damaged on a ramp.

8. If you tow regularly, change your automatic transmission fluid at *half* the recommended mileage. If your owner's manual suggests 30,000 miles, change it every 15,000 miles or if it is discolored or smells burnt.

9. Install an auxiliary transmission cooler to protect the transmission. Typical costs range from $20 to $100.

Safety Belts

About 60 percent of occupants killed or injured in vehicle crashes would have been saved from serious harm had they been wearing safety belts. Yet many Americans do not use these life-saving devices.

Safety belts are particularly important in minivans, 4x4s, and pickups, because there is a greater chance of being killed or seriously injured in a rollover accident. The simple precaution of wearing your belt greatly improves your odds of survival.

Why don't people wear their belts? Sometimes they simply don't know the facts. Once you know the facts, you should be willing to buckle up.

While most safety advocates welcome the passage of safety belt usage laws, the ones passed to date are weak and generally unenforced. In addition, most of the laws are based on "secondary" enforcement—meaning that you cannot be stopped for failing to wear your belt. If you are stopped for another reason and the officer notices you don't have your belt on by the time he or she reaches the vehicle, you may be fined. In states with "primary" enforcement, you can be stopped for not wearing a safety belt. Yet, in many cases the fines are less than a parking ticket. In Arkansas and Wyoming, however, you can get a $5 credit toward a primary violation if you are wearing a seat belt.

Another unusual feature of these laws is that most of them allow drivers to avoid buckling up if they have a doctor's permission. This loophole was inserted to appease those who were not really in favor of the law. However, many doctors are wondering if they will be held responsible for the injuries of unbuckled patients. In fact, the State of New York Medical Society cautions doctors never to give medical dispensation from the law because "no medical condition has yet been found to warrant a medical exemption for seat belt use."

Even though most state laws are weak, they have heightened awareness and raised the level of usage. Belt use in states that have passed a safety belt law tends to rise sharply after the law is enacted. However, after the law has been on the books a few months, safety belt use drops.

The tables on the following pages describe the current safety belt laws. In some cases, the driver is responsible for all or some of the passengers as noted; otherwise, occupants are responsible for themselves. All states are listed, even those that do not yet have safety belt laws. We hope that the blanks following Maine and New Hampshire will soon be filled with new laws.

Safety Belt Myths and Facts

Myth: "I don't want to be trapped by a seat belt. It's better to be thrown free in an accident."

Fact: The chance of being killed is 25 times greater if you're ejected. A safety belt will keep you from plunging through the windshield, smashing into trees, rocks, or other cars, scraping along the ground, or getting run over by your own or another's vehicle. If you are wearing your belt, you're far more likely to be conscious after an accident to free yourself and other passengers.

Myth: "Pregnant women should not wear safety belts."

Fact: According to the American Medical Association, "Both the pregnant mother and the fetus are safer, provided the lap belt is worn as low on the pelvis as possible."

Myth: "I don't need it. In case of an accident, I can brace myself with my hands."

Fact: At 35 mph, the impact of a crash on you and your passengers is brutal. There's no way your arms and legs can brace you against that kind of collision; the speed and force are just too great. The force of impact at only 10 mph is roughly equivalent to the force of catching a 200-pound bag of cement dropped from a first floor window.

Safety Belt Laws

	Law Applies To:	Driver Fined For:	Enforcement	Max. Fine 1st Offense
Alabama	Front seat only	Self only	Secondary	$25
Alaska*	All occupants	0 to 16 year olds	Secondary	$15
Arizona	Front seat only	5 to 16 year olds	Secondary	$10
Arkansas	Front seat only	Self only	Secondary	$25[1]
California*	All occupants	Over 4 years old	Primary	$20
Colorado	Front seat only	Over 4 years old	Secondary	$10
Connecticut	Front seat only	4 to 16 year olds	Primary	$15
Delaware	Front seat only	All occupants	Secondary	$20
Dist. of Columbia	Front seat only	Self only	Secondary	$15
Florida	Front seat only	0 to 16 year olds	Secondary	$20
Georgia	All occupants	4 to 18 year olds	Secondary[2]	$15[2]
Hawaii	Front seat only	4 to 15 year olds	Primary	$20
Idaho	Front seat only	Self only	Secondary	$5
Illinois	Front seat only	6 to 16 year olds	Secondary	$25
Indiana	Front seat only	Self only	Secondary	$25
Iowa	Front seat only	Self only	Primary	$10
Kansas	Front seat only	Self only	Secondary	$10
Kentucky	All occupants	Over 40 inches	Secondary	$25
Louisiana	Front seat only	Self only	Secondary	$25[1]
Maine	No law			
Maryland	Front seat only	0 to 16 year olds	Secondary	$25
Massachusetts	All occupants	12 to 16 year olds	Secondary	$25
Michigan	All occupants	4 to 16 year olds	Secondary	$25
Minnesota	All occupants	4 to 11 year olds[3]	Secondary	$25
Mississippi	Front seat only	Self only	Secondary	$25
Missouri	Front seat only	4 to 16 years olds	Secondary	$10

*In these states driver can be held liable in court for *all* passengers.
See next page for footnotes.

Safety Belt Laws

	Law Applies To:	Driver Fined For:	Enforcement	Max. Fine 1st Offense
Montana*	All occupants	Over 4 years old	Secondary	$20
Nebraska	Front seat	Over 5 years old	Secondary	$25
Nevada*	All occupants	5 to 18 year olds	Secondary	$25
New Hampshire	No law			
New Jersey	Front seat only	5 to 18 year olds	Secondary	$20
New Mexico	Front seat only	Self only	Primary	$25
New York	Front seat[4]	4 to 16 year olds	Primary	$50
North Carolina	Front seat only	6 to 16 year olds	Primary	$25
North Dakota	Front seat	Over 11 years old	Secondary	$20
Ohio	Front seat only	Over 4 year olds	Secondary	$25
Oklahoma	Front seat only	Self only	Secondary	$25
Oregon*	All Occupants	0 to 16 year olds	Primary	$95
Pennsylvania	Front seat only	4 to 18 year olds	Secondary	$10
Rhode Island*	All Occupants	Over 12 years old	Secondary	None
South Carolina	All Occupants[5]	6 to 17 year olds	Secondary	$10
South Dakota	Front seat	5 to 18 year olds	Secondary	$20[7]
Tennessee	Front seat only	4 to 16 year olds	Secondary	$10
Texas	Front seat only	4 to 15 year olds	Primary	$50
Utah	Front seat only	2 to 18 year olds	Secondary	$10
Vermont*	All occupants	Over 13 years old	Secondary	$10
Virginia	Front seat only	4 to 16 year olds	Secondary	$25
Washington*	All occupants	0 to 16 year olds	Secondary	$47
West Virginia	Front seat[6]	All occupants	Secondary	$25
Wisconsin	All occupants[5]	4 to 16 year olds	Secondary	$10
Wyoming	Front seat only	Over 3 years old	Secondary	None[1]

*In these states driver can be held liable in court for *all* passengers.

[1] In Arkansas and Wyoming, reward for buckling up is a $5 reduction in primary violation fine. In Louisiana, 10% reduction in fine for moving violation.

[2] Primary for 14 to 18 year olds; $25 fine if driver is a minor.

[3] Parent driver is responsible for 11 to 15 year olds in front seat.

[4] Driver responsible for 4 to 10 year olds riding in rear seat.

[5] Covers rear seat occupants where shoulder belts are available.

[6] Driver responsible for occupants 0 to 18 years old in rear seat.

[7] Effective 1/1/95.

Child Safety Seats

How many times have you gone out of your way to prevent your children from being injured, taken care to keep household poisons out of reach, or watched carefully while they swam? Probably quite often. Yet, despite our concern about our children's welfare, many parents simply plunk their children in the back of a station wagon or let them roam around in a moving vehicle. Ironically, of all hazards, it is the automobile that poses the greatest threat to your children's health.

After the first weeks of an infant's life, vehicle crashes are the single leading cause of death and serious injury for children. Yet nearly 80 percent of the children who have died in vehicles could have been saved by proper use of child safety seats or safety belts.

Being a safe driver is no excuse for not having everyone in your vehicle buckled up. Quite often crashes or sudden swerves are caused by the recklessness of others. Even in low-speed crashes or swerves, a child can be hurled against the inside of the vehicle with a violent impact.

You simply can't protect children by holding them on your lap. At 30 mph, a crash or sudden braking can wrench your child from your arms with a tremendous force. Your child will continue to fly forward at the speed the vehicle was traveling until he or she hits something. At this speed, even a ten-pound infant would be ripped from your arms with a force of nearly 300 pounds.

If you aren't wearing a safety belt, your own body will be an additional hazard to a child in your lap. You will be thrown forward with enough force to crush your child against the dashboard or the back of the front seat.

The best and only way to protect your child in a vehicle is to use a safety seat. If no seat is available, buckle up the child in the back seat.

By using a child safety seat on every ride, you will help to establish the habit of regular safety belt use . As a lifelong wearer of safety belts, your child reduces his or her chances of being killed or seriously injured in an crash by 50 percent.

Buying Tips: Most consumers find that seats with a three-point automatic retracting harness, such as the Gerry Guard, Nissan, or Fisher Price seats, are the easiest to use. For infants, the Century model is one of the easiest to use. Here are some additional tips:

☑ Make sure the seat you buy can be properly installed in your vehicle. You will find that some car seats cannot be properly buckled into certain vehicles.

☑ Determine how many straps must be fastened to use the seat. The easy-to-use seats require only one.

☑ Make sure the seat is wide enough for growth and bulky winter clothes.

☑ Make sure your child will be comfortable. Can your child move his or her arms freely, sleep in the seat, and, if older, see out the window?

☑ Never use a seat which has restrained a child in a crash—replace it immediately.

Locking Clips

Children are safest if they are restrained in the middle of the back seat of your vehicle. If you put the safety seat somewhere other than the middle, you may need a locking clip. This clip is necessary if the latchplate on the safety belt slides freely along the belt; without it, the safety seat can move or tip over. You should always remove the clip when it is not being used with a safety seat.

Rear-facing Child Safety Seats

Never use a rear-facing child safety seat in a seating position that has an air bag. To deploy fast enough to protect adult occupants, an air bag inflates with enough force to potentially cause serious head and chest injuries to a child in a rear-facing safety seat. And remember, air bags do not take the place of child safety seats.

Seat Types

There are five types of child safety seats: *infant-only, convertible, toddler-only, booster* and *built-in*.

Infant-Only Seat: Infant-only seats can be used from birth until your baby reaches a weight of 17-20 pounds. This type of seat must be installed facing the rear of the car in a semi-reclined position. In a collision, the crash forces are spread over the baby's back, it's strongest body surface. A harness keeps the baby in the seat, which is anchored to the car by the car's safety belt. Look for seats where the height of the harness is adjustable; they will fit the baby better as he or she grows.

One benefit of an infant-only seat, as opposed to a convertible seat that can be used for infants and toddlers, is that you can easily install and remove the seat with the baby in place. Most infant car seats can also be used as indoor baby seats. Caution: Some indoor baby seats look remarkably similar to infant safety seats. These are not crashworthy and should *never* be used as car safety seats.

Convertible Seats: Buying a convertible seat can save you the expense of buying both an infant and a toddler seat. Most convertible seats can be used from birth until the child reaches four years or 40 pounds. When used for an infant, the seat faces rearward in a semi-reclined position. When the child is a year old and over 20 pounds, the frame can be adjusted upright and the seat turned to face forward. The safety harness, which is in the bottom slots when facing rearward, should be moved to the top slots when facing forward. There is one seat that is certified to 32 pounds rear-facing which is useful for kids who reach 20 pounds at earlier ages.

As with any safety seat, it is extremely important that the straps fit snugly over the child's shoulders. A good way to ensure that the straps are adjusted correctly is to buy a seat with an automatically adjusting harness. Like a car safety belt, these models automatically adjust to fit snugly on your child.

Convertible seats come in three basic types:

The *five-point harness* consists of two shoulder and two lap straps that converge at a buckle connected to a crotch strap. These straps are adjustable, allowing for growth and comfort.

The "T-shield" has a small pad joining the shoulder belts. With only one buckle to secure your child, many parents find this the simplest and easiest-to-use type of convertible seat, but it may not fit small infants properly.

The "tray shield," is another convenient model, since the safety harness is attached to the shield. As the shield comes down in front of the child, the harness comes over the child's shoulders. The shield is designed to provide some safety protection, and it is an important part of the restraint system. An additional feature is that the child has a place to rest his or her arms or toys but, like the T-shield, may not fit small infants.

Toddler-only seats and vests: These may take the place of convertible seats when a child is between 20 and 30 pounds or so. Weight and size limits vary greatly.

Booster seats: Booster seats are used when your child is too big for a convertible seat, but too small to use safety belts alone. They can be used for children over 30 pounds. There are three types:

The *shield-type booster seat* has a small, plastic shield with no straps and can be used in seating positions with lap belts only. Typically, the safety belt fastens in front of the shield, anchoring it to the car. The maximum child weight for most of these seats is 60 pounds.

Belt-positioning booster seats use the car's lap and shoulder belt to restrain the child. Most car lap/shoulder belts alone do not adequately fit children shorter than about 50 inches. This type of seat raises the child's relative to the belts and provides a better fit.

The *removable-shield booster seat* can be used either with a lap/shoulder belt, with the shield removed, or can also be used in cars with only a lap belt, with the shield on. This seat's ability to adapt to different cars and seating positions make it a good choice.

Built-in: Chrysler, Ford, GM and Volvo offer the option of a fold-out toddler seat on some of their models. These seats are only for children older than one and can come as either a five-point harness or a booster with 3-point belt. This built-in seat is an excellent feature because the seat is always in the car.

Name of Seat	Price	Harness Type/Comments
Infant Safety Seats		
Century 565	$40-60	3-pt.; tilt-indicator
Century 590	$50-70	3-pt.; tilt indicator; separate base stays in car; can be used in second car without base
Cosco Dream Ride	$59	3-pt.; to 17-20 lbs. (depending on mfg date); use flat as carbed side facing; use as car seat rear facing
Cosco TLC	$25	3-pt.
Evenflo Dyn-O-Mite	$25-35	3-pt.; shoulder belt wraps around front of seat
Evenflo Joy Ride	$30-45	3-pt.; shoulder belt wraps around front of seat
Evenflo Travel Tandem	$45-65	3-pt.; separate base stays in car; can be used in second car without base
Fisher-Price Infant	$50	T-shield; tilt indicator; padded shield; less suitable for very small infants
Gerry Guard with Glide	$49-59	3-pt.; use as glider in house; must be converted to in-car position
Gerry Secure Ride	$39-49	3-pt.; tilt-indicator
Infant Rider (Kolcraft)	$50-60	3-pt.; to 18 lbs. only
Kolcraft Rock 'N Ride	$29-50	3-pt.; up to 18 lbs; no harness height adjustment; separate base stays in car; can be used in second car without base
Convertible Safety Seats		
Babyhood Baby Sitter	$79	5-pt.
Century 1000 STE	$50-90	5-pt.; adjustable crotch strap positions
Century 2000 STE	$60-90	T-shield; adjustable crotch strap positions
Century 3000 STE	$70-100	Tray shield; adjustable crotch strap positions
Century 5000 STE	$70-100	Tray shield; adjustable crotch strap positions
Century Nexus	$89-110	5-pt.; tray shield; adjustable shield grows with child
Cosco 5-pt, Luxury 5-pt	$49-89	5-pt.
Cosco Comfort Ride	$68-89	Tray shield
Cosco Soft Shield	$69	T-shield
Cosco Touriva 5-pt.	$49-59	5-pt.; overhead shield/harness with 2-piece harness retainer
Cosco Touriva LXS	$99	T-shield; 2-piece harness retainer
Cosco Touriva DXO; Luxury Touriva LXO	$69-119	Tray-shield; 2-piece harness retainer; adjustable shield (Luxury model)
Evenflo Champion	$50-70	Tray shield; optional tether available
Evenflo Scout	$40-60	T-shield/5-pt.; optional tether available

Name of Seat	Price	Harness Type/Comments
Convertible Safety Seats cont'd.		
Evenflo Trooper	$50-70	Tray shield
Evenflo Ultra I, Premier	$65-110	Tray shield; adjustable shield
Evenflo Ultra V, Premier	$60-90	5-pt.
Fisher-Price Bolster	$97	Tray shield/Automatic harness adjustment
Fisher-Price Car Seat	$87	T-shield/Automatic; harness adjustment
Gerry Guard SecureLock	$69-89	Tray shield/Automatic/harness adjustment
Gerry Pro-Tech	$59-69	5-pt.; automatic harness adjustment
Kolcraft Auto-Mate	$50-70	5-pt.; requires 2-handed operation
Kolcraft Traveler 700	$50-100	Tray shield; requires 2-handed operation
Renolux GT 2000/3000/4000	$60-80	5-pt.
Renolux GT 5000/5500	$90-100	5-pt.
Turn-a-Tot		
Safeline Sit 'N Stroll	$139-159	5-pt.; converts to stroller
Toddler-Only Vests and Built-In Seats		
Chrysler Built-In Seat	$100-200	5-pt. (20-40 lbs.); built in option in Minivans; one converts; to belt-positioning booster (40 lbs.); in sedan, adjust to fit child (20-65 lbs.)
E-Z-On Vest	$62	4-pt. (25+ lbs.); tether strap must be installed in vehicle
Ford Built-In	$224	5-pt. (1 yr.-60 lbs.); in minivan
GM Built-In	$125-225	5-pt. (20-40 lbs., Booster 40-60 lbs.); manual harness adjustment
Little Cargo Travel Vest	$39-49	5-pt.; (25-40 lbs.); simplified strap-buckle system; auto lap belt attached through padded stress plate

Booster

Name of Seat	Price	Belt Position/Comments
Century Breverra	$60-80	Belt through base when used with shield; belt positioning booster seat with lap/shoulder belt
Cosco Explorer	$25-35	Wrap-around/2 seat heights
Fisher-Price T-Shield	$44	Wrap-around /Belt positioning booster for hip/shoulder belt (30-60 lbs.); shield with crotch post for lap belt (40-60 lbs.)
Gerry Double Guard	$45-55	Wrap-around/Belt through base with shield for lap belt; belt positioning booster for lap shoulder use; internal lap strap
Kolcraft Tot Rider II	$25-35	Wrap-around/Belt positioning booster seat with lap/shoulder belt; shield with crotch post for lap belt

Based on data collected by the American Academy of Pediatrics.

Tips for Using Your Child Safety Seat

The incorrect use of child safety seats has reached epidemic proportions. Problems fall into two categories: incorrect installation of the seat and incorrect use of the seat's straps to secure the child. Over 75 percent of seats in a national survey were incorrectly installed. In the vast majority of these, the vehicle's safety belt was improperly routed through the seat.

The incorrect use of a child safety seat can deny a child life-saving protection and may even contribute to further injury. In addition to following your seat's installation instructions, here are some important usage tips:

☑ The safest place for the seat is the center of the back seat.
☑ Regularly check the seat's safety harness and the car's seat belt for a tight, secure fit.
☑ Don't leave sharp or heavy objects or groceries loose in the car. Anything loose can be deadly in a crash.
☑ In the winter, dress your baby in a legged suit to allow proper attachment of the harness. If necessary, drape an extra blanket over the seat after your baby is buckled.
☑ Be sure all doors are locked.
☑ Do not give your child lollipops or ice cream on a stick while riding. A bump or swerve could jam the stick into his or her throat.

Buckled Up = Better Behavior: Medical researchers have concluded that belted children are better behaved. When not buckled up, children squirm, stand up, complain, fight, and pull at the steering wheel. When buckled into safety seats, however, they displayed 95 percent fewer inci-

dents of bad behavior.

Children behave better when buckled up because they feel secure. In addition, being in a seat can be more fun, because most safety seats are high enough to allow children to see out the window. Also, children are less likely to feel carsick and more likely to fall asleep in a car seat.

Make the car seat your child's own special place, so he or she will enjoy being in it. Pick out some special soft toys or books that can be used only in the car seat to make using the seat a positive experience.

Set a good example for your child by using your own safety belt every time you get in the car.

Buckled Up = Fewer Accidents: Hundreds of car crashes each year are caused when unrestrained children distract the driver. Think of how disconcerting it is when your child falls off the seat, hangs out the window, pulls your hair, or tries to open the door.

Safety Belts for Kids: Normally, children under 40 pounds should always be in a child safety

seat. If no seat is available, use a safety belt if the child is able to sit up unsupported.

When your child outgrows the safety seat, he or she should always use the vehicle's safety belt. The belt should be snug and as low on the hips as possible. If the shoulder belt crosses the face or neck, it is best to use a belt-positioning booster; otherwise, place the shoulder strap behind the child's back. Never use pillows or cushions to boost your child. In an accident, they may let the child slide under the lap belt or allow the child's head to strike the vehicle's interior.

Never put a belt around yourself with a child in your lap. In an accident or sudden stop, both your weight and the child's would be forced into the belt, with the child absorbing a much greater share of the crash force. Most likely, the pressure would push the belt deep into the child's body, causing severe injury or death.

Strapping two children into one belt also can be very dangerous—it makes proper fit impossible.

Register Your Child Seat

Last year, the U.S. Department of Transportation recalled millions of child safety seats for serious safety defects. Tragically, most parents never heard about these recalls and the majority of these problem seats are still being used. You can do two things to protect your children—first, call the Auto Safety Hotline at 800-424-9393 and find out if your seat has been recalled. If so, they will tell you how to contact the manufacturer for a resolution. Second, make sure you fill out the registration card that must come with all new seats. This will enable the company to contact you should there be a recall. If you currently own a seat, ask the Hotline for the address of your seat's manufacturer and send them your name, address and seat model, asking them to keep it on file for recall notices.

Child Restraint Laws

Every state now requires children to be in safety seats or buckled up when riding in vehicles. The following table provides an overview of the requirements and penalties in each state. You will note that most states use the child's age to define the law, although some states have height or weight requirements as well. Also, in most states, the laws are not limited to children riding with their parents, but require that any driver with child passengers makes sure those children in the vehicle are buckled up.

	Law Applies To:	Children Covered Through:	Max. Fine 1st Offense	Safety Belt OK:
Alabama	All drivers	5 yrs.	$10	4-5 yrs.
Alaska	All drivers	15 yrs.	$50	4-15 yrs.
Arizona	All drivers	4 yrs. or 40 lbs	$50	No
Arkansas	All drivers	4 yrs.	$25	3-4 yrs.
California	All drivers	3 yrs. or 40 lbs	$100	No
Colorado	Resident drivers	3 yrs. or 40 lbs	$50	No
Connecticut	All drivers	3 yrs. or 40 lbs.	$90	40 lbs.+
Delaware	All drivers	15 yrs..	$29	4-15 yrs.
Dist. of Columbia	All drivers	15 yrs.	$55	3-15 yrs.
Florida	All drivers	5 yrs.	$155	4-5 yrs.
Georgia	All drivers	4 yrs.	$25	3-4 yrs.
Hawaii	All drivers	3 yrs.	$100	3 yrs. only
Idaho	Resident Parent/Guardian	3 yrs. or 40 lbs	$52	No
Illinois	All drivers	5 yrs.	$25	4-5 yrs.
Indiana	All drivers	4 yrs.	$500	3-4 yrs.
Iowa	All drivers	5 yrs.	$10	3-5 yrs.
Kansas	All drivers	13 yrs.	$20	4-13 yrs.
Kentucky	All drivers	Under 40 inches	$50	No
Louisiana	Resident drivers	4 yrs.	$50	3-4 yrs. in rear
Maine	All drivers	18 yrs.	$55	4-18 yrs.
Maryland	All drivers	9 yrs.	$25	4-10 yrs., over 40 lbs.
Massachusetts	All drivers	11 yrs.	$25	All ages
Michigan	All drivers	3 yrs.	$10	1-3 yrs. in rear
Minnesota	All drivers	3 yrs.	$50	No
Mississippi	All drivers	3 yrs.	$25	No

Child Restraint Laws

	Law Applies To:	Children Covered Through:	Max. Fine 1st Offense	Safety Belt OK:
Missouri	All drivers	3 yrs.	$25	All ages in rear
Montana	Resident Parent/Guardian[1]	3 yrs. or 40 lbs	$25	2-3 yrs.
Nebraska	Resident drivers	4 yrs.	$25	4 yrs., over 40 lbs
Nevada	All drivers	4 yrs. or 40 lbs.	$100	No
New Hampshire	All drivers	11 yrs.	$43	4-11 yrs.
New Jersey	All drivers	4 yrs.	$25	11/2-4 yrs. in rear
New Mexico	All drivers	10 yrs.	$25	1-4 yrs. in rear[2]
New York	All drivers	15 yrs.[3]	$100	4-10 yrs. in rear
North Carolina	All drivers	5 yrs. (11 yrs.)[6]	$25	3-5 yrs.(4-11 yrs.)[6]
North Dakota	All drivers	10 yrs.	$20	3-10yrs.
Ohio	All drivers	3 yrs. or 40 lbs	$100	No
Oklahoma	Resident drivers	5 yrs.	$25	4-5 yrs.[5]
Oregon	All drivers	15 yrs.	$95	4-15 yrs.
Pennsylvania	All drivers	3 yrs.	$25	No
Rhode Island	All drivers	12 yrs.	$30	3-12 yrs.
South Carolina	All drivers	5 yrs.	$25	1-5 yrs. in rear[5]
South Dakota	Resident drivers	4 yrs.	$20	2-4 yrs.
Tennessee	All drivers	3 yrs.	$50	No
Texas	All drivers	3 yrs.	$50	2-3 yrs.
Utah	All drivers	7 yrs.	$20	2-7 yrs.
Vermont	All drivers	12 yrs.	$25	5-12 years
Virginia	Parent/Guardian	3 yrs.	$50	No
Washington	All drivers	9 yrs.	$47	3-9 yrs.
West Virginia	All drivers	8 yrs.	$20	3-8 yrs.
Wisconsin	All drivers	7 yrs.	$75	4-7 yrs.
Wyoming	Parent/Guardian[1]	2 yrs. or 40 inches	$25	1-2 yrs.

**If driver is non-parent, safety belt ok for one to three year olds.
[1]In own vehicle only.
[2]5-10 year olds in all seats
[3] 10 year olds in rear
[4] All children in rear seat
[5] 4-5 year olds in front seat
[6] Effective July 1, 1995

FUEL ECONOMY

Not only does fuel economy affect our wallets and our environment, but the events of the past few years clearly demonstrated its importance in our foreign relations. It's clear that today's vehicles need to be as fuel-efficient as they possibly can be, and there are several ways that consumers can help to achieve this goal. The first and most obvious step is to select a vehicle that gets high mileage, so we've included the Environmental Protection Agency's fuel economy ratings for all 1995 vehicles. This chapter discusses numerous factors that affect your vehicle's fuel efficiency, and cautions you against the many products falsely promising more fuel efficiency.

The EPA ratings provide an excellent means to incorporate fuel efficiency in selecting a new vehicle and it is important to compare these ratings. Even among vehicles of the same size, fuel efficiency varies greatly. One sport utility might get 29 miles per gallon (mpg) while another gets only 15 mpg. If you drive 15,000 miles a year and you pay $1.20 per gallon for fuel, the 29 mpg vehicle will save you $319 a year over the "gas guzzler."

Octane Ratings: Once you've purchased your vehicle you'll be faced with choosing the right gasoline. Oil companies spend millions of dollars trying to get you to buy so-called higher performance or high octane fuels. Because high oc-

tane fuel can add considerably to your gas bill, it is important that you know what you're buying.

The octane rating of a gasoline is *not* a measure of power or quality. It is simply a measure of the gas's resistance to engine knock, which is the pinging sound you hear when the air and fuel mixture in your engine ignites prematurely during acceleration.

The octane rating appears on a yellow label on the fuel pump. Octane ratings vary with different types of gas (premium or regular), in different parts of the country (higher altitudes require lower octane ratings), and even between brands (Texaco's gasolines may have a different rating than Exxon's).

Most vehicles are designed

to run on a posted octane rating of 87. This number is the optimal average derived from testing each gasoline under two different conditions: researched and measured.

Determining the Right Octane Rating for Your Vehicle: Using a lower-rated gasoline saves money. The following procedure can help you select the right octane level for your vehicle.

Step One: Have your engine tuned to exact factory specifications by a competent mechanic, and make sure it is in good working condition.

Step Two: When the gas in your tank is very low, fill it up with your usual gasoline. After driving 10 to 15 miles, come to a complete stop and then accelerate rapidly. (Make sure you do this in a safe place.) If your engine knocks during acceleration, switch to a higher octane rating. If there is no knocking sound, wait until your tank is very low and fill up with a lower rated gasoline. Repeat the test. When you determine the level of octane that causes your engine to knock during the test, use gasoline with the next highest rating.

Note: Your engine may knock when accelerating a heavily loaded vehicle uphill or when the humidity is low. This is normal and does not call for a higher-octane gasoline.

Factors Affecting Fuel Economy

Fuel economy is affected by a number of factors that you should consider before you buy.

Transmission: Manual transmissions are generally more fuel-efficient than automatic transmissions. In fact, a four-speed manual transmission can add up to 6.5 miles per gallon over a three-speed automatic. However, the incorrect use of a manual transmission wastes gas, so choose a transmission that matches your needs *and* experience. Many transmissions now feature an overdrive gear, which can improve a vehicle's fuel economy by as much as 9 percent for an automatic transmission and 3 percent for a manual transmission.

Axle Ratio: The relationship between the revolutions of the drive shaft (or transaxle) and the revolutions of the wheel is called the axle ratio. A low ratio, such as 2.69, means less engine wear and better fuel economy than a higher ratio, such as 3.47. Although a lower axle ratio will result in slower acceleration, it will pay off in increased fuel economy in highway driving. In general, a 10-percent decrease in the axle ratio can improve fuel economy by 4 percent.

Engine: The size of your vehicle's engine greatly affects your fuel economy. The smaller your engine, the better your fuel efficiency. A 10-percent increase in the size of an engine can increase fuel consumption by 6 percent.

Tires: Radial tires can improve mileage by 3 to 7 percent over bias-ply tires. They also last longer and usually improve the way your vehicle handles. For maximum fuel efficiency, tires should be inflated to the top of the pressure range stamped on the sidewall. Check tire pressure when the tires are cold—before you've driven a long distance.

Cruise Control: Cruise control can save fuel because driving at a constant speed uses less fuel than changing speeds frequently. Note: Cruise control has been associated with the problem of sudden, unintended acceleration.

Air Conditioning: Auto air conditioners add weight and require additional horsepower to operate. They can cost up to 3 miles per gallon in city driving. At highway speeds, however, an air conditioner has about the same effect on fuel economy as the air resistance created by opening the windows.

Trim Package: Upgrading a vehicle's trim, installing sound-proofing, and adding undercoating can increase the weight of a typical vehicle by 150 pounds. For each 10 percent increase in weight, fuel economy drops 4 percent.

Power Options: Power steering, brakes, seats, windows, and roofs reduce your mileage by adding weight. Power steering alone can cause a 1-percent drop in fuel economy.

Tune-Up: If you have a 2 to 3 mpg drop over several fill-ups that is not due to a change of driving pattern or vehicle load, first check tire pressure; then consider a tune-up.

Short Trips: Short trips can be expensive because they usually involve a "cold" vehicle. For the first mile or two, a cold vehicle gets 30- to 40-percent of the mileage it gets when fully warm.

Cargo Drag: If the cargo area of your pickup is empty, you'll get less air resistance, and thus better fuel economy, with the tailgate down.

Using Oxyfuels

Today's gasoline contains a bewildering array of ingredients touted as octane boosters or pollution fighters. Some urban areas with carbon monoxide pollution problems are requiring the use of oxygen-containing components (called oxyfuels) such as ethanol and MTBE (methyl-tertiary-butylether). The use of these compounds is controversial. Some auto companies recommend their use; others caution against them. Most companies approve the use of gasoline with up to 10-percent ethanol, and all approve the use of MTBE up to 15-percent. Many companies recommend against using gasoline with methanol, alleging that it will cause poorer driveability, deterioration of fuel system parts, and reduced fuel economy. These companies may not cover the cost of warranty repairs if these additives are used, so check your owner's manual and warranty to determine what additives are covered. Also check the gas pump, as many states now require the pump to display the percentage of methanol and ethanol in the gasoline.

Checking Your MPG

Once you make your purchase, you'll want to keep track of your fuel economy. Here's an easy way to do it:

Step One
The next time you fill your tank, note the mileage on the odometer.

Step Two
When your tank is nearly empty, fill it up completely, and write down the mileage and the number of gallons of gas that you buy.

Step Three
Subtract the first odometer reading from the second, and divide the result by the number of gallons of gas you bought. This gives your miles per gallon.

Current Mileage	25,601
Previous Mileage	-25,301
	300

300÷10 = **30 MPG**

You will get the best estimate of your vehicle's gas mileage by keeping a record over several tankfuls. There may be small differences each time because of changes in weather, where you drive, the truck's condition, and whether your driving is primarily city or highway.

Estimating Your Fuel Costs

TIP

The table below will help you estimate annual fuel costs. First find a vehicle's estimated mpg from the list at the end of this chapter. Next, find the mileage rating on the table below and read across until you reach the column of the amount you typically pay for gas. This price estimates what you can expect to pay for gas during an average year. Multiply this price by the number of years you expect to keep the vehicle. By calculating this number for the vehicles you are considering, you will see how differences in gas mileage will affect your pocketbook.

MPG	1.50	1.40	1.30	1.20	1.10	1.00
50	$450	$420	$390	$360	$330	$300
48	469	438	406	375	344	313
46	489	457	424	391	359	326
44	511	477	443	409	375	341
42	536	500	464	429	393	357
40	563	525	488	450	413	375
38	592	553	513	474	434	395
36	625	583	542	500	458	417
34	662	618	574	529	485	441
32	703	656	609	563	516	469
30	750	700	650	600	550	500
28	804	750	696	643	589	536
26	865	808	750	692	635	577
24	938	875	813	750	688	625
22	1023	955	886	818	750	682
20	1125	1050	975	900	825	750
18	1250	1167	1083	1000	917	833
16	1406	1313	1219	1125	1031	938
14	1607	1500	1393	1286	1179	1071
12	1875	1750	1625	1500	1375	1250
10	2250	2100	1950	1800	1650	1500
8	2813	2625	2438	2250	2063	1875

Price per Gallon

Products That Don't Work

Hundreds of products on the market claim to improve fuel economy. Not only are most of these products ineffective, some may even damage your engine.

Sometimes the name or promotional material associated with these products implies they were endorsed by the federal government. In fact, no government agency endorses *any* gas saving products. Many of the products, however, *have* been tested by the U.S. EPA.

Of the hundreds of so-called gas saving devices on the market, only five tested by the EPA have been shown to *slightly* improve your fuel economy without increasing harmful emissions. Even these, however, offer limited savings because of their cost. They are the Pass Master Vehicle Air Conditioner P.A.S.S. Kit, Idalert, Morse Constant Speed Accessory Drive, Autotherm, and Kamei Spoilers. We don't recommend these products because the increase in fuel economy is not worth the investment in the product.

Do NOT Buy These Devices

Purported gas-saving devices come in many forms. Listed below are the types of products on the market. Under each category are the names of devices actually reviewed or tested by the EPA for which there was *no evidence of any improvement in fuel economy.*

AIR BLEED DEVICES
ADAKS Vacuum Breaker
Air Bleed
Air-Jet Air Bleed
Aquablast Wyman Valve Air Bleed
Auto Miser
Ball-Matic Air Bleed
Berg Air Bleed
Brisko PCV
Cyclone - Z
Econo Needle Air Bleed
Econo-Jet Air Bleed Idle Screws
Fuel Max
Gas Saving Device
Grancor Air Computer
Hot Tip
Landrum Mini-Carb
Landrum Retrofit Air Bleed
Mini Turbocharger Air Bleed*
Monocar HC Control Air Bleed
Peterman Air Bleed*
Pollution Master Air Bleed
Ram-Jet
Turbo-Dyne G.R. Valve

DRIVING HABIT MODIFIERS
Fuel Conservation Device
Gastell

FUEL LINE DEVICES
Fuel Xpander

Gas Meiser I
Greer Fuel Preheater
Jacona Fuel System
Malpassi Filter King
Moleculetor
Optimizer
Petro-Mizer
Polarion-X
Russell Fuelmiser
Super-Mag Fuel Extender
Wickliff Polarizer

FUELS AND FUEL ADDITIVES
Bycosin*
EI-5 Fuel Additive*
Fuelon Power Gasoline Fuel Additive
Johnson Fuel Additive*
NRG #1 Fuel Additive
QEI 400 Fuel Additive*
Rolfite Upgrade Fuel Additive
Sta-Power Fuel Additive
Stargas Fuel Additive
SYNeRGy-1
Technol G Fuel Additive
ULX-15/ULX-15D
Vareb 10 Fuel Additive*
XRG #1 Fuel Additive

IGNITION DEVICES
Autosaver
Baur Condenser*
BIAP Electronic Ignition Unit

Fuel Economizer
Magna Flash Ignition Ctrl. Sys.
Paser Magnum/Paser 500/ Paser 500 HEI
Special Formula Ignition Advance Springs*

INTERNAL ENGINE MODIFICATIONS
ACDS Auto. Cyl. Deactivation Sys.
Dresser Economizer*
MSU Cylinder Deactivation*

LIQUID INJECTION
Goodman Engine Sys. Model 1800*
Waag-Injection System*

MIXTURE ENHANCERS
Basko Enginecoat
Dresser Economizer
Electro-Dyne Superchoke*
Energy Gas Saver*
Environmental Fuel Saver*
Filtron Urethane Foam Filter*
Gas Saving and Emission Control Improvement Device
Glynn-50*
Hydro-Catalyst Pre-Combustion System
Lamkin Fuel Metering Device

Petromizer System
Sav-A-Mile
Smith Power and Deceleration Governor Spritzer*
Turbo-Carb
Turbocarb

OILS AND OIL ADDITIVES
Analube Synthetic Lubricant
Tephguard*

VAPOR BLEED DEVICES
Atomized Vapor Injector
Econo-Mist Vacuum Vapor Injection System
Frantz Vapor Injection System*
Hydro-Vac
Mark II Vapor Injection System*
Platinum Gasaver
POWER FUeL
Scatpac Vacuum Vapor Induction System
Turbo Vapor Injection System*
V-70 Vapor Injector

MISCELLANEOUS
Brake-Ez*
Dynamix
Fuel Maximiser
Gyroscopic Wheel Cover
Kat's Engine Heater
Lee Exhaust and Fuel Gasification EGR*
Mesco Moisture Extraction Sys.
P.S.C.U. 01 Device
Treis Emulsifier

---

* For copies of reports on these products, write Test and Evaluation Branch, U.S. EPA, 2565 Plymouth Rd., Ann Arbor, MI 48105. For the other products, contact the National Technical Information Service, Springfield, VA 22161. (703-487-4650).

Fuel Economy Ratings

Every year the Department of Energy publishes the results of the Environmental Protection Agency's fuel economy tests in a comparative guide. In the past, millions of these booklets have been distributed to consumers who are eager to purchase fuel-efficient vehicles. Recently, however, the government has limited the availability of the guide. Because the success of the EPA program depends on consumers' ability to compare the fuel economy ratings easily, we have reprinted the EPA mileage figures for this year's vehicles.

The mileage estimates below and on the next few pages are the EPA city and highway figures.

A Note about the Ratings: When the EPA figures were first released, they were best used to compare fuel efficiency among vehicles—not to predict expected mileage. Because of changes in how the EPA presents the mileage ratings, these figures should better predict your expected mileage. When buying a vehicle, however, it's still best to use the EPA mileage estimates on a relative basis: if one vehicle is rated at 20 mpg and another at 25, the 25 mpg vehicle will nearly always perform better than the 20 mpg vehicle.

1995 Truck, Van and 4x4 Fuel Economy Winners and Losers

The Misers	MPG City /Highway	Annual Fuel Cost[1]
Suzuki Samurai 4WD (1.3L/4/M5)	28/29	$616
Suzuki Sidekick 2-dr. 2WD (1.6L/4/M5)	25/27	$664
Geo Tracker conv. 2WD (1.6L/4/M5)	25/27	$664
GMC Sonoma 2WD (2.2L/4/M5)*	23/29	$664
Chevy S10 2WD (2.2L/4/M5)*	23/29	$664
Dodge Dakota 2WD (2.5L/4/M5)	23/27	$690
Suzuki Sidekick 16-valve (1.6L/4/M5)	23/26	$719
Geo Tracker conv. 16-valve (1.6L/4/M5)	23/26	$719
Geo Tracker hard top 4WD (1.6L/4/M5)	23/26	$719

The Guzzlers		
Dodge Ram Wagon B3500 2WD (5.9L/8/L4)	11/15	$1327
Dodge Ram Pickup 2500 4WD (5.9L/8/L4)	11/15	$1327
Dodge Ram Pickup 1500 4WD (5.9L/8/L4)	11/15	$1327
GMC Rally Van G35 2WD (5.7L/8/L4)	12/14	$1327
Chevy Sportvan G35 2WD (5.7L/8/L4)	12/14	$1327
Dodge Ram Wagon B1500/2500 2WD (5.2L/8/A3)	12/14	$1437

Based on 1995 EPA figures. (Engine size/number of cylinders/transmission type)

[1] Based on driving 15,000 miles per year.

* These models have "shift indicator" lights.

The following pages contain the EPA mileage ratings and the average annual fuel cost for most of the vehicles sold in the United States. We have arranged the list in alphabetical order. After the vehicle name, we have listed the engine size in liters, the number of cylinders, and some other identifiers: A = automatic transmission; L = lockup transmission; M = manual transmission. The word "Guzz"after the engine description means that buyers will have to pay a "Gas Guzzler" tax.

The table includes the EPA city (first) and highway (second) fuel economy ratings. The city numbers will most closely resemble your expected mileage for everyday driving. The third column presents your average annual fuel cost. Reviewing this number will give you a better idea of how differences in fuel economy can affect your pocketbook. The amount is based on driving the vehicle 15,000 miles per year.

Vehicle (eng./trans.)	City	Hwy	Cost
Chevy Astro 2wd (cargo) (4.3L/6/L4)	17	22	$ 1065
Chevy Astro 2wd (Pass.) (4.3L/6/L4)	16	21	$ 1126
Chevy Astro AWD (cargo) (4.3L/6/L4)	16	21	$ 1126
Chevy Astro AWD (Pass.) (4.3L/6/L4)	15	19	$ 1266
Chevy Blazer 2wd (4.3L/6/M5)	17	23	$ 1065
Chevy Blazer 2wd (4.3L/6/L4)	17	22	$ 1065
Chevy Blazer 4wd (4.3L/6/M5)	17	22	$ 1065
Chevy Blazer 4wd (4.3L/6/L4)	16	21	$ 1126
Chevy G10/20 Sportvan 2wd (5.0L/8/L4)	14	16	$ 1151
Chevy G10/20 Sportvan 2wd (5.7L/8/L4)	12	15	$ 1327
Chevy G10/20 Sportvan 2wd (6.5L/8/L4)	16	20	$ 1102
Chevy G10/20 Sportvan 2wd (4.3L/6/L4)	14	16	$ 1151
Chevy G10/20 Van 2wd (4.3L/6/L4)	16	21	$ 959
Chevy G10/20 Van 2wd (5.0L/8/L4)	14	17	$ 1151
Chevy G10/20 Van 2wd (5.7L/8/L4)	12	15	$ 1327
Chevy G10/20 Van 2wd (6.5L/8/L4)	17	21	$ 1042
Chevy G30 Sportvan 2wd (5.7L/8/L4)	12	14	$ 1327
Chevy G30 Van 2wd (4.3L/6/L4)	14	16	$ 1151
Chevy G30 Van 2wd (5.7L/8/L4)	12	15	$ 1327
Chevy Lumina Minivan 2wd (3.1L/6/L3)	19	23	$ 862
Chevy Lumina Minivan 2wd (3.8L/6/L4)	17	25	$ 862
Chevy PU C1500 2wd (4.3L/6/L4)	16	21	$ 959
Chevy PU C1500 2wd (4.3L/6/M5C)	16	22	$ 959
Chevy PU C1500 2wd (4.3L/6/M5)	16	21	$ 959
Chevy PU C1500 2wd (5.0L/8/L4)	14	18	$ 1078
Chevy PU C1500 2wd (5.0L/8/M5)	14	19	$ 1078
Chevy PU C1500 2wd (5.7L/8/L4)	14	18	$ 1151
Chevy PU C1500 2wd (5.7L/8/M5C)	14	18	$ 1078
Chevy PU C1500 2wd (5.7L/8/M5)	13	18	$ 1151
Chevy PU C1500 2wd (6.5L/8/L4)	17	22	$ 986
Chevy PU C1500 2wd (6.5L/8/M5)	19	23	$ 938
Chevy PU C1500 2wd (6.5L/8/L4)	16	21	$ 1042
Chevy PU C2500 2wd (4.3L/6/M5C)	16	22	$ 959
Chevy PU C2500 2wd (4.3L/6/M5)	16	21	$ 959
Chevy PU C2500 2wd (4.3L/6/L4)	16	21	$ 959
Chevy PU C2500 2wd (5.0L/8/L4)	14	17	$ 1151
Chevy PU C2500 2wd (5.0L/8/M5)	14	19	$ 1078
Chevy PU C2500 2wd (5.7L/8/M5)	13	18	$ 1151
Chevy PU C2500 2wd (5.7L/8/L4)	12	15	$ 1232
Chevy PU C2500 2wd (5.7L/8/M5C)	14	18	$ 1151
Chevy PU C2500 2wd (6.5L/8/L4)	15	19	$ 1102
Chevy PU C2500 2wd (6.5L/8/L4)	17	22	$ 986
Chevy PU C2500 2wd (6.5L/8/M5C)	19	23	$ 938
Chevy PU K1500 4wd (4.3L/6/M5C)	15	18	$ 1078
Chevy PU K1500 4wd (4.3L/6/L4)	15	19	$ 1014
Chevy PU K1500 4wd (4.3L/6/M5)	14	19	$ 1078
Chevy PU K1500 4wd (5.0L/8/M5)	13	17	$ 1232
Chevy PU K1500 4wd (5.0L/8/L4)	13	16	$ 1232
Chevy PU K1500 4wd (5.7L/8/M5C)	13	17	$ 1151
Chevy PU K1500 4wd (5.7L/8/M5)	12	16	$ 1232

Vehicle (eng./trans.)	City	Hwy	Cost
Chevy PU K1500 4wd (5.7L/8/L4)	12	16	$ 1232
Chevy PU K1500 4wd (6.5L/8/L4)	16	20	$ 1102
Chevy PU K1500 4wd (6.5L/8/M5C)	16	19	$ 1102
Chevy PU K1500 4wd (6.5L/8/L4)	15	18	$ 1172
Chevy PU K2500 4wd (4.3L/6/M5C)	15	17	$ 1078
Chevy PU K2500 4wd (4.3L/6/L4)	14	18	$ 1078
Chevy PU K2500 4wd (4.3L/6/M5)	14	18	$ 1151
Chevy PU K2500 4wd (5.0L/8/L4)	13	16	$ 1232
Chevy PU K2500 4wd (5.0L/8/M5)	13	16	$ 1232
Chevy PU K2500 4wd (5.7L/8/L4)	12	16	$ 1232
Chevy PU K2500 4wd (5.7L/8/M5)	12	16	$ 1232
Chevy PU K2500 4wd (5.7L/8/M5C)	13	16	$ 1232
Chevy PU K2500 4wd (6.5L/8/M5C)	16	19	$ 1102
Chevy PU K2500 4wd (6.5L/8/L4)	16	20	$ 1102
Chevy PU K2500 4wd (6.5L/8/L4)	14	18	$ 1172
Chevy S10 PU 2wd (2.2L/4/M5)	23	29	$ 664
Chevy S10 PU 2wd (2.2L/4/L4)	20	26	$ 785
Chevy S10 PU 2wd (4.3L/6/L4)	18	24	$ 862
Chevy S10 PU 2wd (4.3L/6/L4)	17	23	$ 1065
Chevy S10 PU 2wd (4.3L/6/M5)	17	23	$ 862
Chevy S10 PU 2wd (4.3L/6/M5)	18	25	$ 964
Chevy S10 PU 4wd (4.3L/6/L4)	16	22	$ 1126
Chevy S10 PU 4wd (4.3L/6/M5)	16	21	$ 959
Chevy S10 PU 4wd (4.3L/6/L4)	17	21	$ 959
Chevy S10 PU 4wd (4.3L/6/M5)	17	22	$ 1065
Chevy Suburban C1500 2wd (5.7L/8/L4)	13	17	$ 1151
Chevy Suburban K1500 4wd (5.7L/8/L4)	12	15	$ 1327
Chevy Tahoe K1500 4wd (5.7L/8/L4)	12	15	$ 1327
Chevy Tahoe K1500 4wd (5.7L/8/M5)	12	16	$ 1232
Chevy Tahoe K1500 4wd (6.5L/8/L4)	14	17	$ 1172
Chrysler T&C 2wd (3.8L/6/L4)	17	23	$ 907
Chrysler T&C 4wd (3.8L/6/L4)	16	22	$ 959
Dodge Caravan 2wd (2.5L/4/L3)	21	25	$ 785
Dodge Caravan 2wd (2.5L/4/M5)	22	28	$ 719
Dodge Caravan 2wd (3.0L/6/L3)	20	24	$ 785
Dodge Caravan 2wd (3.0L/6/L4)	19	25	$ 821
Dodge Caravan 2wd (3.3L/6/L4)	17	22	$ 907
Dodge Caravan 2wd (3.3L/6/L4)	18	23	$ 900
Dodge Caravan 2wd (3.8L/6/L4)	17	23	$ 907
Dodge Caravan 4wd (3.3L/6/L4)	17	21	$ 959
Dodge Caravan 4wd (3.8L/6/L4)	16	22	$ 959
Dodge Caravan C/v 2wd (2.5L/4/L3)	21	25	$ 785
Dodge Caravan C/v 2wd (3.0L/6/L3)	20	24	$ 785
Dodge Caravan C/v 2wd (3.3L/6/L4)	17	22	$ 907
Dodge Caravan C/v 2wd (3.3L/6/L4)	18	23	$ 900
Dodge Dak. Cab Chas. 2wd (3.9L/6/L4)	15	19	$ 1078
Dodge Dak. Cab Chas. 2wd (5.2L/8/L4)	13	17	$ 1151
Dodge Dak. PU 2wd (2.5L/4/M5)	23	27	$ 690
Dodge Dak. PU 2wd (3.9L/6/L4)	16	20	$ 959
Dodge Dak. PU 2wd (3.9L/6/M5)	17	23	$ 907

Vehicle (eng./trans.)	City	Hwy	Cost
Dodge Dak. PU 2wd (5.2L/8/M5)	15	20	$ 1078
Dodge Dak. PU 2wd (5.2L/8/L4)	14	18	$ 1078
Dodge Dak. PU 4wd (3.9L/6/M5)	15	19	$ 1014
Dodge Dak. PU 4wd (3.9L/6/L4)	15	19	$ 1078
Dodge Dak. PU 4wd (5.2L/8/M5)	13	17	$ 1232
Dodge Dak. PU 4wd (5.2L/8/L4)	14	17	$ 1151
Dodge Ram B1500/B2500 Van (5.2L/8/L4)	13	17	$ 1151
Dodge Ram B1500/B2500 Van (5.2L/8/A3)	13	14	$ 1327
Dodge Ram B1500/B2500 Van (5.9L/8/L4)	12	16	$ 1232
Dodge Ram B1500/B2500 Van (3.9L/6/L3)	15	17	$ 1078
Dodge Ram B1500/B2500 Wgn. (3.9L/6/L3)	15	17	$ 1078
Dodge Ram B1500/B2500 Wgn. (5.2L/8/A3)	12	14	$ 1327
Dodge Ram B1500/B2500 Wgn. (5.2L/8/L4)	13	17	$ 1151
Dodge Ram B1500/B2500 Wgn. (5.9L/8/L4)	12	16	$ 1327
Dodge Ram B3500 Van (5.2L/8/L4)	13	17	$ 1151
Dodge Ram B3500 Van (5.9L/8/L4)	12	16	$ 1327
Dodge Ram B3500 Wgn. (5.2L/8/L4)	12	16	$ 1327
Dodge Ram B3500 Wgn. (5.9L/8/L4)	11	15	$ 1437
Dodge Ram PU 1500 2wd (3.9L/6/M5)	16	21	$ 959
Dodge Ram PU 1500 2wd (5.2L/8/L4)	13	17	$ 1151
Dodge Ram PU 1500 2wd (5.2L/8/M5)	14	19	$ 1078
Dodge Ram PU 1500 2wd (3.9L/6/L4)	15	19	$ 1078
Dodge Ram PU 1500 2wd (5.9L/8/L4)	12	16	$ 1232
Dodge Ram PU 1500 4wd (5.2L/8/L4)	12	16	$ 1327
Dodge Ram PU 1500 4wd (5.2L/8/M5)	13	17	$ 1232
Dodge Ram PU 1500 4wd (5.9L/8/L4)	11	15	$ 1327
Dodge Ram PU 2500 2wd (5.2L/8/L4)	13	17	$ 1151
Dodge Ram PU 2500 2wd (5.2L/8/M5C)	13	16	$ 1232
Dodge Ram PU 2500 2wd (5.9L/8/L4)	12	16	$ 1327
Dodge Ram PU 2500 2wd (5.9L/8/M5C)	13	16	$ 1232
Dodge Ram PU 2500 4wd (5.2L/8/M5C)	13	15	$ 1232
Dodge Ram PU 2500 4wd (5.2L/8/L4)	12	16	$ 1327
Dodge Ram PU 2500 4wd (5.9L/8/M5C)	12	15	$ 1327
Dodge Ram PU 2500 4wd (5.9L/8/L4)	11	15	$ 1327
Ford Aerostar wgn. Rwd (3.0L/6/L4)	17	23	$ 907
Ford Aerostar wgn. Rwd (4.0L/6/L4)	16	22	$ 907
Ford Bronco 4wd (5.0L/8/L4)	14	19	$ 1078
Ford Bronco 4wd (5.0L/8/M5)	14	17	$ 1151
Ford Bronco 4wd (5.8L/8/L4)	13	17	$ 1232
Ford E150 Club wgn. (4.9L/6/L4)	13	17	$ 1232
Ford E150 Club wgn. (5.0L/8/L4)	13	18	$ 1151
Ford E150 Club wgn. (5.8L/8/L4)	12	16	$ 1232
Ford E150 Econoline 2wd (4.9L/6/A3)	14	16	$ 1151
Ford E150 Econoline 2wd (4.9L/6/L4)	14	18	$ 1151
Ford E150 Econoline 2wd (5.0L/8/L4)	13	18	$ 1151
Ford E150 Econoline 2wd (5.8L/8/L4)	13	17	$ 1232
Ford E250 Econoline 2wd (4.9L/6/L4)	13	17	$ 1232
Ford E250 Econoline 2wd (4.9L/6/A3)	13	14	$ 1327
Ford E250 Econoline 2wd (5.8L/8/L4)	12	16	$ 1327
Ford F150 Lightning PU 2wd (5.8L/8/L4)	12	16	$ 1327
Ford F150 PU 2wd (4.9L/6/M5)	15	20	$ 1014
Ford F150 PU 2wd (4.9L/6/L4)	15	20	$ 1014
Ford F150 PU 2wd (5.0L/8/L4)	15	20	$ 1078
Ford F150 PU 2wd (5.0L/8/M5)	14	18	$ 1078
Ford F150 PU 2wd (5.8L/8/L4)	13	17	$ 1151
Ford F150 PU 4wd (4.9L/6/M5)	15	18	$ 1078
Ford F150 PU 4wd (4.9L/6/L4)	15	19	$ 1078
Ford F150 PU 4wd (5.0L/8/M5)	14	17	$ 1151
Ford F150 PU 4wd (5.0L/8/L4)	14	19	$ 1078
Ford F150 PU 4wd (5.8L/8/L4)	13	17	$ 1232
Ford F250 PU 2wd (4.9L/6/M5)	14	18	$ 1078
Ford F250 PU 2wd (4.9L/6/L4)	14	18	$ 1151
Ford F250 PU 2wd (5.0L/8/M5)	14	18	$ 1151
Ford F250 PU 2wd (5.0L/8/L4)	13	18	$ 1151
Ford F250 PU 2wd (5.8L/8/L4)	13	17	$ 1232
Ford Windstar Fwd Van (3.8L/6/L4)	17	24	$ 862
Ford Windstar Fwd wgn. (3.8L/6/L4)	17	24	$ 862
Geo Tracker conv. 4x2 (1.6L/4/L3)	23	24	$ 750
Geo Tracker conv. 4x2 (1.6L/4/L3)	23	24	$ 750
Geo Tracker conv. 4x2 (1.6L/4/M5)	25	27	$ 664
Geo Tracker conv. 4x2 (1.6L/4/M5)	23	26	$ 719
Geo Tracker conv. 4x4 (1.6L/4/L3)	23	24	$ 750
Geo Tracker conv. 4x4 (1.6L/4/M5)	23	26	$ 719
Geo Tracker Hard Top 4x4 (1.6L/4/L3)	23	24	$ 750
Geo Tracker Hard Top 4x4 (1.6L/4/M5)	23	26	$ 719
GMC G15/25 Rally 2wd (4.3L/6/L4)	14	16	$ 1151
GMC G15/25 Rally 2wd (6.5L/8/L4)	16	20	$ 1102
GMC G15/25 Rally 2wd (5.7L/8/L4)	12	15	$ 1327
GMC G15/25 Rally 2wd (5.0L/8/L4)	14	16	$ 1151
GMC G15/25 Vandura 2wd (5.0L/8/L4)	14	17	$ 1151
GMC G15/25 Vandura 2wd (5.7L/8/L4)	12	15	$ 1327
GMC G15/25 Vandura 2wd (6.5L/8/L4)	17	21	$ 1042
GMC G15/25 Vandura 2wd (4.3L/6/L4)	16	21	$ 959
GMC G35 Rally 2wd (4.7L/8/L4)	12	14	$ 1437
GMC G35 Vandura 2wd (4.3L/6/L4)	14	16	$ 1151
GMC G35 Vandura 2wd (5.7L/8/L4)	12	15	$ 1327
GMC Jimmy 2wd (4.3L/6/L4)	17	22	$ 1065
GMC Jimmy 2wd (4.3L/6/M5)	17	23	$ 1065
GMC Jimmy 4wd (4.3L/6/M5)	17	22	$ 1065
GMC Jimmy 4wd (4.3L/6/L4)	16	21	$ 1126
GMC Safari 2wd (cargo) (4.3L/6/L4)	17	22	$ 1065
GMC Safari 2wd (pass.) (4.3L/6/L4)	16	21	$ 1126
GMC Safari AWD (cargo) (4.3L/6/L4)	16	21	$ 1126
GMC Safari AWD (pass.) (4.3L/6/L4)	15	19	$ 1266
GMC Sierra C1500 2wd (4.3L/6/M5C)	16	22	$ 959
GMC Sierra C1500 2wd (4.3L/6/M5)	16	21	$ 959
GMC Sierra C1500 2wd (4.3L/6/L4)	16	21	$ 959
GMC Sierra C1500 2wd (5.0L/8/L4)	14	18	$ 1078
GMC Sierra C1500 2wd (5.0L/8/M5)	14	19	$ 1078
GMC Sierra C1500 2wd (5.7L/8/M5C)	14	18	$ 1078
GMC Sierra C1500 2wd (5.7L/8/M5)	13	18	$ 1151
GMC Sierra C1500 2wd (5.7L/8/L4)	14	18	$ 1151
GMC Sierra C1500 2wd (6.5L/8/L4)	17	22	$ 986
GMC Sierra C1500 2wd (6.5L/8/M5C)	19	23	$ 938
GMC Sierra C1500 2wd (6.5L/8/L4)	16	21	$ 1042
GMC Sierra C2500 2wd (4.3L/6/L4)	16	21	$ 959
GMC Sierra C2500 2wd (4.3L/6/M5)	16	21	$ 959
GMC Sierra C2500 2wd (4.3L/6/M5C)	16	22	$ 959
GMC Sierra C2500 2wd (5.0L/8/M5)	14	19	$ 1078
GMC Sierra C2500 2wd (5.0L/8/L4)	14	17	$ 1151
GMC Sierra C2500 2wd (5.7L/8/M5C)	14	18	$ 1151
GMC Sierra C2500 2wd (5.7L/8/L4)	12	15	$ 1232
GMC Sierra C2500 2wd (5.7L/8/M5)	13	18	$ 1151
GMC Sierra C2500 2wd (6.5L/8/L4)	17	22	$ 986
GMC Sierra C2500 2wd (6.5L/8/L4)	16	19	$ 1102
GMC Sierra C2500 2wd (6.5L/8/M5C)	19	23	$ 938
GMC Sierra K1500 4wd (4.3L/6/M5C)	15	18	$ 1078
GMC Sierra K1500 4wd (4.3L/6/M5)	14	19	$ 1078
GMC Sierra K1500 4wd (4.3L/6/L4)	15	19	$ 1014
GMC Sierra K1500 4wd (5.0L/8/M5)	13	17	$ 1232
GMC Sierra K1500 4wd (5.0L/8/L4)	13	16	$ 1232
GMC Sierra K1500 4wd (5.7L/8/M5C)	13	17	$ 1151
GMC Sierra K1500 4wd (5.7L/8/M5)	12	16	$ 1232
GMC Sierra K1500 4wd (5.7L/8/L4)	12	16	$ 1232
GMC Sierra K1500 4wd (6.5L/8/L4)	15	18	$ 1172
GMC Sierra K1500 4wd (6.5L/8/L4)	16	20	$ 1102
GMC Sierra K1500 4wd (6.5L/8/M5C)	16	19	$ 1102
GMC Sierra K2500 4wd (4.3L/6/L4)	15	18	$ 1078
GMC Sierra K2500 4wd (4.3L/6/M5)	14	18	$ 1151
GMC Sierra K2500 4wd (4.3L/6/M5C)	15	17	$ 1078
GMC Sierra K2500 4wd (5.0L/8/M5)	13	16	$ 1232
GMC Sierra K2500 4wd (5.0L/8/L4)	13	16	$ 1232

Vehicle (eng./trans.)	City	Hwy	Cost	Vehicle (eng./trans.)	City	Hwy	Cost
GMC Sierra K2500 4wd (5.7L/8/L4)	12	15	$ 1327	Mits. Montero (3.0L/6/L4)	15	18	$ 1078
GMC Sierra K2500 4wd (5.7L/8/M5C)	13	16	$ 1232	Mits. Montero (3.0L/6/L4)	15	18	$ 1078
GMC Sierra K2500 4wd (5.7L/8/M5)	12	16	$ 1232	Mits. Montero (3.0L/6/M5)	16	18	$ 1014
GMC Sierra K2500 4wd (6.5L/8/M5C)	16	19	$ 1102	Mits. Montero (3.0L/6/M5)	15	18	$ 1014
GMC Sierra K2500 4wd (6.5L/8/L4)	14	18	$ 1172	Mits. Montero (3.5L/6/L4)	14	17	$ 1351
GMC Sierra K2500 4wd (6.5L/8/L4)	16	20	$ 1102	Nissan Pathfinder 4x2 (3.0L/6/L4)	15	19	$ 1014
GMC Sonoma 2wd (2.2L/4/L4)	20	26	$ 785	Nissan Pathfinder 4x2 (3.0L/6/M5)	15	18	$ 1078
GMC Sonoma 2wd (2.2L/4/M5)	23	29	$ 664	Nissan Pathfinder 4x4 (3.0L/6/L4)	15	18	$ 1078
GMC Sonoma 2wd (4.3L/6/M5)	18	25	$ 964	Nissan Pathfinder 4x4 (3.0L/6/M5)	15	18	$ 1078
GMC Sonoma 2wd (4.3L/6/M5)	17	23	$ 862	Nissan Pathfinder Cargo (3.0L/6/M5)	15	18	$ 1078
GMC Sonoma 2wd (4.3L/6/L4)	17	23	$ 1065	Nissan PU 4x2 (2.4L/4/L4)	21	25	$ 750
GMC Sonoma 2wd (4.3L/6/L4)	18	24	$ 862	Nissan PU 4x2 (2.4L/4/M5)	22	26	$ 719
GMC Sonoma 4wd (4.3L/6/M5)	17	22	$ 1065	Nissan PU 4x2 (3.0L/6/M5)	18	22	$ 862
GMC Sonoma 4wd (4.3L/6/M5)	16	21	$ 959	Nissan PU 4x2 (3.0L/6/L4)	17	22	$ 907
GMC Sonoma 4wd (4.3L/6/L4)	17	21	$ 959	Nissan PU 4x4 (2.4L/4/M5)	18	20	$ 907
GMC Sonoma 4wd (4.3L/6/L4)	16	22	$ 1126	Nissan PU 4x4 (3.0L/6/M5)	15	18	$ 1078
GMC Suburban C1500 2wd (5.7L/8/L4)	13	17	$ 1151	Nissan PU 4x4 (3.0L/6/L4)	15	18	$ 1078
GMC Suburban K1500 4wd (5.7L/8/L4)	12	15	$ 1327	Nissan Quest (3.0L/6/L4)	17	23	$ 907
GMC Yukon K1500 4wd (5.7L/8/L4)	12	15	$ 1327	Olds Silhouette 4x2 (3.1L/6/L3)	19	23	$ 862
GMC Yukon K1500 4wd (5.7L/8/M5)	12	16	$ 1232	Olds Silhouette 4x2 (3.8L/6/L4)	17	25	$ 862
GMC Yukon K1500 4wd (6.5L/8/L4)	14	17	$ 1172	Plymouth Voyager 4x2 (2.5L/4/M5)	22	28	$ 719
Honda Passport 4x2 (2.6L/4/M5)	18	22	$ 907	Plymouth Voyager 4x2 (2.5L/4/L3)	21	25	$ 785
Honda Passport 4x2 (3.2L/6/L4)	16	19	$ 1014	Plymouth Voyager 4x2 (3.0L/6/L4)	19	25	$ 821
Honda Passport 4x2 (3.2L/6/M5)	16	19	$ 1014	Plymouth Voyager 4x2 (3.0L/6/L3)	20	24	$ 785
Honda Passport 4x4 (3.2L/6/M5)	16	19	$ 1014	Plymouth Voyager 4x2 (3.3L/6/L4)	17	22	$ 907
Honda Passport 4x4 (3.2L/6/L4)	15	18	$ 1014	Plymouth Voyager 4x2 (3.3L/6/L4)	18	23	$ 900
Isuzu PU 4x2 (2.3L/4/M5)	22	25	$ 750	Plymouth Voyager 4x2 (3.8L/6/L4)	17	23	$ 907
Isuzu PU 4x4 (2.6L/4/M5)	17	20	$ 959	Plymouth Voyager 4x4 (3.3L/6/L4)	17	21	$ 959
Isuzu Rodeo 4x2 (2.6L/4/M5)	18	22	$ 907	Plymouth Voyager 4x4 (3.8L/6/L4)	16	22	$ 959
Isuzu Rodeo 4x2 (3.2L/6/M5)	16	19	$ 1014	Pontiac Trans Sport 2wd (3.1L/6/L3)	19	23	$ 862
Isuzu Rodeo 4x2 (3.2L/6/L4)	16	19	$ 1014	Pontiac Trans Sport 2wd (3.8L/6/L4)	17	25	$ 862
Isuzu Rodeo 4x4 (3.2L/6/L4)	15	18	$ 1014	Suzuki Samurai (1.3L/4/M5)	28	29	$ 616
Isuzu Rodeo 4x4 (3.2L/6/M5)	16	19	$ 1014	Suzuki Sidekick 2dr 2wd (1.6L/4/L3)	23	24	$ 750
Isuzu Trooper (3.2L/6/L4)	14	17	$ 1151	Suzuki Sidekick 2dr 2wd (1.6L/4/M5)	23	26	$ 719
Isuzu Trooper (3.2L/6/L4)	15	18	$ 1078	Suzuki Sidekick 2dr 2wd (1.6L/4/M5)	25	27	$ 664
Isuzu Trooper (3.2L/6/M5)	16	18	$ 1014	Suzuki Sidekick 2dr 2wd (1.6L/4/L3)	23	24	$ 750
Isuzu Trooper (3.2L/6/M5)	14	17	$ 1151	Suzuki Sidekick 2dr 4wd (1.6L/4/M5)	23	26	$ 719
Jeep Cherokee 4x2 (2.5L/4/M5)	20	23	$ 821	Suzuki Sidekick 2dr 4wd (1.6L/4/L3)	23	24	$ 750
Jeep Cherokee 4x2 (2.5L/4/L3)	17	19	$ 1014	Suzuki Sidekick 4dr 2wd (1.6L/4/L4)	22	26	$ 719
Jeep Cherokee 4x2 (4.0L/6/M5)	17	21	$ 959	Suzuki Sidekick 4dr 2wd (1.6L/4/M5)	23	26	$ 719
Jeep Cherokee 4x2 (4.0L/6/L4)	15	20	$ 1014	Suzuki Sidekick 4dr 4wd (1.6L/4/M5)	23	26	$ 719
Jeep Cherokee 4x4 (2.5L/4/M5)	19	22	$ 862	Suzuki Sidekick 4dr 4wd (1.6L/4/L4)	22	26	$ 719
Jeep Cherokee 4x4 (2.5L/4/L3)	17	19	$ 1014	Toyota 4Runner 4x2 (2.4L/4/M5)	19	21	$ 862
Jeep Cherokee 4x4 (4.0L/6/M5)	17	21	$ 959	Toyota 4Runner 4x2 (3.0L/6/L4)	17	21	$ 959
Jeep Cherokee 4x4 (4.0L/6/L4)	14	19	$ 1078	Toyota 4Runner 4x4 (3.0L/6/M5)	15	18	$ 1078
Jeep Gr. Cherokee 4x2 (4.0L/6/L4)	15	21	$ 1014	Toyota 4Runner 4x4 (3.0L/6/L4)	14	16	$ 1151
Jeep Gr. Cherokee 4x4 (4.0L/6/M5)	15	20	$ 1014	Toyota Previa (2.4L/4/L4)	17	22	$ 907
Jeep Gr. Cherokee 4x4 (4.0L/6/L4)	15	20	$ 1014	Toyota Previa (2.4L/4/L4)	18	22	$ 907
Jeep Gr. Cherokee 4x4 (5.2L/8/L4)	14	18	$ 1151	Toyota Previa All-Trac (2.4L/4/L4)	17	21	$ 907
Jeep Wrangler 4x4 (2.5L/4/M5)	19	20	$ 907	Toyota Previa All-Trac (2.4L/4/L4)	17	21	$ 907
Jeep Wrangler 4x4 (2.5L/4/L3)	17	18	$ 1014	Toyota PU 4x2 (2.4L/4/A4)	22	25	$ 750
Jeep Wrangler 4x4 (4.0L/6/M5)	15	18	$ 1078	Toyota PU 4x2 (2.4L/4/M5)	22	27	$ 719
Jeep Wrangler 4x4 (4.0L/6/L3)	15	17	$ 1151	Toyota PU 4x2 (3.0L/6/L4)	18	22	$ 862
Kia Sportage 4x2 (2.0L/4/M5)	19	23	$ 821	Toyota PU 4x2 (3.0L/6/M5)	18	23	$ 862
Kia Sportage 4x4 (2.0L/4/M5)	20	24	$ 784	Toyota PU 4x4 (2.4L/4/L4)	18	19	$ 959
Land Rover Defender 90 (3.9L/8/M5)	12	16	$ 1446	Toyota PU 4x4 (2.4L/4/M5)	19	22	$ 862
Land Rover Discovery (3.9L/8/L4)	13	16	$ 1446	Toyota PU 4x4 (3.0L/6/L4)	14	17	$ 1151
Land Rover Range Rover (4.3L/8/L4)	12	15	$ 1557	Toyota PU 4x4 (3.0L/6/M5)	15	18	$ 1078
Mazda MPV 4x2 (2.6L/4/L4)	18	24	$ 821	Toyota T100 4x2 (2.7L/4/L4)	20	23	$ 785
Mazda MPV 4x2 (3.0L/6/L4)	16	22	$ 959	Toyota T100 4x2 (2.7L/4/M5)	21	25	$ 785
Mazda MPV 4x4 (3.0L/6/L4)	15	19	$ 1014	Toyota T100 4x2 (3.4L/6/L4)	17	20	$ 907
Mercury Villager Van (3.0L/6/L4)	17	23	$ 862	Toyota T100 4x2 (3.4L/6/M5)	17	20	$ 959
Mercury Villager wgn. (3.0L/6/L4)	17	23	$ 862	Toyota T100 4x4 (3.4L/6/L4)	16	18	$ 1014
Mits. Mighty Max 4x2 (2.4L/4/L4)	19	23	$ 821	Toyota T100 4x4 (3.4L/6/M5)	17	19	$ 959
Mits. Mighty Max 4x2 (2.4L/4/M5)	21	25	$ 785				
Mits. Mighty Max 4x4 (3.0L/6/M5)	17	22	$ 907				

MAINTENANCE

After you buy a vehicle, maintenance costs will be a significant portion of your operating expenses. This chapter allows you to consider and compare some of these costs *before* deciding which vehicle to purchase. These costs include preventive maintenance servicing—such as changing the oil and filters—as well as the cost of repairs after your warranty expires. On the following pages, we compared the costs of preventive maintenance and of nine likely repairs for the 1995 models. Since the cost of a repair also varies, depending on the shop and the mechanic, this chapter includes tips for finding a good shop and for communicating effectively with a mechanic.

Preventive maintenance is the periodic servicing, specified by the manufacturer, that keeps your vehicle running properly. For example, regularly changing the oil and oil filter. Every owner's manual specifies a schedule of recommended servicing for at least the first 50,000 miles, and the tables on the following pages estimate the cost of following this preventive maintenance schedule.

If, for some reason, you do not have an owner's manual with the preventive maintenance schedule, contact the manufacturer to obtain one.

Note: Some dealers and repair shops create their own maintenance schedules, which call for more frequent (and thus more expensive) servicing than the manufacturer's recommendations. If the servicing recommended by your dealer or repair shop doesn't match what the car maker recommends, make sure you understand and agree to the extra items.

The tables also list the costs for nine repairs that typically occur during the first 100,000 miles. There is no precise way to predict exactly when a repair will be needed. But if you keep a vehicle for 75,000 to 100,000 miles, it is likely that you will experience most of these repairs at least once. The last column provides a relative indication of how expensive these nine repairs are for many vehicles. Repair cost is rated as *Very Good* if the total for nine repairs is in the bottom fifth of all the vehicles rated, and *Very Poor* if the total is in the top fifth.

Most repair shops use "flat-rate manuals" to estimate repair costs. These manuals list the approximate time required for repairing many items. Each automobile manufacturer publishes its own manual, and there are several independent manuals as well. For many repairs, the time varies from one manual to another, and some repair shops even use different manuals for different repairs. To determine a repair bill, a shop multiplies the time listed in its manual by its hourly labor rate and then adds the cost of parts.

Our cost estimates are based on flat-rate manual repair times multiplied by a nationwide average labor rate of $45 per hour. All estimates also include the cost of replaced parts and related adjustments.

Prices on the following tables may not predict the exact costs of these repairs. For example, the labor rate for your area may be more or less than the national average. However, the prices will provide you with a relative comparison of maintenance costs for various automobiles.

	PM Costs to 50,000 Miles	Water Pump	Alternator	Front Brake Pads	Starter	Fuel Injection	Fuel Pump	Struts	Lower Ball Joints	CVJ or Univ. Joint	Relative Maint. Cost
Minivan											
Chevrolet Astro	640	164	218	108	282	288	130	130	191	95	Vry. Gd.
Chevy Lumina Minivan	475	130	211	109	295	156	149	264	263	235	Good
Chry. Town and Country	590	108	296	117	189	89	242	223	128	291	Vry. Gd.
Dodge Caravan	590	108	296	117	189	89	242	223	128	291	Vry. Gd.
Ford Aerostar	570	163	411	120	245	143	225	147	340	350	Ave.
Ford Windstar	570	175	403	125	297	148	227	135	360	350	Ave.
GMC Safari	640	164	218	108	282	288	130	130	191	95	Vry. Gd.
Honda Odyssey	885	195	363	325	112	125	477	290	233	310	Poor
Mazda MPV	750	114	247	104	223	264	350	231	535	254	Ave.
Mercury Villager	595	216	310	140	274	226	208	247	176	254	Good
Nissan Quest	595	216	310	140	274	226	208	247	176	254	Good
Oldsmobile Silhouette	475	130	211	109	295	156	149	264	263	235	Good
Plymouth Voyager	590	108	296	117	189	89	242	223	128	291	Vry. Gd.
Pontiac Trans Sport	475	130	211	109	295	156	149	264	263	235	Good
Toyota Previa	765	133	487	99	406	203	353	416	185	106	Poor
Volkswagen Eurovan	380	251	582	142	506	221	305	291	148	362	Vry. Pr.
Full Size Van											
Chevy Van/Sport Van	725	178	222	100	300	195	126	148	184	93	Vry. Gd.
Dodge Ram Van/Wagon	810	159	330	117	320	115	377	116	295	75	Good
Ford Econoline/Club Wgn	630	195	320	101	253	187	247	128	271	46	Vry. Gd.
GMC Vandura/Rally	725	178	222	100	300	195	126	148	184	93	Vry. Gd.
Small Sport Utility											
Geo Tracker	620	249	402	119	472	209	470	307	226	74	Poor
Isuzu Amigo	725	185	278	106	298	130	339	132	177	96	Vry. Gd.
Jeep Wrangler	685	122	316	127	245	92	241	95	388	57	Vry. Gd.
Average	733	194	378	111	325	175	284	290	291	234	

Maintenance Costs

	PM Costs to 50,000 Miles	Water Pump	Alternator	Front Brake Pads	Starter	Fuel Injection	Fuel Pump	Struts	Lower Ball Joints	CVJ or Univ. Joint	Relative Maint. Cost
Small Sport Utility (cont.)											
Kia Sportage	680	205	505	85	350	110	360	198	220	155	Ave.
Land Rover Defender 90	1390	298	534	130	648	205	450	193	398	134	Vry. Pr.
Suzuki Samurai	535	233	420	109	482	209	452	175	216	78	Ave.
Suzuki Sidekick	620	249	402	119	472	209	470	307	226	74	Poor
Mid-Size Sport Utility											
Chevrolet Blazer	670	158	226	112	329	144	188	99	239	153	Vry. Gd.
Ford Explorer	630	225	349	104	280	130	203	118	242	38	Vry. Gd.
GMC Jimmy	670	158	226	112	329	144	188	99	239	153	Vry. Gd.
Isuzu Trooper	725	212	343	106	349	155	339	143	177	96	Good
Jeep Cherokee	685	170	325	133	197	182	164	135	339	72	Vry. Gd.
Land Rover Discovery	1390	298	534	130	648	205	450	193	398	134	Vry. Pr.
Nissan Pathfinder	780	230	389	95	394	258	297	110	175	84	Good
Toyota 4Runner	780	149	473	110	327	256	340	78	313	115	Ave.
Large Sport Utility											
Chevrolet Suburban	735	166	221	108	397	249	144	92	202	76	Vry. Gd.
Chevrolet Tahoe	735	160	136	108	341	271	144	100	159	83	Vry. Gd.
Ford Bronco	630	164	337	101	279	176	333	88	391	76	Good
GMC Suburban	735	166	221	108	397	249	144	92	202	76	Vry. Gd.
GMC Yukon	735	160	136	108	341	271	144	100	159	83	Vry. Gd.
Honda Passport	725	234	288	116	298	142	445	94	194	94	Good
Isuzu Rodeo	725	234	288	116	298	142	445	94	194	94	Good
Jeep Grand Cherokee	685	184	307	108	182	88	317	135	303	80	Vry. Gd.
Land Rover Range Rover	1390	345	575	140	702	225	490	220	398	290	Vry. Pr.
Mazda Navajo	720	193	251	118	228	115	211	145	322	115	Vry. Gd.
Mitsubishi Montero	905	262	301	114	416	235	423	156	226	110	Ave.
Average	733	194	378	111	325	175	284	290	291	234	

	PM Costs to 50,000 Miles	Water Pump	Alternator	Front Brake Pads	Starter	Fuel Injection	Fuel Pump	Struts	Lower Ball Joints	CVJ or Univ. Joint	Relative Maint. Cost
Large Sport Utility (cont.)											
Toyota Land Cruiser	780	199	508	110	396	275	344	105	243	115	Ave.
Compact Pickup											
Chevrolet S-Series	745	151	166	108	291	152	121	240	190	93	Vry.Gd.
Dodge Dakota	699	137	302	146	215	110	300	65	273	57	Vry.Gd.
Ford Ranger	630	143	312	104	285	149	243	124	284	59	Vry.Gd.
GMC Sonoma	745	151	166	108	291	152	121	240	190	93	Vry.Gd.
Isuzu Pickup	730	153	290	106	320	112	431	95	194	84	Good
Mazda B-Series	802	182	220	83	166	264	303	88	174	100	Vry.Gd.
Mitsubishi Mighty Max	905	206	536	114	282	228	322	112	165	76	Good
Nissan Pickup	780	157	270	92	184	173	349	98	221	80	Vry.Gd.
Toyota Pickup	770	130	469	110	328	263	340	91	292	107	Ave.
Standard Pickup											
Chevrolet CK Series	735	144	217	116	288	195	185	107	170	84	Vry.Gd.
Dodge Ram	810	152	390	110	290	135	195	102	310	69	Vry.Gd.
Ford F-Series	630	180	313	106	282	180	339	88	300	72	Good
GMC Sierra	735	144	217	116	288	195	185	107	170	84	Vry.Gd.
Toyota T100	770	168	461	110	357	231	344	127	289	111	Ave.
Average	733	194	378	111	325	175	284	290	291	234	

Service Contracts

Each year nearly 50 percent of new vehicle buyers buy "service contracts." Ranging from $400 to $1500 in price, a service contract is one of the most expensive options you can buy. In fact, service contracts are a major source of profit for many dealers.

A service contract is not a warranty. It is more like an insurance plan that, in theory, covers repairs that are not covered by your warranty or that occur after the warranty runs out.

Service contracts are generally a very poor value. The companies who sell contracts are very sure that, on average, your repairs will cost considerably less than what you pay for the contract—if not, they wouldn't be in business.

One alternative to buying a service contract is to deposit the cost of the contract into a savings account. If the vehicle needs a major repair, not covered by your warranty, chances are good that the money in your account will cover the cost. Most likely, you'll be building up your down payment for your next vehicle!

If you believe that you really need a service contract, contact an insurance company, such as GEICO. You can save up to 50-percent by buying from an insurance company.

Here are some important questions to ask before buying a service contract:

How reputable is the company responsible for the contract? If the company offering the contract goes out of business, you will be out of luck. Recently, a number of independent service contract companies have gone under, so be very careful about who you buy from. Check with your Better Business Bureau or office of consumer affairs if you are not sure of a company's reputation. Service contracts from car and insurance companies are more likely to remain in effect than those from independent companies.

Exactly what does the contract cover and for how long? Service contracts vary considerably—different items are covered and different time limits are offered. This is true even among service contracts offered by the same company. For example, Ford's plans range from 3 years/50,000 miles maximum coverage to 6 years/100,000 miles maximum coverage, with other options for only powertrain coverage.

If you plan to resell your vehicle in a few years, you won't want to purchase a long-running service contract. Some service contracts automatically cancel when you resell the vehicle, while others require a hefty transfer fee before extending privileges to the new owner.

Some automakers offer a "menu" format which lets you pick the items you want covered in your service contract. Find out if the contract pays for preventive maintenance, towing, and rental car expenses. If not written into the contract, assume they are not covered.

Finally, think twice before purchasing travel services offered in the contract. Such amenities are offered by auto clubs, and you should compare prices before adding them into your contract cost.

How will the repair bills be paid? It is best to have the service contractor pay bills directly. Some contracts require you to pay the repair bill, and reimburse you later.

Where can the vehicle be serviced? Can you take the vehicle to any mechanic if you have trouble on the road? What if you move?

What other costs can be expected? Most service contracts will have a deductible expense. Compare deductibles on various plans. Also, some companies charge the deductible for each individual repair while other companies charge per visit, regardless of the number of repairs made.

Turbocharging

A turbocharger is an air pump that forces more air into the engine for combustion. Most turbochargers consist of an air compressor driven by a small turbine wheel that is powered by the engine's exhaust. The turbine takes advantage of energy otherwise lost and forces increased efficiency from the engine. Turbochargers are often used to increase the power and sometimes the fuel efficiency of small engines. Engines equipped with turbochargers are more expensive than standard engines. The extra power may not be necessary when you consider the added expense and the fact that turbocharging adds to the complexity of the engine.

Tips for Dealing with a Mechanic

Call around. Don't choose a shop simply because it's nearby. Calling a few shops may turn up estimates cheaper by half.

Don't necessarily go for the lowest price. A good rule is to eliminate the highest and lowest estimates; the mechanic with the highest estimate is probably charging too much, and the lowest may be cutting too many corners.

Check the shop's reputation. Call your local consumer affairs agency and the Better Business Bureau. They don't have records on every shop, but if their reports on a shop aren't favorable, you can disqualify it.

Look for certification. Mechanics can be certified by the National Institute for Automotive Service Excellence, an industry-wide yardstick for competence. Certification is offered in eight areas of repair, and shops with certified mechanics are allowed to advertise this fact. However, make sure the mechanic working on your car is certified for the repair.

Take a look around. A well-kept shop reflects pride in workmanship. A skilled and efficient mechanic would probably not work in a messy shop.

Don't sign a blank check. Your service order should have specific instructions or describe your vehicle's symptoms. Signing a vague work order could make you liable to pay for work you didn't want. Be sure you are called for approval before the shop does extra work.

Show interest. Ask about the repair. A mechanic may become more helpful just knowing that you're interested. But don't act like an expert if you really don't understand what's wrong. Demonstrating your ignorance, on the other hand, may set you up to be taken by a dishonest mechanic, so strike a balance.

Express your satisfaction. If you're happy with the work, compliment the mechanic and ask for him or her the next time you come in. You'll get to know each other, and the mechanic will get to know your vehicle.

Develop a "sider." If you know a mechanic, ask about work on the side—evenings or weekends. The labor will be cheaper.

Test drive, then pay! Before you pay for a major repair, you should take the vehicle for a test drive. The few extra minutes that you spend checking out the repair could save you a trip back to the mechanic. If you find that the problem still exists, there will be no question that the repair wasn't properly completed. It is much more difficult to prove the repair wasn't properly made after you've left the shop.

Repair Protection By Credit Card

TIP

Paying your auto repair bills by credit card can provide a much-needed recourse if you are having problems with an auto mechanic. According to federal law, you have the right to withhold payment for sloppy or incorrect repairs. Of course, you may withhold no more than the amount of the repair in dispute.

In order to use this right, you must first try to work out the problem with the mechanic. Also, unless the credit card company owns the repair shop (this might be the case with gasoline credit cards used at gas stations), two other conditions must be met. First, the repair shop must be in your home state (or within 100 miles of your current address), and second, the cost of repairs must be over $50. Until the problem is settled or resolved in court, the credit card company cannot charge you interest or penalties on the amount in dispute.

If you decide to take action, send a letter to the credit card company and a copy to the repair shop, explaining the details of the problem and what you want as settlement. Send the letter by certified mail with a return receipt requested.

Sometimes the credit card company or repair shop will attempt to put a "bad mark" on your credit record if you use this tactic. Legally, you can't be reported as delinquent if you've given the credit card company notice of your dispute. But, a creditor can report that you are disputing your bill, which goes in your record. However, you have the right to challenge any incorrect information and add your side of the story to your file.

For more information write to the Federal Trade Commission, Credit Practices Division, 601 Pennsylvania Avenue, NW, Washington, D.C. 20580.

Keeping It Going

With the popularity of self-service gasoline stations, many of us overlook the simplest and most vital maintenance task of all: checking various items to prevent serious problems down the road. In about fifteen minutes a month, you can make the following checks yourself. *Warning:* Many new vehicles have electric cooling fans that operate when the engine is off. Be sure to keep your hands away from the fan if the engine is warm.

Coolant: We'll start with the easiest fluid to check. Most vehicles have a plastic reservoir next to the radiator. This bottle will have "full hot" and "full cold" marks on it. If coolant is below "full cold" mark, add water to bring it up to that mark. (Antifreeze should be used if you want extra protection in cold weather.) *Caution:* If vehicle is hot, do not open the radiator cap. Pressure and heat that can cause a severe burn may be released.

Brakes: The most important safety item on the vehicle is the most ignored. A simple test will signal problems. (With power brakes, turn on engine to test.) Push the brake pedal down and hold it down. It should stop firmly and stay about halfway to the floor. If the stop is mushy or the pedal keeps moving to the floor, you should have your brakes checked. Checking the brake fluid on most vehicles is also very easy. Your owner's manual tells you where to find the fluid reservoir, which indicates minimum and maximum fluid levels. If you add your own brake fluid, buy it in small cans

and keep them tightly sealed. Brake fluid absorbs moisture, and excess moisture can damage your brake system. Have the brakes checked if you need to replace brake fluid regularly.

Oil: A few years ago, the phrase "fill it up and check the oil" was so common that it seemed like one word. Today, checking the oil often is the responsibility of the driver. To check your oil, first turn off the engine. Find the dipstick (look for a loop made of flat wire located on the side of the engine). If the engine has been running, be careful, because the dipstick and surrounding engine parts will be hot. Grab the loop, pull out the dipstick, clean it off, and reinsert it into the engine. Pull it out again and observe the oil level. "Full" and "add" are marked at the end of the stick. If the level is between "add" and "full," you are OK. If it is below "add," you should add enough oil until it reaches the "full" line. To add oil, remove the cap at the top of the engine. You may have to add more than one quart. Changing your oil regularly (every 3000 miles) is the single most important way to protect your engine. Many owner's manuals also contain directions for doing so. Change the oil filter whenever you change the oil.

Transmission Fluid: An automatic transmission is a very complicated and expensive item. Checking your transmission fluid level is easy and can prevent a costly repair job. As in the oil check, you must first find the transmission fluid dipstick. Usually it is at the rear of the engine

and looks like a smaller version of the oil dipstick. To get an accurate reading, the engine should be warmed up and running. If fluid is below the "add" line, pour in one pint at a time, but do not overfill reservoir.

While you check the fluid, also note its color. It should be a bright, cherry red. If it is a darker, reddish brown, the fluid needs changing. If it is very dark, nearly black, and has a burnt smell (like varnish), your transmission may be damaged. You should take it to a specialist.

Automatic transmission fluid is available at most department stores; check your owner's manual for the correct type for your vehicle.

Power Steering: The power steering fluid reservoir is usually connected by a belt to the engine. To check it, simply unscrew the cap and look in the reservoir. There will be markings inside; some vehicles have a little dipstick built in to the cap.

Belts: You may have one or more belts connected to your engine. A loose belt in the engine can lead to electrical, cooling, or even air conditioning problems. To check, simply push down on the middle of each belt. It should feel tight. If you can push down more than half an inch, the belt needs tightening.

Battery: If your battery has caps on the top, lift off the caps and check that fluid comes up to the bottom of the filler neck. If it doesn't, add water (preferably distilled). If it is very cold outside, add water only if you are planning to drive the vehicle immediately. Otherwise the newly added water can freeze and damage your battery.

Also, look for corrosion around the battery connections. It can prevent electrical circuits from being completed, leading you to assume your perfectly good battery is "dead." If cables are corroded, remove and clean with fine sandpaper or steel wool. The inside of the connection and the battery posts should be shiny when you put the cables back on. *Caution:* Do not smoke or use any flame when checking the battery.

Tires: Improperly inflated tires are a major cause of premature tire failure. Check for proper inflation at least once a month. The most fuel-efficient inflation level is the maximum pressure listed on the side of the tire. Because many gas station pumps do not have gauges, and those that do are generally inaccurate, you should invest in your own tire gauge.

Air Filter: Probably the easiest item to maintain is your air filter. You usually can check the filter just by looking at it. If it appears dirty, change it—it's a simple task. If you are not sure how clean your filter is, try the following: Once the engine warms up, put the vehicle in park or neutral and, with the emergency brake on, let the vehicle idle. Open filter lid and remove the filter. If the engine begins to run faster, change the filter.

Battery Safety

Almost all motorists have had to jump start a vehicle because of a dead battery. But that innocent-looking battery can cause some serious injuries.

Batteries produce hydrogen gas when they discharge or undergo heavy use (such as cranking the engine for a long period of time). A lit cigarette or a spark can cause this gas to explode. Whenever you work with the battery, always remove the negative (or ground) cable first and reconnect it last; it is usually marked with a minus sign. This precaution will greatly reduce the chance of causing a spark that could ignite any hydrogen gas present.

For a safe jump start:

1. Connect each end of the red cable to the positive (+) terminal on each battery.

2. Connect one end of the black cable to the negative (-) terminal of the *good* battery.

3. Connect the other end of the black cable to the engine block (or exposed metal away from the battery) of the vehicle being started.

4. To avoid damaging electrical parts of the vehicle being jump started, make sure the engine is idling before disconnecting the cables.

Saving Gasoline

TIP

A cold-running engine dramatically reduces fuel economy. Most engines operate efficiently at 180 degrees, and an engine running at 125 degrees can waste one out of every ten gallons of gas. Your engine temperature is controlled by a thermostat valve. A faulty thermostat can be a major cause of poor fuel economy. If you feel that your vehicle should be getting better mileage, have your thermostat checked. They are inexpensive and relatively easy to replace.

WARRANTIES

Along with your new vehicle comes a warranty, which is a promise from the manufacturer that the vehicle will perform as it should. Most of us never read the warranty—until it is too late. In fact, because warranties are often difficult to read and understand, most of us don't really know what our warranties offer. This chapter will help you understand what to look for in a new vehicle warranty, tip you off to secret warranties and provide you with the best and worst among the 1995 vehicles.

There are two types of warranties: one provided by the manufacturer and one implied by law.

Manufacturers' warranties are either "full" or "limited." The best warranty you can get is a full warranty, because it must meet the standards set by federal law and must cover all aspects of the product's performance. Any other guarantee is called a limited warranty, which is what most manufacturers offer. If the warranty is limited, it must be clearly marked as such, and you must be told exactly what the warranty covers.

Warranties implied by law are defined by the Uniform Commercial Code (UCC). All states have passed a version of the UCC, although Louisiana has not passed the portion that gives warranty protection. The UCC provides an implied warranty of merchantability and a warranty of fitness. The "warranty of merchantability" ensures that your new vehicle will be fit for the purpose for which it is used—that means safe, efficient, and trouble-free transportation. The "warranty of fitness" guarantees that if the dealer says that a vehicle can be used for a specific purpose, it will perform for that purpose.

Any claims made by the salesperson are considered warranties. They are called expressed warranties, and you should have them put in writing if you consider them to be important. If the vehicle does not live up to promises made to you in the showroom, you may have a case against the seller.

The manufacturer can restrict the amount of time the limited warranty is in effect. And in most states, the manufacturer can also limit the time that the warranty implied by law is in effect.

Be careful not to confuse your warranty with a service contract. The service contract must be purchased separately; the warranty is yours at no extra cost when you buy the vehicle. (See page 51 for more on service contracts.)

Through the warranty, the manufacturer is promising that the way the vehicle was made and the materials used to make the vehicle are free from defects, provided that the vehicle is used in a normal fashion for a certain period after you buy it. This period of time is usually measured in both months and miles— whichever comes first is the limit.

While the warranty is in effect, the manufacturer will perform, at no charge to the owner, repairs that are necessary because of defects in materials or in the way the vehicle was manufactured.

The warranty does not cover parts that have to be replaced because of normal wear, such as filters, fuses, bulbs, wiper blades, clutch linings, brake pads, or the addition of oil, fluids, coolants, and lubricants. Tires, batteries, and the emission control system are covered by separate warranties. Options, such as a stereo system, should have their own warranties as well. Service should be provided through the dealer. A separate rust (corrosion) warranty also is included.

The costs for required maintenance, which are listed in the owner's manual, are not covered by the warranty. Problems resulting from misuse, negligence, changes you make in the vehicle, accidents, or lack of required maintenance are also not covered.

Any implied warranties, including the warranties of merchantability and of fitness, are limited to 12 months or 12,000 miles. Also, the manufacturer is not responsible for consequential damages, such as the loss of time or use of your vehicle, or any expenses they might cause.

Some states do not allow the implied warranties to be limited to a specific time or the consequential damages to be limited or excluded. If this is true in your state, the above limitations do not apply. In addition to the rights granted to you in the warranty, you may have other rights under your state laws.

To keep your warranty in effect, you must operate and maintain your car according to the instructions in your owner's manual. As such, it is important to keep a record of all maintenance performed on your vehicle.

To have your car repaired under the warranty, take it to an authorized dealer or service center. The work should be done in a reasonable amount of time during normal business hours.

Corrosion Warranty: All manufacturers warrant against corrosion. The typical corrosion warranty lasts for seven years or 100,000 miles, whichever comes first.

Some dealers offer extra rust protection at an additional cost.

Before you purchase this option, compare the extra protection offered to the corrosion warranty already included in the price of the vehicle—it probably already provides sufficient protection against rust. (See pg. 93 for more important information on rust-proofing.)

Emission System Warranty: The emission system is warranted by federal law. Any repairs required during the first two years or 24,000 miles will be paid for by the manufacturer if an original engine part fails because of a defect in materials or workmanship, and the failure causes your car to exceed federal emissions standards. Major components, such as an on board computer emissions control unit, are covered for eight years or 80,000 miles.

Using leaded fuel in a vehicle designed for unleaded fuel will void your emission system warranty and may prevent the vehicle from passing your state's inspection. Because an increasing number of states are requiring an emissions test before a vehicle can pass inspection, you may have to pay to fix the system if you used the wrong type of fuel. Repairs to emission systems are usually very expensive.

Dealer Options & Your Warranty

Make sure that "dealer-added" options will not void your warranty. For example, some consumers who have purchased cruise control as an option to be installed by the dealer have found that their warranty is void when they take the car in for engine repairs. Also, some manufacturers warn that dealer-supplied rustproofing will void your corrosion warranty. If you are in doubt, contact the manufacturer before you authorize the installation of dealer-supplied options. If the manufacturer says that adding the option will not void your warranty, get it in writing.

Getting Warranty Service

Ford dealers are finally offering better warranty service to their customers! Now, any Ford dealer must perform warranty work on all Ford vehicles, regardless of where the vehicle was purchased. Previously, only the selling dealer was required to perform repairs under warranty. GM, Japanese and European car dealers also provide this service to their customers, and Chrysler "recommends" that dealers follow this policy.

If dealers report a number of complaints about a certain part and the manufacturer determines that the problem is due to faulty design or assembly, the manufacturer may permit dealers to repair the problem at no charge to the customer even though the warranty is expired. In the past, this practice was often reserved for customers who made a big fuss. The availability of the free repair was never publicized, which is why we call these *secret* warranties.

Manufacturers deny the existence of secret warranties. They call these free repairs "policy adjustments" or "goodwill service." Whatever they are called, most consumers never find out about them.

Many secret warranties are disclosed in service bulletins that the manufacturers send to dealers. These bulletins outline free repair or reimbursement programs, as well as other problems and their possible causes and solutions.

Because of problems with secret warranties in the past, three companies are now required to make many of their bulletins available to the public. *Ford* was required to disclose both bulletins and goodwill adjustments under an FTC Consent Order through 1988. Now Ford's toll-free "defect line," 800-241-3673, provides information only on goodwill adjustments. *General Motors* bulletins from the past three years

(which may cover models made earlier) and indexes to the bulletins are available at GM dealers. You may also call 800-551-4123 to obtain a form to order them directly from GM. The indexes are free, but there is a charge for the bulletins. *Volkswagen* is also required to make this information available to consumers. You can order an index of all service bulletins, which includes information on obtaining the actual bulletins, by calling 800-544-8021.

Service bulletins from other manufacturers may be on file at the National Highway Traffic Safety Administration. For copies of the bulletins on file, send a letter with the make, model and year of the vehicle and the year you believe the service bulletin was issued to the NHTSA's Technical Reference Library, Room 5108, NHTSA, Washington, DC, 20590. If you write to the government, ask for "service bulletins" rather than "secret warranties."

If you find that a secret warranty is in effect and repairs are being made at no charge after the warranty has expired, contact the Center for Auto Safety, 2001 S Street NW, Washington, D.C. 20009-1160. They will publish the information so others can benefit.

Disclosure Laws: Spurred by the proliferation of secret warranties and the failure of the FTC to take action, California, Connecticut, Virginia, and Wisconsin have

passed legislation that requires consumers to be notified of secret warranties on their cars. Several other states have introduced similar warranty bills.

Typically, the laws require the following: Direct notice to consumers within a specified time after the adoption of a warranty adjustment policy; Notice of the disclosure law to new car buyers; Reimbursement, within a number of years after payment, to owners who paid for covered repairs before they learned of the extended warranty service; and dealers must inform consumers who complain about a covered defect that it is eligible for repair under warranty.

New York's bill has another requirement—the establishment of a toll-free number for consumer questions. Consumer groups, such as the Center for Auto Safety, support this requirement, but it has met opposition from Ford, GM, Toyota, and other auto manufacturers.

Unlike the other states' laws, California's law does not give consumers the right to sue for damages or attorney's fees. The bill itself does not deter manufacturers from violating the law.

If you live in a state with a secret warranty law already in effect, write your state attorney general's office (in care of your state capitol) for information. To encourage passage of such a bill, contact your state representative (in care of your state capitol).

Uncovered Secret Warranties

Secret warranties are, by nature, difficult to find out about. However, following are a few examples recently uncovered by the Center for Auto Safety. If you think you may be covered, first contact your dealer. If they are unwilling to help, write to vehicle's manufacturer.

Ford is liable for up to $1 billion for bad paint—mainly on blue, silver, and grey 1985-92 F-Series trucks. The Center is also aware of paint problems on the Aerostar, Bronco, Bronco II, Econoline, Escort, EXP, LTD, Mustang, Probe, Ranger, Sable, Taurus, Tempo, Thunderbird and Tracer. If your Ford has had problems with peeling paint, voice your complaint to the Center for Auto Safety, the Federal Trade Commission or your local attorney general's office or state representative.

At the Center for Auto Safety's urging, General Motors has adopted the most comprehensive paint policy in the industry. GM will repaint vehicles with defective paint at no cost within the first six years of the vehicle's life, regardless of mileage or whether you bought the vehicle new or used. GM will pay repair costs except for normal wear including bumps, scrapes and dents. If the paint on your vehicle is peeling or blistering, contact the service manager at your local dealership, who has the authorization to make the repair free of charge. For further information or for a refund of a previous paint job, contact the GM official responsible for the program: Elizabeth A. Marsh, Associate Coordinator, Legal Staff, General Motors Corp., New Center One Building, 3031 West Grand Boulevard, P.O.Box 33130, Detroit, MI, 48232. Or call your respective GM customer assistance division.

Honda has recently attempted to evade Connecticut's secret warranty law by conducting a free repair program through its regional offices and declaring it a "goodwill adjustment." The defect involves the misalignment, and subsequent premature tire wear, on 1989-90 Honda Civics. As the Center for Auto Safety learned, the defect involved was serious enough to cause at least one accident. That particular instance fell under the secret warranty category, as only the VIN number was verified, without the usual review of repair records, purchase history or vehicle inspection, before the work was performed. Again, if you think your vehicle may be involved, contact a local dealership's service manager or the regional office of Honda.

To find out more about secret warranties and other items the manufacturers don't want you to know about, the Center for Auto Safety's recently released book "Little Secrets of the Auto Industry" is available by sending a check for $11.95 to the Center for Auto Safety, 2001 S Street, NW, Washington, D.C. 20009-1160.

Comparing Warranties

Warranties are difficult to compare because they contain lots of fine print and confusing language. The following table will help you understand this year's new car warranties. Because the table does not contain all the details about each warranty, you should review the actual warranty to make sure you understand its fine points. Remember, you have the right to inspect a warranty before you buy—it's the law.

The table provides information on five areas covered by a typical warranty:

The **Basic Warranty** covers most parts of the car against manufacturer's defects. The tires, batteries, and items you may add to the car are covered under separate warranties. The table describes coverage in terms of months and miles; for example, 36/36,000 means the warranty is good for 36 months or 36,000 miles, whichever comes first. This is the most important part of your warranty.

The **Powertrain Warranty** usually lasts longer than the basic warranty. Because each manufacturer's definition of the powertrain is different, it is important to find out exactly what your warranty will cover. Powertrain coverage should include parts of the engine, transmission, and drivetrain. The warranty on some luxury vehicles will often cover some additional systems such as steering, suspension, and electrical systems.

The **Corrosion Warranty** usually applies only to actual holes due to rust. Read this section carefully, because many corrosion warranties *do not* apply to what the manufacturer may describe as cosmetic rust or bad paint.

The **Roadside Assistance** column indicates whether or not the warranty includes a program for helping with problems on the road. Typically, these programs cover such things as lock outs, jump starts, flat tires, running out of gas and towing. Most of these are offered for the length of the basic warranty. Some have special limitations or added features, which we have pointed out. Because each one is different, check your's out carefully.

The last column contains the **Warranty Rating Index,** which provides an overall assessment of this year's warranties. The higher the Index number, the better the warranty. The Index number incorporates the important features of each warranty. In developing the Index, we gave the most weight to the basic and powertrain components of the warranties. The corrosion warranty was weighted somewhat less, and the roadside assistance feature received the least weight. We also considered special features such as whether you had to bring the vehicle in for corrosion inspections, or if rental vehicles were offered when warranty repairs were being done.

After evaluating all the features of the new warranties, here are this year's best and worst ratings.

1995 Warranties: The Best and The Worst

The Best		The Worst	
Isuzu	1328	Suzuki Soft Tops	524
Nissan	1086	Suzuki	702
Mazda	1061	Ford	942
Land Rover	1059	Chevrolet/Geo	956
Volkswagen	1058	GMC	956
		Oldsmobile	956
		Pontiac	956

The higher the index number, the better the warranty. See the following table for complete details.

Manufacturer	Basic Warranty	Powertrain Warranty	Corrosion Warranty	Roadside Assistance	Index	Warranty Rating
Chevrolet	36/36,000	36/36,000	72/100,000	36/36,000	956	Very Poor
Chrysler	36/36,000	36,36,000	84/100,000	36/36,000	980	Poor
Dodge	36/36,000	36,36,000	84/100,000	36/36,000	980	Poor
Ford	36/36,000	36/36,000	60/unlimited	36/36,000	942	Very Poor
Geo	36/36,000	36/36,000	72/100,000	36/36,000	956	Very Poor
GMC	36/36,000	36/36,000	72/100,000	36/36,000	956	Very Poor
Isuzu	36/50,000	60/60,000	72/100,000	60/60,000	1328	Very Good
Jeep	36/36,000	36,36,000	84/100,000	36/36,000	980	Poor
Kia	36/36,000	60/60,000	36/50,000	36/36,000[1]	978	Poor
Land Rover	36/42,000	36/42,000	72/unlimited	36/42,000	1059	Average
Mazda	36/50,000	36/50,000	60/unlimited	36/50,000	1061	Average
Mitsubishi	36/36,000	60/60,000	60/unlimited	36/36,000	980	Poor
Nissan	36/36,000	60/60,000	60/unlimited	36/36,000	1086	Average
Oldsmobile	36/36,000	36/36,000	72/100,000	36/36,000	956	Very Poor
Plymouth	36/36,000	36,36,000	84/100,000	36/36,000	980	Poor
Pontiac	36/36,000	36/36,000	72/100,000	36/36,000	956	Very Poor
Suzuki	36/36,000	36/36,000	36/unlimited	None	702	Very Poor
Suzuki Soft Tops	24/24,000	24/24,000	36/unlimited	None	524	Very Poor
Toyota	36/36,000	60/60,000	60/unlimited	Optional	978	Poor
Volkswagen	24/24,000	120/100,000	72/unlimited	24/24,000	1058	Average

[1] Covers trip interruption expenses.

INSURANCE

Insurance is an often overlooked expense of owning a vehicle. As you shop, remember that the vehicle's design and accident history may affect your insurance rates. Some vehicles cost less to insure because experience has shown that they are damaged less, less expensive to fix after a collision, or stolen less.

This chapter provides you with the information you need to make a wise and economical insurance purchase. We discuss the different types of insurance, offer special tips on reducing this cost and include information on occupant injury and theft—factors that can affect your insurance.

More and more consumers are saving considerable amounts of money by shopping around for insurance. In order to be a good comparison shopper, you need to know a few things about automobile insurance. First, there are six basic types of coverage:

Property Damage Liability: This pays claims and defense costs if your vehicle damages someone else's property.

Uninsured Motorists Protection: This pays for injuries caused by an uninsured or a hit-and-run driver.

Collision Insurance: This pays for the damage to your vehicle after an accident.

Bodily Injury Liability: This provides money to pay claims against you and to pay for the cost of your legal de-fense if your vehicle injures or kills someone.

Comprehensive Physical Damage Insurance: This pays for damages when your vehicle is stolen or damaged by fire, floods, or other perils.

Medical Payments Insurance: This pays for your vehicle's occupants' medical expenses resulting from an accident.

A number of factors determine what these coverages will cost you. A vehicle's design can affect both the chances and severity of an accident. A vehicle with a well-designed bumper may escape damage altogether in a low-speed crash. Some vehicles are easier to repair than others or may have less expensive parts. Vehicles with four doors tend to be dam-aged less than vehicles with two doors.

The reason one vehicle may get a discount on insurance while another receives a sur-charge also depends upon the way it is traditionally driven. Sports cars, for example, are usually surcharged due, in part, to the typical driving habits of their owners. Four-door sedans and station wagons generally merit discounts.

Insurance companies use this and other information to determine whether to offer a *discount* on insurance premiums for a particular vehicle, or whether to levy a *surcharge*.

Not all companies offer discounts or surcharges, and many vehicles receive neither. Some companies offer a discount or impose a surcharge on collision premiums only. Others apply discounts and surcharges on both collision and comprehensive coverage. Discounts and surcharges usually range from 10 to 30 percent. Allstate offers discounts of up to 35 percent on certain vehicles. Remember that one company may offer a discount on a particular vehicle while another may not.

Check with your insurance agent to find out whether your company has a rating program. The Truck Rating pages at the end of the book indicate the expected insurance rates for each of the 1995 models.

No-Fault Insurance

One of the major expenses of vehicular accidents has been the cost of determining who is "at fault." Often, both parties hire lawyers and wait for court decisions, which can take a long time. Another problem with this system is that some victims receive considerably less than others for equivalent losses.

To resolve this, many states have instituted "no-fault" vehicle insurance. The concept is that each person's losses are covered by his or her personal insurance protection, regardless of who is at fault. Lawsuits are permitted only under certain conditions.

While the idea is the same from state to state, the details of the no-fault laws vary. These variations include the amounts paid in similar situations, conditions of the right to sue, and the inclusion or exclusion of property damage.

The concept of no-fault means that your insurance company pays for your losses regardless of who is responsible and that lawsuits are restricted. Ironically some no-fault states still permit lawsuits to determine who is at fault.

Although the laws in each state may vary, the following is a list of states with and without no-fault laws.

No-Fault States

Colorado	Massachusetts	New York
Florida	Michigan	North Dakota
Hawaii	Minnesota	Pennsylvania*
Kansas	New Jersey*	Utah
Kentucky*		

States Without No-Fault

Alabama	Louisiana	Oregon
Alaska	Maine	Rhode Island
Arizona	Maryland	South Carolina
Arkansas	Mississippi	South Dakota
California	Missouri	Tennessee
Connecticut	Montana	Texas
Delaware	Nebraska	Vermont
District of Columbia	Nevada	Virginia
Georgia	New Hampshire	Washington
Idaho	New Mexico	West Virginia
Illinois	North Carolina	Wisconsin
Indiana	Ohio	Wyoming
Iowa	Oklahoma	

*NJ, KY, PA have a policy option for choosing no-fault.

Insurance Industry Statistics

TIP

The insurance industry regularly publishes information about the accident history of cars currently on the road. The most reliable source of this rating information is the Highway Loss Data Institute (HLDI). These ratings, which range from very good to very poor, are based on the frequency of medical claims under personal injury protection coverages. A few companies will charge you more to insure a car rated poor than for one rated good.

A car's accident history may not match its crash test performance. Such discrepancies arise because the accident history includes driver performance. A sports car, for example, may have good crash test results but a poor accident history because its owners tend to drive relatively recklessly.

If you want more information about the injury history, bumper performance, and theft rating of today's cars, write to HLDI, 1005 North Glebe Road, Arlington, VA 22201.

Reducing Insurance Costs

After you have shopped around and found the best deal by comparing the costs of different coverages, consider these other factors that will affect your final insurance bill.

Your Annual Mileage: The more you drive, the more your vehicle will be "exposed" to a potential accident. The insurance cost for a vehicle rarely used will be less than the cost for a frequently used one.

Where You Drive: If you regularly drive and park in the city, you will most likely pay more than if you drive in rural areas.

Youthful Drivers: Usually the highest premiums are paid by male drivers under the age of 25. Whether or not the under-25-year-old male is married also affects insurance rates. (Married males pay less.) As the driver gets older, rates are lowered.

In addition to shopping around, take advantage of certain discounts to reduce your insurance costs. Most insurance companies offer discounts of 5 to 30 percent on various parts of your insurance bill. The availability of discounts varies among companies and often depends on where you live. Many consumers do not benefit from these discounts simply because they don't ask about them.

To determine whether you are getting all the discounts that you're entitled to, ask your insurance company for a complete list of the discounts that it offers.

Here are some of the most common insurance discounts:

Driver Education/Defensive Driving Courses: Many insurance companies offer (and in some cases mandate) discounts to young people who have successfully completed a state-approved driver education course. Typically, this can mean a $40 reduction in the cost of coverage. Also, a discount of 5-15% is available in some states to those who complete a defensive driving course.

Good Student Discounts: Many insurance companies offer discounts of up to 25 percent on insurance to full-time high school or college students who are in the upper 20 percent of their class, on the dean's list, or have a B or better average.

Good Driver Discounts: Many companies offer discounts to drivers with an accident and violation-free record.

Mature Driver Credit: Drivers ages 50 and older may qualify for up to a 10 percent discount, or a lower price bracket.

Sole Female Driver: Some companies offer discounts of 10 percent for females, ages 30 to 64, who are the only driver in a household, citing favorable claims experience.

Non-Drinkers and Non-Smokers: A limited number of companies offer incentives ranging from 10-25% to those who abstain.

Farmer Discounts: Many companies offer farmers either a discount of 10-30% or a lower price bracket.

Car Pooling: Commuters sharing driving may qualify for discounts of 5-25% or a lower price bracket.

Insuring Driving Children: Children away at school don't drive the family car very often, so it's usually less expensive to insure them on the parents' policy rather than separately. If you do insure them separately, discounts of 10-40% or a lower price bracket are available.

Desirable Vehicles: Premiums are usually much higher for vehicles with high collision rates or that are the favorite target of thieves.

Passive Restraints/Anti-Lock Brake Credit: Many companies offer discounts (from 10 to 30 percent) for automatic belts and air bags. Some large companies are now offering a 5 percent discount to owners of vehicles with anti-lock brakes.

Anti-Theft Device Credits: Discounts of 5 to 15 percent are offered in some states for vehicles equipped with a hood lock and an alarm or a disabling device (active or passive) that prevents the vehicle from being started.

Multi-Car Discount: Consumers insuring more than one vehicle in the household with the same insurer can save up to 20 percent.

Account Credit: Some companies offer discounts of up to 10 percent for insuring your home and auto with the same company.

Long-Term Policy Renewal: Although not available in all states, some companies offer price breaks of 5-20% to customers who renew a long-term policy.

First Accident Allowance: Some insurers offer a "first accident allowance," which guarantees that if a customer achieves five accident-free years, his or her rates won't go up after the first at-fault accident.

Deductibles: Opting for the largest reasonable deductible is the obvious first step in reducing premiums. Increasing your deductible to $500 from $200 could cut your collision premium about 20 percent. Raising the deductible to $1,000 from $200 could lower your premium about 45 percent. Discounts may vary by company.

Collision Coverage: The older the vehicle, the less the need for collision insurance. Consider dropping collision insurance entirely on an older vehicle. Regardless of how much coverage you carry, the insurance company will only pay up to the vehicle's "book value." For example, if your vehicle requires $1,000 in repairs but its "book value" is only $500, the insurance company is required to pay only $500.

Uninsured Motorist Coverage/Optional Coverage: The necessity of both of these policies depends upon the extent of your health insurance coverage. In states where they are not required, consumers with applicable health insurance may not want uninsured motorist coverage. Also, those with substantial health insurance coverage may not want an optional medical payment policy.

Rental Cars: If you regularly rent cars, special coverage on your personal auto insurance can cover you while renting for far less than rental agencies offer.

Tip: Expensive fender bender repairs can add up for both you and your insurance company. To reduce repairs, look for a vehicle with bumpers that can withstand a 5-mph impact without damage.

Vehicle Theft

The risk of your vehicle being stolen is an important factor in the cost of your insurance. In fact, each year over 1.5 million vehicles are stolen. As a result, the market is flooded with expensive devices designed to prevent theft. Before you spend a lot of money on anti-theft devices, consider this: Of the vehicles stolen, nearly 80 percent were unlocked and 40 percent actually had the keys in the ignition. Most of these thefts are by amateurs. While the most important way to protect your vehicle is to keep it locked and remove the keys, this precaution will not protect you from the pros. If you live or travel in an area susceptible to auto thefts or have a high-priced vehicle, here are some steps you can take to prevent theft.

Inexpensive Theft Prevention:

☑ Replace door lock buttons with tapered tips. They make it difficult to hook the lock with a wire hanger. (But it will also keep you from breaking into your own vehicle!)

☑ Buy an alarm sticker (even if you don't have an alarm) for one of your windows.

☑ Buy an electric etching tool (about $15) and write your driver's license number in the lower corners of the windows and on unpainted metal items where it can be seen. Many police departments offer this service at no charge.

They provide a sticker and enter the number into their records. The purpose of these identifying marks is to deter the professional thief who is planning to take the vehicle apart and sell the components. Since the parts can be traced, your vehicle becomes much less attractive.

☑ Remove the distributor wire. This is a rather inconvenient but effective means of rendering your vehicle inoperable. If you are parking in a particularly suspect place or leaving your vehicle for a long time you may want to try this. On the top of the distributor, there is a short wire running to the coil. Removing the wire makes it impossible to start the vehicle.

A recently popular anti-theft device is a long rod that locks the steering wheel into place, sold under a variety of names. It costs $50 and requires a separate key without which the car can only be driven straight, if the ignition will engage at all. Beware, however, that thieves now use a spray can of freon to freeze the lock, making it brittle enough to be smashed open with a hammer.

More Serious Measures:

☑ Cutting off the fuel to the engine will keep someone from driving very far with your vehicle. For around $125, you can have a fuel cutoff device installed that enables you to open or close the gasoline line to the engine. One drawback is that the thief will be able to drive a few blocks before running out of gas. If your vehicle is missing, you'll have to check your neighborhood first!

☑ Another way to deter a pro is to install a second ignition switch for about $150. To start your vehicle, you activate a hidden switch. The device is wired in such a complicated manner that a thief could spend hours trying to figure it out. Time is the thief's worst enemy, and the longer it takes to start your vehicle, the more likely the thief is to give up.

☑ The most common anti-theft devices on the market are alarms. These cost from $100 to $500 installed. Their complexity ranges from simply sounding your horn when someone opens your door to setting off elaborate sirens when someone merely approaches the vehicle. Alarms require an exterior key-operated switch to turn them off and on. Some people buy the switch, mount it on their vehicle, and hope that its presence will intimidate the thief.

The Highway Loss Data Institute regularly compiles statistics on motor vehicle thefts. In rating vehicles, they consider the frequency of theft and the loss resulting from the theft. The result is an index based on "relative average loss payments per insured vehicle year." The next page indicates the current theft ratings of some popular vehicles.

Theft Ratings

Vehicle	Theft Rate Index	Vehicle	Theft Rate Index	Vehicle	Theft Rate Index
Mercury Villager Wagon	19	Ford F-250 2wd	97	Suzuki Samurai 2wd	207
Nissan Quest Wagon	23	Dodge W250 4wd	98	Toyota 4Runner Wagon, 4dr	209
Ford Aerostar 4wd	34	GMC S15 Sonoma 2wd	100	Chrysler Town & Country	210
Dodge Dakota 2wd	35	GMC Sierra 2500 4wd	111	GMC Vandura 2500	221
Ford Ranger 4wd	35	Dodge B250 Cargo Van	112	Chevrolet 1500 4wd	227
Ford Aerostar 2wd	36	Nissan Reg/Ext Cab 2wd	112	Chevrolet 2500 2wd	237
Ford Ranger 2wd	38	Nissan Reg/Ext Cab 4wd	115	Isuzu Amigo 2wd	249
GMC Safari 4wd	41	Chevrolet Astro 2wd	115	Jeep Cherokee 4dr	250
Mazda MPV 2wd	43	GMC Safari 2wd	116	GMC Sierra 1500 2wd	250
Isuzu Trooper 4dr, 4wd	45	Isuzu Rodeo 4dr	117	Jeep Cherokee 4dr, 4wd	253
Dodge Dakota 4wd	46	Chevrolet 2500 4wd	118	Chevrolet Chevy Van 20	255
Dodge W150 4wd	47	Chevrolet Astro 4wd	128	Isuzu Amigo 4wd	261
Dodge Caravan 2wd	53	GMC Safari Cargo Van	131	Suzuki Samurai 4wd	269
Toyota Previa 4wd	59	Ford F-250 4wd	132	Chevrolet K1500	270
Plymouth Voyager 2wd	60	Pontiac Trans Sport	134	Nissan Pathfinder 4dr	271
Isuzu Reg/Ext Cab 2wd	70	Ford F-350 2wd	136	Suzuki Sidekick 2dr, 4wd	272
Dodge Caravan 4wd	74	Oldsmobile Silhouette	136	Jeep Wrangler	285
Ford F-150 2wd	75	Chevrolet Lumina APV	139	Chevrolet 1500 2wd	293
Ford F-150 4wd	76	Jeep Cherokee 2dr	142	GMC T15 Sonoma 4wd	306
Mazda Navajo 2dr, 4wd	78	Isuzu Rodeo 4dr, 4wd	143	Chevy Suburban 1500 4wd	311
Toyota Previa 2wd	79	Ford Bronco	157	Jeep Gr. Cherokee 4dr, 4wd	329
Ford E-150 Econoline	85	GMC Sierra1500 4wd	177	Olds Bravada 4dr, 4wd	386
Ford F-350 4wd	88	Geo Tracker 2wd	189	Chevy Suburban 1500 2wd	403
Mazda MPV 4wd	88	Chevrolet T10 4wd	191	Chevrolet 3500	406
Plymouth Voyager 4wd	91	Jeep Cherokee 2dr, 4wd	196	Toyota 4Runner W,4dr,4wd	444
Mitsubishi Reg/Ext Cab 2wd	95	Geo Tracker 4wd	199	Nissan Pathfinder 4dr, 4wd	748
Suzuki Sidekick 4dr, 4wd	95	Chevrolet Astro Cargo Van	204	Toyota Land Cruiser	1178

Note: Lower numbers indicate a lower likelihood of being stolen.

TIRES

For most of us, buying tires has become an infrequent task. The reason—most vehicles now come with radial tires, which last much longer than the bias and bias-belted tires of the past. However, when we do get around to buying tires, making an informed purchase is not easy. The tire has to perform more functions simultaneously than any other part of the vehicle (steering, bearing the load, cushioning the ride, and stopping). And not only is the tire the hardest-working item on the vehicle, but there are nearly 1,800 tire lines to choose from. With only a few major tire manufacturers selling all those tires, the difference in many tires may only be the brand name.

This chapter contains all the information you need to select the best tires for your vehicle.

Because it is so difficult to compare tires, it is easy to understand why many consumers mistakenly use price and brand name to determine quality. The difficulty in comparing one tire to another is compounded by the advertising terminology that is used to describe tires. One company's definition of "first line" or "premium" may be entirely different from another's. But there is help. The U.S. government now requires tires to be rated according to their safety and expected mileage.

A little-known system grades tires on their *treadwear*, *traction*, and *heat resistance*. The grades are printed on the sidewall and also attached to the tire on a paper label. In addition, every dealer can provide you with the grades of the tires he or she sells.

Treadwear: The treadwear grade gives you an idea of the mileage you can expect from a tire. It is shown in numbers—300, 310, 320, 330 and so forth. A tire graded 400 should give you 33 percent more mileage than one graded 300. In order to *estimate* the expected actual mileage, multiply the treadwear grade by 200. Under average conditions a tire graded 300 should last 60,000 miles. Because individual driving habits vary considerably, it is best to use the treadwear as a *relative* basis of comparison rather than an absolute predictor of mileage. Also remember that tire wear is affected by regional differences in the level of abrasive material used in road surfaces.

Traction: Traction grades of A, B, and C describe the tire's ability to stop on wet surfaces. Tires graded A will stop on a wet road in a shorter distance than tires graded B or C. Tires rated C have poor traction. If you drive frequently on wet roads, buy a tire with a higher traction grade.

Heat Resistance: Heat resistance is also graded A, B, and C. This grading is important because hot-running tires can result in blowouts or tread separation. An A rating means the tire will run cooler than one rated B or C, and it is less likely to fail if driven over long distances at highway speeds. In addition, tires that run cooler tend to be more fuel efficient. If you do a lot of high speed driving, a high heat resistance grade is best.

The tables at the end of this section give you a list of the highest rated tires on the market. For a complete listing of all the tires on the market, you can call the Auto Safety Hotline, toll free, at 800-424-9393 or 800-424-9153 (TTY). (In Washington, D.C., the number is 202-366-7800.)

Tire Pricing: Getting the Best Value

There are few consumer products on the market today as price competitive as tires. While this situation provides a buyer's market, it does require some price shopping.

The price of each tire is based on the size of the tire, and tires may come in as many as nine sizes. For example, the list price of the same Goodyear Arriva tire can range from $74.20 to $134.35, depending on its size. Some manufacturers do not provide list prices, leaving the appropriate markup to the individual retailer. Even when list prices are provided, dealers rarely use them. Instead, they offer tires at what is called an "everyday low price," which can range from 10 to 25 percent below list.

The following tips can help you get the best buy.

1 Check to see which manufacturer makes the least expensive "offbrand." Only twelve major manufacturers produce the over 1,800 types of tires sold in the U.S. So you can save money and still get high quality.

2 Remember, generally the wider the tire, the higher the price. (Tire width is described by the aspect ratio, which is the height-to-width ratio of a tire's cross section. The lower the profile number, the wider the tire.)

3 Don't forget to inquire about balancing and mounting costs when comparing tire prices. In some stores the extra charges for balancing, mounting and valve stems can add up to more than $25. Other stores may offer them as a customer service at little or no cost. That good buy in the newspaper may turn into a poor value when coupled with these extra costs. Also, compare warranties; they do vary from company to company.

4 Never pay list price for a tire. A good rule of thumb is to pay at least 30 to 40 percent off the suggested list price.

5 Use the treadwear grade the same way you would the "unit price" in a supermarket. It is the best way to ensure that you are getting the best tire value. The tire with the lowest cost per grade point is the best value. For example, if tire A costs $100 and has a treadwear grade of 300, and tire B costs $80 and has a treadwear grade of 200:

Tire A:
$100÷300 = $.33 per point

Tire B:
$80÷200 = $.40 per point

Since 33 cents is less than 40 cents, tire A is the better buy.

New Tire Registration

You may be missing out on free or low-cost replacement tires or, worse, driving on potentially hazardous ones, if you don't fill out the tire registration form when you buy tires. The law once required all tire sellers to submit buyers' names automatically to the manufacturer, so the company could contact them if the tires were ever recalled. While this is still mandatory for tire dealers and distributors owned by tire manufacturers, it is not required of independent tire dealers. A recent government study found that 70 percent of independent tire dealers had not registered a single tire purchase. Ask for the tire registration card when you buy tires, and remember to fill it out and send it in. This information will allow the company to notify you if the tire is ever recalled.

Tire Grades

America's Top-Rated Tires

Brand Name	Model	Description	Grades			Expected Mileage		
			Trac.	Heat	Tred.	High	Medium	Low
Dunlop	Elite 65	15 & 16	A	B	540	162,000	108,000	81,000
Toyo	800 Plus	15	A	B	540	162,000	108,000	81,000
Vogue	CBR VII 65/70/75 S	14 & 15	A	B	540	162,000	108,000	81,000
Cooper	Grand Classic STE SR	All	A	B	520	156,000	104,000	78,000
Dunlop	Elite 65	14	A	B	520	156,000	104,000	78,000
Falls	Mark VII	All	A	B	520	156,000	104,000	78,000
Michelin	XH4	14 & 15	A	B	520	156,000	104,000	78,000
Toyo	800 Plus	14	A	B	520	156,000	104,000	78,000
Pirelli	P300 60/65	All	A	A	500	15,0000	1,00000	75,000
Atlas	Pinnacle TE 70	13	A	B	500	15,0000	1,00000	75,000
Atlas	Pinnacle TE 70/75	14 & 15	A	B	500	15,0000	1,00000	75,000
Dayton	Touring 70	All	A	B	500	15,0000	1,00000	75,000
Dayton	Touring 70/75s	All	A	B	500	15,0000	1,00000	75,000
Duralon	Touring Plus IV	All	A	B	500	15,0000	1,00000	75,000
Duralon	IV Plus	All	A	B	500	15,0000	1,00000	75,000
Gillette	Kodiak LE	All	A	B	500	15,0000	1,00000	75,000
Peerless	Permasteel LE	All	A	B	500	15,0000	1,00000	75,000
Pirelli	P300 80	All	A	B	500	15,0000	1,00000	75,000
Sumitomo	SC890 75	15	A	B	500	15,0000	1,00000	75,000
Cordovan	Grand Prix ST	All	A	B	480	144,000	96,000	72,000
Douglas	Premium Touring	All	A	B	480	144,000	96,000	72,000
Dunlop	Elite 65	13	A	B	480	144,000	96,000	72,000
Hallmark	Ultimate Touring	All	A	B	480	144,000	96,000	72,000
Kelly	Voyager 1,000 Touring	All	A	B	480	144,000	96,000	72,000
Lee	STL Trak	All	A	B	480	144,000	96,000	72,000
Michelin	XH4	13	A	B	480	144,000	96,000	72,000
Monarch	Ultra Touring GT	All	A	B	480	144,000	96,000	72,000
Multi-Mile	Grand Am ST	All	A	B	480	144,000	96,000	72,000
Sigma	Supreme ST	All	A	B	480	144,000	96,000	72,000
Star	Centurion Touring	All	A	B	480	144,000	96,000	72,000
Vanderbilt	Turbo Tech Tour G/T	All	A	B	480	144,000	96,000	72,000
Winston	Signature Premium	All	A	B	480	144,000	96,000	72,000
Big-O	Legacy 70/75	15	A	B	460	138,000	92,000	69,000
Big-O	Legacy 65	P205/65R15	A	B	460	138,000	92,000	69,000
Brigadier	Touring 65	P205/65R15	A	B	460	138,000	92,000	69,000
Brigadier	Touring 70/75	15	A	B	460	138,000	92,000	69,000
General	GS	All	A	B	460	138,000	92,000	69,000
General	Ameri Tech ST	P215,P225/75R15	A	B	460	138,000	92,000	69,000
General	Ameri Tech ST	15	A	B	460	138,000	92,000	69,000
General	Ameri Tech 4 75	15	A	B	460	138,000	92,000	69,000
Pirelli	P300 70/75	All	A	B	460	138,000	92,000	69,000
Reynolds	Touring 65	P205/65R15	A	B	460	138,000	92,000	69,000
Reynolds	Touring 70/75	15	A	B	460	138,000	92,000	69,000
Sonic	Sentinel 70/75	15	A	B	460	138,000	92,000	69,000
Sonic	Sentinel 65	P205/65R15	A	B	460	138,000	92,000	69,000
Touring	65	P205/65R15	A	B	460	138,000	92,000	69,000
Touring	70/75	15	A	B	460	138,000	92,000	69,000
Toyo	800 Plus	13	A	B	460	138,000	92,000	69,000
Vogue	CBR VII 60 V	16	A	A	440	132,000	88,000	66,000
Atlas	Pinnacal TE 80	13	A	B	440	132,000	88,000	66,000
Big-O	Legacy 70/75	14 & 15	A	B	440	132,000	88,000	66,000
Brigadier	Touring 70//75	14	A	B	440	132,000	88,000	66,000
Delta	Supreme 70/75	15	A	B	440	132,000	88,000	66,000
General	Ameri Tech 4 75	14	A	B	440	132,000	88,000	66,000
General	Ameri Tech 4 70	P205/70R14	A	B	440	132,000	88,000	66,000
General	Ameri Tech ST 70	14	A	B	440	132,000	88,000	66,000
Medalist	Precept 70/75	15	A	B	440	132,000	88,000	66,000
Montgomery Ward	Yokohama	14 & 15	A	B	440	132,000	88,000	66,000

Brand Name	Model	Description	Grades			Expected Mileage		
			Trac.	Heat	Tred.	High	Medium	Low
National	XT6,000 70/75	15	A	B	440	132,000	88,000	66,000
Reynolds	Touring 70/75	14	A	B	440	132,000	88,000	66,000
Sonic	Sentinel 70/75	14	A	B	440	132,000	88,000	66,000
Sumitomo	SC890 75	14	A	B	440	132,000	88,000	66,000
Touring	70/75	14	A	B	440	132,000	88,000	66,000
Armstrong	Evolution	14 & 15	A	B	420	126,000	84,000	63,000
Continental	CS24 70/75	All	A	B	420	126,000	84,000	63,000
Cooper	Lifeline, Touring	15 & 16	A	B	420	126,000	84,000	63,000
Cordovan	Grand Prix 70	15	A	B	420	126,000	84,000	63,000
Cordovan	Grand Prix SE70	15	A	B	420	126,000	84,000	63,000
Cordovan	Grand Prix STE	All	A	B	420	126,000	84,000	63,000
Dean	Quasar	15 & 16	A	B	420	126,000	84,000	63,000
Dean	Cheetah 70	15	A	B	420	126,000	84,000	63,000
Delta	Supreme 70/75	14	A	B	420	126,000	84,000	63,000
Douglas	Premium WTE	All	A	B	420	126,000	84,000	63,000
Dorado	Marquis SR	All	A	B	420	126,000	84,000	63,000
El Dorado	Crusader	15 & 16	A	B	420	126,000	84,000	63,000
Falls	P-70 SR	15	A	B	420	126,000	84,000	63,000
Falls	P-60/65 SR	15 & 16	A	B	420	126,000	84,000	63,000
Firestone	Widetrack SR	P205/65R15	A	B	420	126,000	84,000	63,000
Hallmark	Prestige PWR4	All	A	B	420	126,000	84,000	63,000
Kelly	Navigator 800S	All	A	B	420	126,000	84,000	63,000
Laramie	Touring	All	A	B	420	126,000	84,000	63,000
Laramie	LTD 1011	15 & 16	A	B	420	126,000	84,000	63,000
Lee	GT VI Trak	All	A	B	420	126,000	84,000	63,000
Medalist	Precept 70/75	14	A	B	420	126,000	84,000	63,000
Monarch	Ultra Trak	All	A	B	420	126,000	84,000	63,000
Montgomery Ward	Road Tamer 900	4 & 15	A	B	420	126,000	84,000	63,000
Montgomery Ward	Road Tamer LX	4 & 15	A	B	420	126,000	84,000	63,000
Multi-Mile	Grand Am STE	All	A	B	420	126,000	84,000	63,000
Multi-Mile	Grand Am SE70	15	A	B	420	126,000	84,000	63,000
Multi-Mile	Grand Am RWL 70	15	A	B	420	126,000	84,000	63,000
National	XT6,000 70/75	14	A	B	420	126,000	84,000	63,000
Pos-A-Trac	Performance	All	A	B	420	126,000	84,000	63,000
Road King	Regency Touring	All	A	B	420	126,000	84,000	63,000
Sigma	Supreme STE	All	A	B	420	126,000	84,000	63,000
Sigma	Supreme 70	15	A	B	420	126,000	84,000	63,000
Sigma	Grand Sport RWL 70	15	A	B	420	126,000	84,000	63,000
Star	Imperial	All	A	B	420	126,000	84,000	63,000
Starfire	Spectrum SR	15 & 16	A	B	420	126,000	84,000	63,000
Vanderbilt	Turbo Tech Tour A/S	All	A	B	420	126,000	84,000	63,000
Vogue	Premium	All	A	B	420	126,000	84,000	63,000
Winston	Classic 70/75	All	A	B	420	126,000	84,000	63,000
Armstrong	Evolution	P235/75R15	A	C	420	126,000	84,000	63,000
Cordovan	Grand Prix STE	XL	A	C	420	126,000	84,000	63,000
Hallmark	Prestige PWR4	235/75R15	A	C	420	126,000	84,000	63,000
Kelly	Navigator 800S	235/75R15	A	C	420	126,000	84,000	63,000
Lee	GT VI Trak	235/75R15	A	C	420	126,000	84,000	63,000
Monarch	Ultra Trak	235/75R15	A	C	420	126,000	84,000	63,000
Multi-Mile	Grand Am STE	XL	A	C	420	126,000	84,000	63,000
Sigma	Supreme STE	XL	A	C	420	126,000	84,000	63,000
Star	Imperial	235/75R15	A	C	420	126,000	84,000	63,000
Cooper	Monogram	All	B	B	420	126,000	84,000	63,000
Cordovan	Centron	All	B	B	420	126,000	84,000	63,000
Falls	Solitare SR	All	B	B	420	126,000	84,000	63,000
Multi-Mile	Matrix	All	B	B	420	126,000	84,000	63,000
Sumitomo	SC890 80	All	B	B	420	126,000	84,000	63,000
Cooper	Monogram	P235/75R15	B	C	420	126,000	84,000	63,000
Falls	Solitare SR	235/75R15	B	C	420	126,000	84,000	63,000

COMPLAINTS

Americans spend billions of dollars on motor vehicle repairs every year. While many of those repairs are satisfactory, there are times when getting your vehicle fixed can be a very difficult process. In fact, vehicle defects and repairs are the number one cause of consumer complaints in the U.S., according to the Federal Trade Commission.

This chapter is designed to help you resolve your complaint, whether it's for a new vehicle still under warranty or for one you've had for years. In addition, we offer a guide to arbitration, the names and addresses of consumer groups, federal agencies, and the manufacturers themselves. Finally, we tell you how to take the important step of registering your complaint with the National Highway Traffic Safety Administration.

No matter what your complaint, keep accurate records. Copies of the following items are indispensable in helping to resolve your problems:

- your service invoices
- bills you have paid
- letters you have written to the manufacturer or the repair facility owner
- written repair estimates from your independent mechanic.

Complaint Resolution Checklist: If you are having trouble, here are some basic steps to help you resolve your problem.

First, return your vehicle to the repair facility that did the work. Bring a written list of the problems, and make sure that you keep a copy of the list. Give the repair facility a reasonable opportunity to examine your vehicle and attempt to fix it. Speak directly to the service manager (not to the service writer who wrote up your repair order), and ask him or her to test drive the vehicle with you so that you can point out the problem.

If you can't get the problem resolved, take the vehicle to another mechanic for an independent examination. This may cost $45 to $60. Get a written statement defining the problem and outlining how it may be fixed. Give your repair shop a copy. If your vehicle is under warranty, do not allow any warranty repair by an independent mechanic; you may not be reimbursed by the manufacturer.

If your repair shop does not respond to the independent assessment, present your problem to a mediation panel. These panels hear both sides of the story and try to come to a resolution.

If the problem is with a new vehicle dealer, or if you feel that the manufacturer is responsible, you may be able to use one of the manufacturer's mediation programs discussed on page 74.

If the problem is solely with an independent dealer, a local Better Business Bureau (BBB) may be able to mediate your complaint. It may also offer an arbitration hearing. In any case, the BBB should enter your complaint into its files on that establishment.

When contacting any mediation program, determine how long the process takes, who makes the final decision, whether you are bound by that decision, and whether the program handles all problems or only warranty complaints.

If there are no mediation programs in your area, contact private consumer groups, local government agencies, or your local "action line" newspaper columnist, newspaper editor, or radio or TV broadcaster. A phone call or letter from them may persuade a repair facility to take action. Send a copy of your letter to the repair shop.

One of your last resorts is to bring a law suit against the dealer, manufacturer, or repair facility in small claims court. The fee for filing such an action is usually small, and you generally act as your own attorney, saving attorney's fees. There is a monetary limit on the amount you can claim, which varies from state to state. Your local consumer affairs office, state attorney general's office, or the clerk of the court can tell you how to file such a suit.

Finally, talk with an attorney. It's best to select an attorney who is familiar with handling automotive problems. If you don't know of one, call the lawyer referral service listed in the telephone directory and ask for the names of attorneys who deal with automobile problems. If you can't afford an attorney, contact the Legal Aid Society.

Warranty Complaints: If your vehicle is under warranty or you are having problems with a factory-authorized dealership here are some special guidelines:

Have the warranty available to show the dealer. Make sure you call the problem to the dealer's attention before the end of the warranty period.

If you are still unsatisfied after giving the dealer a reasonable opportunity to fix your vehicle, contact the manufacturer's representative (also called the zone representative) in your area. This person can authorize the dealer to make repairs or take other steps to resolve the dispute. Your dealer will have your zone representative's name and telephone num-

ber. Explain the problem and ask for a meeting and a personal inspection of your vehicle.

If you can't get satisfaction from the zone representative, call or write the manufacturer's owner relations department. Your owner's manual contains this phone number and address. In each case, as you move up the chain, indicate the steps you have already taken.

Your next option is to present your problem to a complaint-handling panel or to the arbitration program in which the manufacturer of your vehicle participates. See page 76 for additional information.

If you complain of a problem during the warranty period, you have a right to have the problem fixed even after the warranty runs out. If your warranty has not been honored, you may be able to "revoke acceptance," which means

that you return the vehicle to the dealer. If you are successful, you may be entitled to a replacement vehicle or to a full refund of the purchase price and reimbursement of legal fees, under the Magnuson-Moss Warranty Act. Or, if you are covered by one of the state Lemon Laws, you may be able to return the vehicle and receive a refund or replacement from the manufacturer. For more information on Lemon Laws, see page 82.

You may also contact the Center for Auto Safety, 2001 S St. NW, Washington, DC 20009. The Center can provide the names of lawyers in your area who handle consumer automobile problems. The Center also has published *The Lemon Book*, a detailed, 368-page guide to resolving automobile complaints. The book is available for $15.95 from the Center.

Legal Aid

If you need legal assistance with your repair problem, the Center for Auto Safety has a list of lawyers who specialize in helping consumers with auto repair problems. For the names of some attorneys in your area, send a stamped, self-addressed envelope to: Center for Auto Safety, 2001 S Street, NW, Washington, D.C. 20009-1160.

Attorneys Take Note: For information on litigation assistance provided by the Center for Auto Safety, including The Lemon Law Litigation Manual, please contact the Center for Auto Safety at the above address.

One of the most valuable but often unused services of the government is the Auto Safety Hotline. By calling the Hotline to report safety problems, your particular concern or problem will become part of the National Highway Traffic Safety Administration's (NHTSA) complaint database. This complaint program is extraordinarily important to government decision makers who often take action based on this information. In addition, it provides consumer groups, like the Center for Auto Safety, with the evidence they need to force the government to act. Unless government engineers or safety advocates have evidence of a wide-scale problem, little can be done to get the manufacturers to correct the defect.

Few government services have the potential to do as much for the consumer as this complaint database, so we encourage you to voice your concerns to the government.

Your letter can be used as the basis of safety defect investigations and recall campaigns. Be sure to write on the NHTSA complaint to make it public, otherwise NHTSA will keep it confidential.

Hotline Complaints: When you call the Hotline to report a safety problem, you will be mailed a questionnaire asking for information that the agency's technical staff will need to evaluate the problem. *Note: A copy of the actual questionnaire appears on the last page of this book. If you like, you can remove and use this questionnaire.*

After you complete and return the questionnaire, the following things will happen:
1. A copy will go to NHTSA's safety defect investigators.
2. A copy will be sent to the manufacturer of the vehicle or equipment, with a request for help in resolving the problem.
3. You will be notified that your questionnaire has been received.

The questionnaire asks for information that the agency's technical staff will need to evaluate the problem. This information also gives the government an indication of which vehicles are causing consumers the most problems.

You can also use this questionnaire to report defects in tires and child safety seats. In fact, we strongly encourage you to report problems with child safety seats. Now that they are required by law in all fifty states, we have noticed that numerous design and safety problems have surfaced. If the government knows about these problems, they will be more likely to take action so that modifications are made to these life-saving devices.

Hotline Services: Hotline operators can also provide information on recalls. If you want recall information on a particular automobile, simply tell the Hotline operator the make, model, and year of the vehicle, or the type of equipment involved. You will receive any recall information that NHTSA has about that vehicle or item. This information can be very important if you are not sure whether your vehicle has ever been recalled. If you want a printed copy of the recall information, it will be mailed within twenty-four hours at no charge.

If you have other vehicle-related problems, the Hotline operators can refer you to the appropriate federal, state, and local government agencies. If you need information about federal safety standards and regulations, you'll be referred to the appropriate experts.

You may call the Hotline day or night, seven days a week. If you call when no operators are available, a recorded message will ask you to leave your name and address and a description of the information you want. The appropriate materials will be mailed to you.

Complaints and Safety Information

Auto Safety Hotline
800-424-9393
(in Washington, D.C.: 202-366-0123)
TTY for hearing impaired:
800-424-9153
(in Washington, D.C.: 202-366-7800)

The toll-free Auto Safety Hotline can provide information on recalls, record information about safety problems, and refer you to the appropriate government experts on other vehicle related problems. You can even have recall information mailed to you within 24 hours of your call at no charge.

Arbitration

An increasingly popular method of resolving automobile repair problems is through arbitration. This procedure requires that both parties present their cases to a mediator or panel that makes a decision based on the merits of the complaint. You can seek repairs, reimbursement of expenses, or a refund or replacement for your vehicle through arbitration.

In theory, arbitration can be an effective means of resolving disputes. It is somewhat informal, relatively speedy, and you do not need a lawyer to present your case. If you resolve your problem through arbitration, you avoid the time and expense of going to court.

Almost all manufacturers now offer some form of arbitration, usually for problems that arise during the warranty period. Some companies run their own and others subscribe to programs run by groups like the Better Business Bureau or the American Automobile Association. Your owner's manual will identify which programs you can use. Also, contact your state attorney general to find out what programs your state offers.

How it works: Upon receiving your complaint, the arbitration program will attempt to mediate a resolution between you and the manufacturer or dealer. If you are not satisfied with the proposed solution, you have the right to have your case heard at an arbitration hearing.

These hearings vary among the programs. In the BBB program, each party presents its case in person to a volunteer arbitrator. The other programs will decide your case based on written submissions from both you and the manufacturer.

If an arbitration program is incorporated into your warranty, you may have to use that program before filing a legal claim. However, you may always go to small claims court instead of using arbitration. Federal law requires that arbitration programs incorporated into a warranty be nonbinding on the consumer. That is, if you do not like the result, you can seek other remedies.

Arbitration programs have different eligibility requirements, so be sure you are eligible for the program you are considering.

Let the Federal Trade Commission, the Center for Auto Safety (their addresses are on pages 82 and 81, respectively), and your state attorney general (c/o your state capitol) know of your experience with arbitration. It is particularly important to contact these offices if you have a complaint about how your case was handled.

Ford Dispute Settlement Board: This was one of the first panels established by a manufacturer. Each case is considered by a four-person panel that includes one dealer, who has no vote. In most cases, no oral presentations are given. Only cases under warranty are reviewed. For information, call 800-392-3673.

Chrysler Customer Arbitration Board: No oral presentations are allowed under this program—decisions are based on written submissions by each party. A Chrysler zone representative and dealer are on the panel but cannot vote. The panel will only hear cases under warranty. (In Maryland, Chrysler will sometimes hear cases beyond the warranty.) For information, call 800-992-1997.

Better Business Bureau Arbitration Programs (Auto Line): The BBB always tries to mediate a dispute before recommending arbitration. Fewer than 10 percent of the disputes it handles actually go to arbitration. Theoretically, each party receives a list of potential arbitrators with a background description of each person and then ranks them according to preference. The arbitrator with the most votes handles the case. But in actual fact, the consumer rarely has a voice in the selection of an arbitrator.

The arbitrators are volunteers from the local community and sometimes are not automobile experts. This can both help and harm your case. As a result, it is important to be well prepared when participating in the BBB program. If you're not, the potential exists for the dealer or manufacturer to appear as the "expert" on automobiles. For more information, contact your local BBB or 800-955-5100.

Automobile Consumer Action Program: AUTOCAP was established by the National Automobile Dealers Association to assist consumers in resolving auto sales or service disputes with dealers and manufacturers. The program is sponsored on a voluntary basis by state and local dealer associations. Currently, most AUTOCAPs do not operate under the FTC guidelines required for warranty cases. Sixty-five percent of the cases that

AUTOCAP considers are resolved in preliminary mediation. Of those cases that go to arbitration, 45 percent are resolved in favor of the consumer, 22 percent are a compromise, and 33 percent are in favor of the company. For more information and the name of your local panel, contact: AUTOCAP, 8400 Westpark Drive, McLean, Virginia 22102; 703-821-7144.

State-Run Arbitration

State-run arbitration programs are often more fair to consumers than national programs. The following states have set up state programs (or guidelines) which are far better than their national counterparts. If you live in one of these areas, contact your attorney general's office for information. Even if your state is not listed below, you can contact your state attorney general's office (in care of your state capitol) for advice on arbitration.

Connecticut	Hawaii	New Jersey	South Carolina
D. C.	Massachusetts	New Hampshire	Texas
Florida	Maine	New York	Vermont
Georgia	Montana	Rhode Island	Washington

Ten Tips for Arbitration

Arbitration is designed to be easier and less intimidating than going to court. However, the process can still be nerve-racking, especially if you've never been through it before. Here are some tips to help make the process as simple and straightforward as possible.

1 Before deciding to go to arbitration, get a written description of how the program works, and make sure you understand the details. If you have any questions, contact the local representatives of the program. Remember, the manufacturer or dealer probably has more experience with this process than you do.

2 Make sure the final decision is nonbinding on you. If the decision is binding, you give up your right to appeal.

3 Determine whether the program allows you to appear at the hearing. If not, make sure your written statement is complete and contains all the appropriate receipts and documentation. If you think of something that you want considered after you have sent in your material, send it and specifically request that the additional information be included.

4 Make sure the program follows the required procedures. If the arbitration program is incorporated into the vehicle's warranty, for example, the panel must make a decision on your case within 40 days of receiving your complaint.

5 Contact the manufacturer's zone manager and request copies of any technical service bulletins that apply to your vehicle. (See "Secret Warranties" on page 57 for a description of technical service bulletins and how to get them.) Service bulletins may help you prove that your vehicle is defective.

6 Well before the hearing, ask the program representative to send you copies of all material submitted by the other party. You may want to respond to this information.

7 Make sure all your documents are in chronological order, and include a brief outline of the events. Submit copies of all material associated with your problem and a copy of your warranty.

8 Even though you may be very angry about the situation, try to present your case in a calm, logical manner.

9 If you are asking for a refund or a replacement for your vehicle in accordance with your state's Lemon Law, do not assume that the arbitrator is completely familiar with the law. Be prepared to explain how it entitles you to your request.

10 In most programs, you have to reject the decision in order to go to court to pursue other action. If you accept the decision, you may limit your rights to pursue further action. You will, however, have additional claims if the manufacturer or dealer does not properly follow through on the decision or if your vehicle breaks down again.

Complaint Index

Thanks to the efforts of the Center for Auto Safety, we are able to provide you with the vehicle complaints on file with the National Highway Traffic Safety Administration (NHTSA). Each year, thousands of Americans call the government to register complaints about their vehicles. The government collects this information but has never released it to the public.

The complaint index is the result of our analysis of these complaints. It is based on a ratio of the number of complaints for each vehicle to the sales of that vehicle. In order to predict the expected complaint performance of the 1995 models, we have examined the complaint history of that car's *series*. The term series refers to the fact that when a manufacturer introduces a new model, that vehicle remains essentially unchanged for 4-6 years. For example, the Chevrolet Lumina Minivan was introduced in 1990 and remains essentially the same vehicle for 1995. As such, we have compiled the complaint experience for that series in order to give you some additional information to use in deciding which car to buy. For those vehicles just introduced in 1994 or 1995, we do not yet have enough data to develop a complaint index.

The following table presents the complaint indices for the best and worst 1995 models. Higher index numbers mean the vehicle generated a greater number of complaints. Lower numbers indicate fewer complaints. After calculating the indices, we compared the results among all 1995 vehicles.

1995 Complaint Ratings

The Best		The Worst	
Vehicle	Index	Vehicle	Index
Isuzu Pickup	470	Jeep Grand Cherokee	14548
Nissan Pickup	688	Chevy Suburban	12697
Toyota Pickup	1043	Chry. T & C	12179
Dodge Ram Van/Wgn.	1107	GMC Yukon	12052
Toyota T100	1222	Mercury Villager	11096
Chevy Van/Sport Van	1376	GMC Suburban	11037
Suzuki Samurai	1484	Nissan Quest	8604
GMC Vandura Rally	1624	Toyota Land Cruiser	8399
GMC Sierra	1647	Plymouth Voyager	7670
Chevy CK Pickup	1832	Dodge Caravan	7610
Ford F-Series Pickup	1883	Mazda MPV	6284
Nissan Pathfinder	2062	Jeep Cherokee	6122
Chevy Lumina Minivan	2154	Isuzu Rodeo	5781
Geo Tracker	2258	Jeep Wrangler	5708
Mits. Mighty Max	2469	Toyota Previa	4604
Isuzu Trooper	2627	Olds Silhouette	4576
Suzuki Sidekick	2731	Ford Aerostar	4538
Chevy Astro	2900	Land Rover Range Rover	4532
Toyota 4Runner	2968	Ford Ranger	3917
Ford Econol./Club Wgn.	3010	Isuzu Amigo	3875
GMC Safari	3206	Ford Bronco	3826
Dodge Dakota	3578	Pontiac Trans Sport	3694

Center for Auto Safety

Every year automobile manufacturers spend millions of dollars making their voices heard in government decision making. For example, General Motors and Ford have large staffs in Detroit and Washington that work solely to influence government activity. But who looks out for the consumer?

For over twenty years, the non-profit Center for Auto Safety (CAS) has told the consumer's story to government agencies, to Congress and to the courts. Its efforts focus on all consumers rather than only those with individual complaints.

The Center for Auto Safety was established in 1970 by Ralph Nader and Consumers Union. As consumer concerns about auto safety issues expanded, so did the work of CAS. It became an independent group in 1972, and the original staff of two has grown to fourteen attorneys and researchers. CAS' activities include:

Initiating Safety Recalls: CAS analyzes over 50,000 consumer complaints each year. By following problems as they develop, CAS requests government investigations and recalls of defective vehicles. CAS was responsible for the Ford Pinto faulty gas tank recall, the Firestone 500 steel-belted radial tire recall, and more recently the record recall of over 3 million Evenflo One Step child seats.

Representing the Consumer in Washington: CAS follows the activities of federal agencies and Congress to ensure that they carry out their responsibilities to the American taxpayer. CAS brings a consumer's point of view to vehicle safety policies and rule-mak-

ing. Since 1970, CAS has submitted more than 450 petitions and comments on federal safety standards.

One major effort in this area has been the successful fight for adoption of automatic crash protection in passenger cars. These systems are a more effective and less intrusive alternative to crash protection than mandatory safety belt laws or belts that must be buckled in order to start the car.

Three years ago, the Center for Auto Safety uncovered a fire defect that dwarfed the highly publicized flammability of the Ford Pinto. It had to do with the side-saddle gas tanks on full size 1973-87 GM pickups and 1988-90 crew cabs that tend to explode on impact. Over 1,200 people have been killed in fire crashes involving these trucks. After mounting a national campaign to warn consumers to steer clear of these GM fire hazards, the U.S. Department of Transportation granted CAS' petition and conducted one of its biggest defect investigations in history. The result—GM was asked to recall its pickups. GM, sadly, is fighting this request.

Thanks to a petition originally filed by CAS, NHTSA adopted a new registration system to better enable manufacturer notification to parents with defective child seats. This will enable more parents to find out about potentially hazardous safety seats.

Exposing Secret Warranties: CAS played a prominent role in the disclosure of secret warranties, "policy adjustments," as they are called by manufacturers. These occur when an auto maker agrees to pay for repair of certain defects

beyond the warranty period but refuses to notify consumers. (See "Secret Warranties" in the Warranty Chapter.)

Improving Rust Warranties: Rust and corrosion cost American car owners up to $14 billion annually. CAS has been successful in its efforts to get domestic and foreign auto companies to lengthen their all-important rust warranties.

Lemon Laws: CAS work on Lemon Laws aided in the enactment of state laws which make it easier to return a defective new automobile and get money back.

Tire Ratings: After a suspension between 1982-84, consumers have reliable treadwear ratings to help them get the most miles for their dollar. CAS' lawsuit overturned DOT's revocation of this valuable new tire information program.

Initiating Legal Action: When CAS has exhausted other means of obtaining relief for consumer problems, it will initiate legal action. For example, in 1978 when the Department of Energy attempted to raise the price of gasoline 4 cents per gallon without notice or comment, CAS succeeded in stopping this illegal move through a lawsuit, thus saving consumers $2 billion for the six month period that the action was delayed.

A Center for Auto Safety lawsuit against the Environmental Protection Agency, in 1985, forced the EPA to recall polluting cars, rather than let companies promise to make cleaner cars in the future. As part of the settlement, GM (which was responsible for the polluting cars) funded a $7.

millioncomplete description of all of the CAS' publications, send a separate stamped, self-addressed, business-sized envelope with 52 cents postage to the address below. Unless otherwise noted, the packets listed cover all known major problems for the models indicated and explain what to do about them. Requests for information should include make, model and year of vehicle (with VIN number) as well as the type of problem you are experiencing. (Allow 2 to 3 weeks for delivery.)

Airbag Deployment Fact Sheet (1993)
Audi Defects (1978-92)
Cadillac (1982-94)
Child Seat Recalls/Recommendations (1995)
Chrysler Paint/Water Leaks (1983-1992)
Chrysler Ultradrive Transmission (1989-94)
Chrysler Front-Wheel-Drive Cars/ Vans (1981-94)
Ford Aerostar (1986-94)
Ford Crown Victoria/Grand Marquis/Lincoln Continental/Town Car/Mark Series (1983-94)
Ford Escort/Lynx/Tracer (1981-94)
Ford F-Series Pickup Truck/Van Defects (1981-94)
Ford Taurus/Sable (1986-94)
Ford Tempo/Topaz (1984-94)
Ford Mustang/Capri/Probe (1979-94)
Ford Paint (1985-94)
GM Automatic Transmission: front-wheel-drive (1981-93)
GM Automatic Transmission: rear-wheel-drive (1981-92)
GM Beretta/Corsica (1987-94)
GM Cutlass Supreme/Grand Prix/ Lumina/Regal (1988-94)

GM Celebrity/6000/Century/Cutlass Ciera & Cruiser (1982-94)
GM Camaro/Firebird (1982-94)
GM Citation/Omega/Phoenix/ Skylark (1981-85)
GM Achieva/Calais/Grand Am/ Skylark/Somerset Regal (1985-94)
GM Buick Roadmaster/Chevrolet Caprice (1981-94)
GM Cavalier/Cimarron/Firenza/ Skyhawk/Sunbird/J2000 (1982-94)
GM LeSabre/Delta 88 & 98/ Bonneville/Electra & Park Avenue (1986-94)
GM Power Steering Failure (1980-88)
GM Large Pickup/Suburban & Blazer/Jimmy Utility Vehicle (1984-94)
GM S-series Truck/Blazer/Jimmy (1982-94)
GM Big Vans/Astro/Safari/APVs (1980-94)
GM Pontiac Fiero (1984-88)
GM Paint (1985-94)
Honda/Acura Defects (1979-94)

Hyundai Defects (1986-93)
Jeep–all models (1984-94)
Lemon Law Fact Sheet and Chart (1995)
Lemon Lawyer Recommendations (1995)
Mazda Defects (1977-94)
Minivan Safety (1995)
Mitsubishi Defects (1983-94)
Nissan Defects (1983-94)
Renault/Eagle/Dodge Defects (1981-94)
Toyota Defects (1983-94)
Volkswagen Defects (1980-94)
Volvo Defects (1980-94)

The Center for Auto Safety depends on the public for its support. Annual consumer membership is $15 ($20 for overseas). All contributions to this nonprofit organization are tax-deductible. Annual membership includes a quarterly newsletter called "LEMON TIMES." To join, send a check to:

Center for Auto Safety
2001 S St. NW, Suite 410, Washington, D.C. 20009-1160

Lemon Aid

TIP

The Center for Auto Safety has published *The Lemon Book,* a detailed, 368 page guide to resolving automobile complaints. Co-authored by Ralph Nader and the CAS Executive Director, Clarence Ditlow, this handbook is designed to help car buyers avoid lemons and tells you what to do if you wind up with one. To obtain this valuable book, send $15.95 to the Center for Auto Safety, 2001 S St., NW, Washington, DC 20009-1160. CAS is a non-profit consumer group supported, in part, by the sales of its publications.

Consumer Groups and Government

Here are the names of additional consumer groups which you may find helpful:

Consumer Action San Francisco
116 New Montgomery St., #233
San Francisco, CA 94105
(415) 777-9635
Focus: General problems of California residents.

Consumers Education and Protective Association
6048 Ogontz Avenue
Philadelphia, PA 19141
(215) 424-1441
Focus: Pickets on behalf of members to resolve auto purchase and repair problems.

Motor Voters
1500 W. El Camino Ave, #419
Sacramento, CA 95833-1945
(916) 920-5464
Focus: Auto safety, air bags, and lemon laws.

SafetyBelt Safe, U.S.A.
P.O. Box 553
Altadena, CA 91003
(800) 745-SAFE or
(310) 673-2666
Focus: Provides excellent information and training on child safety seats and safety belt usage.

VIGOR (Victims Group Opposed to Unsafe Restraint Systems)
9413 Ives Street
Bellflower, CA 90706
(310) 866-6680
Focus: Promotes the replacement of lap-only seat belts in existing vehicles and prevents their use in new vehicles.

Several federal agencies conduct automobile-related programs. Listed below is each agency with a description of the type of work it performs as well as the address and phone number for its headquarters in Washington, D.C.

National Highway Traffic Safety Administration
400 7th Street, SW, NOA-40
Washington, D.C. 20590
202-366-9550

NHTSA issues safety and fuel economy standards for new motor vehicles; investigates safety defects and enforces recall of defective vehicles and equipment; conducts research and demonstration programs on vehicle safety, fuel economy, driver safety, and automobile inspection and repair; provides grants for state highway safety programs in areas such as police traffic services, driver education and licensing, emergency medical services, pedestrian safety, and alcohol abuse.

Environmental Protection Agency
401 M Street, SW
Washington, D.C. 20460
202-260-2090

EPA is responsible for the control and abatement of air, noise, and toxic substance pollution. This includes setting and enforcing air and noise emission standards for motor vehicles and measuring fuel economy in new vehicles (EPA Fuel Economy Guide).

Federal Trade Commission
PA Avenue & 6th Street, NW
Washington, D.C. 20580
202-326-2000

FTC regulates advertising and credit practices, marketing abuses, and professional services and ensures that products are properly labeled (as in fuel economy ratings). The commission covers unfair or deceptive trade practices in motor vehicle sales and repairs, as well as in non-safety defects.

Federal Highway Administration
400 7th Street, SW,
Room 3401, HHS1
Washington, D.C. 20590
202-366-1153

FHA develops standards to ensure highways are constructed to reduce occurrence and severity of accidents.

Department of Justice
Consumer Litigation
Civil Division
5510 11th Street, NW
Washington, D.C. 20530
202-514-6786

The Department of Justice enforces the federal law that requires manufacturers to label new automobiles and forbids removal or alteration of labels before delivery to consumers. Labels must contain the make, model, vehicle identification number, dealer's name, suggested base price, manufacturer option costs, and manufacturer's suggested retail price.

Manufacturers

Mr. Robert Eaton
Chairman and CEO
Chrysler Corporation
12000 Chrysler Drive
Highland Park, MI 48288
(313) 956-5741
(313) 956-5143 (fax)

Mr. Alex Trotman
Chairman, President and CEO
Ford Motor Company
The American Road
Dearborn, MI 48103
(313) 322-3000
(313) 446-9475 (fax)

Mr. John F. Smith, Jr.
CEO and President
General Motors Corporation
General Motors Building
Detroit, MI 48202
(313) 556-5000
(313) 556-5108 (fax)

Mr. K. Amemiya
President
American Honda Motor Co.
1919 Torrance Blvd.
Torrance, CA 90501-2746
(310) 783-2000
(310) 783-3900 (fax)

Mr. Kozo Sakaino
President
American Isuzu Motors Inc.
P.O. Box 2480
City of Industry, CA 91746
(310) 699-0500
(310) 692-7135 (fax)

Mr. H.R. Park
President
Kia Motors America Inc.
2 Cromwell
Irvine, CA 92619-2410
(714) 470-7000
(714) 470-2800 (fax)

Mr. Charles R. Hughes
President
Land Rover of America
4390 Parliament Place
Lanham, MD 20706
(301) 731-9040
(301) 731-9054 (fax)

Mr. Yoji Toyama
President
Mazda (North America), Inc.
22000 Gibraltar Rd.
Flat Rock, MI 48134
(714) 727-1990
(714) 727-6529 (fax)

Mr. Tohei Takeuchi
President
Mitsubishi Motor Sales
6400 Katella
Cypress, CA 90630
(714) 372-6000
(714) 373-1019 (fax)

Mr. Robert Thomas
President and CEO
Nissan Motor Corp. U.S.A.
P.O. Box 191
Gardena, CA 90248-0191
(310) 532-3111
(310) 719-3343 (fax)

Mr. Yoshinori Fujii
President
American Suzuki Motor Corp.
3251 E. Imperial Hwy.
Brea, CA 92621-6722
(714) 996-7040
(714) 524-2512 (fax)

Mr. Shinji Sakai
President and CEO
Toyota Motors Sales, U.S.A., Inc.
19001 S. Western Avenue
Torrance, CA 90509
(310) 618-4000
(310) 618-7800 (fax)

Mr. John Kerr
President
Volkswagen of America, Inc.
3800 Hamlin Road
Auburn Hills, MI 48326
(810) 340-5000
(810) 340-4643 (fax)

Lemon Laws

Sometimes, despite our best efforts, we buy a vehicle that just doesn't work right. There may be little problem after little problem, or perhaps one big problem that never seems to be fixed. Because of the bad taste that such vehicles leave in the mouths of consumers who buy them, these vehicles are known as "lemons."

In the past, it's been difficult to obtain a refund or replacement if a vehicle was a lemon. The burden of proof was left to the consumer. Because it is hard to define exactly what constitutes a lemon, many lemon owners were unable to win a case against a manufacturer. But things are changing. As of 1993, all states have passed "Lemon Laws."

Although there are some important state-to-state variations, all of the laws have similarities: They establish a period of coverage, usually one year from delivery or the written warranty period, whichever is shorter; they may require some form of noncourt arbitration; and most importantly they define a lemon. In most states a lemon is a new car, truck, or van that has been taken back to the shop at least four times for the same repair or is out of service for a total of 30 days during the covered period.

This time does not mean consecutive days. In some states the total time must be for the same repair; in others, it can be based on different repair problems.

Be sure to keep careful records of your repairs since some states now require only one of the three or four repairs to be within the specified time period.

Specific information about laws in your state can be obtained from your state attorney general's office (c/o your state capitol) or your local consumer protection office. The following table offers a general description of the Lemon Law in your state and what you need to do to set it in motion (*Notification/Trigger*). An **L** indicates that the law covers leased vehicles and we indicate where state-run arbitration programs are available. State-run programs are the best type of arbitration.

Alabama	**Qualification:** 3 unsuccessful repairs or 30 calendar days out of service within shorter of 24 months or 24,000 miles, provided 1 repair attempt or 1 day out of service is within shorter of 1 year or 12,000 miles. **Notification/Trigger:** Certified mail notice to manufacturer, who has 14 calendar days to make final repair.
Alaska	**Qualification:** 3 unsuccessful repairs or 30 business days out of service within shorter of 1 year or warranty. **Notification/Trigger:** Certified mail notice to manufacturer and dealer, or agent within 60 days after expiration of warranty or 1 year. Consumer must demand refund or replacement to be delivered within 60 days after mailing the notice. Final repair attempt within 30 days of receipt of notice.
Arizona	**Qualification:** 4 unsuccessful repairs or 30 calendar days out of service within shorter of 1 year or warranty. **Notification/Trigger:** Written notice to manufacturer and opportunity to repair.
Arkansas	**Qualification:** 3 unsuccessful repairs, or 1 unsuccessful repair of a problem likely to cause death or serious bodily injury within longer of 24 months or 24,000 miles. **Notification/Trigger:** Certified or registered mail notice to manufacturer. Manufacturer has 10 days to notify consumer of repair facility. Facility has 10 days to repair.
California	**Qualification:** 4 unsuccessful repairs or 30 calendar days out of service within shorter of 1 year or 12,000 miles. **Notification/Trigger:** Written notice to manufacturer and delivery of car to repair facility for repair attempt within 30 days. *State has certified guidelines for arbitration.* **L**
Colorado	**Qualification:** 4 unsuccessful repairs or 30 business days out of service within shorter of 1 year or warranty. **Notification/Trigger:** Prior certified mail notice for each defect occurance and opportunity to repair.
Conn.	**Qualification:** 4 unsuccessful repairs or 30 calendar days out of service within shorter of 2 years or 18,000 miles, or 2 repairs of problem likely to cause death or serious bodily injury within shorter of 1 year or warranty. **Notification/Trigger:** Report to manufacturer, agent or dealer. Written notice to manufacturer only if required in owner's manual or warranty. *State-run arbitration program is available.* **L**

Delaware	**Qualification:** 4 unsuccessful repairs or 30 calendar days out of service within shorter of 1 year or warranty. **Notification/Trigger:** Written notice to manufacturer and opportunity to repair. L
D.C.	**Qualification:** 4 unsuccessful repairs or 30 calendar days out of service or 1 unsuccesful repair of a safety-related defect, within shorter of 2 years or 18,000 miles. **Notification/Trigger:** Report of each defect occurance to manufacturer, agent or dealer. *State-run arbitration program is available.* L
Florida	**Qualification:** 3 unsuccessful repairs or 20 calendar days out of service within shorter of 12 months or 12,000 miles. **Notification/Trigger:** Written notice by certified or express mail to manufacturer who has 14 calendar days (10 if vehicle has been out of service 20 cumulative calendar days) for final repair attempt after delivery to designated dealer. *State-run arbitration program is available.* L
Georgia*	**Qualification:** 3 unsuccessful repair attempts or 30 calendar days out of service within shorter of 24,000 miles or 24 months, with 1 repair or 15 days out of service within shorter or 1 year or 12,000 miles; or one unsuccessful repair of a serious safety defect in the braking or steering system within shorter of 1 year or 12,000 miles. **Notification/Trigger:** Certified mail notice return receipt requested. Manufacturer has 7 days to notify consumer of repair facility. Facility has 14 days to repair. *State-run arbitration program is available.* L
Hawaii	**Qualification:** 3 unsuccessful repairs, or 1 unsuccessful repair of a nonconformity likely to cause death or serious bodily injury, or out of service within shorter of 2 years or 24,000 miles. **Notification/Trigger:** Written notice to manufacturer and opportunity to repair. *State-run arbitration program is available.* L
Idaho	**Qualification:** 4 repair attempts or 30 business days out of service within shorter of 12 months or 12,000 miles. **Notification/Trigger:** Written notice to manufacturer or dealer.
Illinois*	**Qualification:** 4 unsuccessful repairs or 30 business days out of service within shorter of 1 year or 12,000 miles. **Notification/Trigger:** Written notice to manufacturer and opportunity to repair.
Indiana	**Qualification:** 4 unsuccessful repairs or 30 business days out of service within the shorter of 18 months or 18,000 miles. **Notification/Trigger:** Written notice to manufacturer only if required in warranty. L
Iowa	**Qualification:** 3 unsuccessful repairs, or 1 unsuccessful repair of a nonconformity likely to cause death or serious bodily injury, or 20 calendar days out of service within shorter of 2 years or 24,000 miles. **Notification/Trigger:** Written notice to manufacturer and final opportunity to repair within 10 calendar days of receipt of notice. *State has certified guidelines for arbitration.* L
Kansas	**Qualification:** 4 unsuccessful repairs of the same problem or 30 calendar days out of service or 10 total repairs of any problem within shorter of 1 year or warranty. **Notification/Trigger:** Actual notice to manufacturer.
Kentucky	**Qualification:** 4 unsuccessful repairs or 30 calendar days out of service within shorter of 1 year or 12,000 miles. **Notification/Trigger:** Written notice to manufacturer.
Louisiana	**Qualification:** 4 unsuccessful repairs or 30 calendar days out of service within shorter of 1 year or warranty. **Notification/Trigger:** Report to manufacturer or dealer. L
Maine	**Qualification:** 3 unsuccessful repairs (when at least 2 times the same agent attempted the repair) or 15 business days out of service within shorter of 2 years or 18,000 miles. **Notification/Trigger:** Written notice to manufacturer or dealer only if required in warranty or owner's manual. Manufacturer has 7 business days after receipt for final repair attempt. *State has certified guidelines for arbitration.* L

Maryland	**Qualification:** 4 unsuccessful repairs, 30 calendar days out of service or 1 unsuccessful repair of braking or steering system within shorter of 15 months or 15,000 miles. **Notification/Trigger:** Certified mail notice, return receipt requested to manu. or factory branch and opportunity to repair within 30 calendar days of receipt of notice. L
Mass.	**Qualification:** 3 unsuccessful repairs or 15 business days out of service within shorter of 1 year or 15,000 miles. **Notification/Trigger:** Notice to manufacturer or dealer who has 7 business days to attempt a final repair. *State-run arbitration program is available*
Michigan	**Qualification:** 4 unsuccessful repairs or 30 calendar days out of service within shorter of 1 year or warranty. **Notification/Trigger:** Certified mail notice, return receipt requested, to manufacturer who has 5 business days to repair after delivery.
Minn.	**Qualification:** 4 unsuccessful repairs or 30 business days out of service or 1 unsuccessful repair of total braking or steering loss likely to cause death or serious bodily injury within shorter of 2 years or warranty. **Notification/Trigger:** At least one written notice to manufacturer, agent or dealer and opportunity to repair. L
Miss.	**Qualification:** 3 unsuccessful repairs or 15 business days out of service within shorter of 1 year or warranty. **Notification/Trigger:** Written notice to manufacturer who has 10 business days to repair after delivery to designated dealer.
Missouri	**Qualification:** 4 unsuccessful repairs or 30 business days out of service within shorter of 1 year or warranty. **Notification/Trigger:** Written notice to manufacturer who has 10 calendar days to repair after delivery to designated dealer.
Montana	**Qualification:** 4 unsuccessful repairs or 30 business days out of service after notice within shorter of 2 years or 18,000 miles. **Notification/Trigger:** Written notice to manufacturer and opportunity to repair. *State-run arbitration program is available.*
Nebraska	**Qualification:** 4 unsuccessful repairs or 40 calendar days out of service within shorter of 1 year or warranty. **Notification/Trigger:** Certified mail notice to manufacturer and opportunity to repair.
Nevada	**Qualification:** 4 unsuccessful repairs or 30 calendar days out of service within shorter of 1 year or warranty. **Notification/Trigger:** Written notice to manufacturer.
N. H.	**Qualification:** 3 unsuccessful repairs by same dealer or 30 business days out of service within warranty. **Notification/Trigger:** Report to manufacturer, distributor, agent or dealer (on forms provided by manufacturer) and final opportunity to repair before arbitration. *State-run arbitration program is available.* L
N. J.	**Qualification:** 3 unsuccessful repairs or 20 calendar days out of service within shorter of 2 years or 18,000 miles. **Notification/Trigger:** Certified mail notice, return receipt requested to manufacturer who has 10 days to repair. L
N. M.	**Qualification:** 4 unsuccessful repairs or 30 business days within shorter of 1 year or warranty. **Notification/Trigger:** Written notice to manufacturer, agent or dealer and opportunity to repair.
N. Y.	**Qualification:** 4 unsuccessful repairs or 30 calendar days out of service within shorter of 2 years or 18,000 miles. **Notification/Trigger:** Certified notice to manufacturer, agent or dealer. *State-run arbitration program is available.* L

N. C.	**Qualification:** 4 unsuccessful repairs within the shorter of 24 months, 24,000 miles or warranty or 20 business days out of service during any 12 month period of the warranty. **Notification/Trigger:** Written notice to manufacturer and opportunity to repair within 15 calendar days of receipt only if required in warranty or owner's manual. **L**
N. D.	**Qualification:** 4 unsuccessful repairs or 30 business days out of service within shorter of 1 year or warranty. **Notification/Trigger:** Direct written notice and opportunity to repair to manufacturer.
Ohio	**Qualification:** 3 unsuccessful repairs of same nonconformity, 30 calendar days out of service, 8 total repairs of any problem, or 1 unsuccessful repair of problem likely to cause death or serious bodily injury within shorter of 1 year or 18,000 miles. **Notification/Trigger:** Report to manufacturer, its agent or dealer.
Okla.	**Qualification:** 4 unsuccessful repairs or 45 calendar days out of service within shorter of 1 year or warranty. **Notification/Trigger:** Written notice to manufacturer and opportunity to repair.
Oregon	**Qualification:** 4 unsuccessful repairs or 30 business days out of service within shorter of 1 year or 12,000 miles. **Notification/Trigger:** Direct written notice to manufacturer and opportunity to repair. **L**
Penn.	**Qualification:** 3 unsuccessful repairs or 30 calendar days out of service within shorter of 1 year, 12,000 miles, or warranty. **Notification/Trigger:** Delivery to authorized service and repair facility. If delivery impossible, written notice to manufacturer or its repair facility obligates them to pay for delivery.
R. I.	**Qualification:** 4 unsuccessful repairs or 30 calendar days out of service within shorter of 1 year or 15,000 miles. **Notification/Trigger:** Report to dealer or manufacturer who has 7 days for final repair opportunity. **L**
S. Carol.	**Qualification:** 3 unsuccessful repairs or 30 calendar days out of service within shorter of 1 year or 12,000 miles. **Notification/Trigger:** Written notice to manufacturer by certified mail and oppportunity to repair only if manufacturer informed consumer of such at time of sale. Manufacturer has 10 days to notify consumer of repair facility. Facility has 10 days to repair. *State-run arbitration program is available.* **L**
S.Dakota	**Qualification:** 4 unsuccessful repairs, at least 1 of which occurred during the shorter of 1 year or 12,000 miles, or 30 calendar days out of service during the shorter of 24 months or 24,000 miles. **Notification/Trigger:** Certified mail notice to manufacturer and final opportunity to repair. Manufacturer has 7 calendar days to notify consumer of repair facility. Facility has 14 days to repair. If manufacturer has established a state recognized informal dispute settlement procedure, consumer must use program before instituting a cause of action.
Tenn.	**Qualification:** 4 unsuccessful repairs or 30 calendar days out of service within shorter of 1 year or warranty. **Notification/Trigger:** Certified mail notice to manufacturer and final opportunity to repair within 10 calendar days. **L**
Texas	**Qualification:** 4 unsuccessful repairs when 2 occured within shorter of 1 year or 12,000 miles, and other 2 occur within shorter of 1 year or 12,000 miles from date of 2nd repair attempt; or 2 unsuccessful repairs of a serious safety defect when 1 occured within shorter of 1 year or 12,000 miles and other occured within shorter of 1 year or 12,000 miles from date of 1st repair; or 30 calendar days out of service within shorter of 2 years or 24,000 miles and at least 2 attempts were made within shorter of 1 year or 12,000 miles. **Notification/Trigger:** Written notice to manufacturer. *State-run arbitration program is available.* **L**
Utah	**Qualification:** 4 unsuccessful repairs or 30 business days out of service within shorter of 1 year or warranty. **Notification/Trigger:** Report to manufacturer, agent or dealer. **L**

Vermont	**Qualification:** 3 unsuccessful repairs when at least 1st repair was within warranty, or 30 calendar days within warranty **Notification/Trigger:** Written notice to manufacturer (on provided forms) after 3rd repair attempt, or 30 days. Arbitration must be held within 45 days after notice, during which time manufacturer has 1 final repair. *State-run arbitration program is available.* **L**
Virginia	**Qualification:** 3 unsuccessful repairs, or 1 repair attempt of a serious safety defect, or 30 calendar days out of service within 18 months. **Notification/Trigger:** Written notice to manufacturer. If 3 unsuccessful repairs or 30 days already exhausted before notice, manufacturer has 1 more repair attempt not to exceed 15 days.
Wash.	**Qualification:** 4 unsuccessful repairs, 30 calendar days out of service (15 during warranty period), or 2 repairs of serious safety defects, first reported within shorter of the warranty or 24 months or 24,000 miles. One repair attempt and 15 of the 30 days must fall within manufacturer's express warranty of at least 1 year or 12,000 miles. **Notification/Trigger:** Written notice to manufacturer. *State-run arbitration program is available.* **L** *Note: Consumer should receive replacement or refund within 40 calendar days of request.*
W. V.	**Qualification:** 3 unsuccessful repairs or 30 calendar days out of service or 1 unsuccessful repair of problem likely to cause death or serious bodily injury within shorter of 1 year or warranty. **Notification/Trigger:** Prior written notice to manufacturer and at least one opportunity to repair. *State-run arbitration program is available.*
Wisc.	**Qualification:** 4 unsuccessful repairs or 30 calendar days out of service within shorter of 1 year or warranty. **Notification/Trigger:** Report to manufacturer or dealer. **L** *Note: Consumer should receive replacement or refund within 30 calendar days after offer to return title.*
Wyoming	**Qualification:** 3 unsuccessful repairs or 30 business days out of service within 1 year. **Notification/Trigger:** Direct written notice to manufacturer and opportunity to repair.

SHOWROOM STRATEGIES

Buying a vehicle means matching wits with a seasoned professional. But if you know what to expect, you'll have a much better chance of getting a really good deal! This chapter offers practical advice on buying a vehicle, tips on getting the best price, and information on buying vs. leasing, avoiding lemons and options for the future that will increase driving safety.

For most of us, the auto showroom can be an intimidating environment, and for good reason. We're matching wits with seasoned, professional negotiators over a very complex product. Being prepared is the best way to turn a potentially intimidating showroom experience into a profitable one. Here's some general advice about what to expect in the showroom.

Beware of silence. Silence is often used to intimidate, so be prepared for long periods of time when the salesperson is "talking with the manager." This tactic is designed to make you want to "just get the negotiation over with." Instead of becoming a victim, do something that indicates you are serious about looking elsewhere. Bring the classified section of the newspaper with you and begin circling other vehicles or review brochures from other manufacturers. By sending the message that you have other options, you increase your bargaining power and speed the process.

Don't fall in love with a vehicle. Never look too interested in any particular vehicle. Advise family members who go with you against being too enthusiastic about any one vehicle. *Tip:* Beat the dealers at their own game—bring along a friend who tells you that the price is "too much compared to the *other* deal."

Keep your wallet in your pocket. Don't leave a deposit, even if it's refundable. You'll feel pressure to rush your shopping, and you'll have to return and face the salesperson again, perhaps before you are ready.

Shop at the end of the month. Salespeople anxious to meet sales goals are more willing to negotiate a lower price at this time.

Buy last year's model. The majority of new vehicles are the same as the previous year, with minor cosmetic changes. You can save considerably by buying in early fall when dealers are clearing space for "new" models. The important trade-off you make using this technique is that the car maker may have added air bags or anti-lock brakes to an otherwise unchanged vehicle.

Buying from stock. You can often get a better deal on a vehicle that the dealer has on the lot. However, these vehicles usually have expensive options that you may not want or need. Do not hesitate to ask the dealer to remove an option (and its accompanying charge) or sell you the vehicle without charging for the option. Another advantage of buying from stock is that the longer the vehicle sits there, the more interest the dealer pays on the vehicle, which increases the dealer's incentive to sell.

Ordering a vehicle. Domestic vehicles can be ordered from the manufacturer. Simply offering a fixed amount over invoice may be attractive because it's a sure sale and the dealership has not invested in the vehicle. All the salesperson has to do is take your order.

If you do order a vehicle, make sure when it arrives that it includes only the options you requested. Don't fall for the trick where the dealer offers you unordered options at a "special price," because it was their mistake. If you didn't order the option, don't pay for it.

Don't trade in. Although it is more work, you can almost always do better by selling your old vehicle yourself than by trading it in. To determine what you'll gain by selling your vehicle yourself, check the NADA "Blue Book" at your credit union or library. The difference between the trade-in price (what the dealer will give you) and the retail price (what you typically can sell it for) is your extra payment for selling the vehicle yourself.

If you do decide to trade your car in at the dealership, *keep the buying and selling separate.* First, negotiate the best price for your new vehicle, then find out how much the dealer will give you for your old vehicle. Keeping the two deals separate ensures that you know what you're paying for your new vehicle and simplifies the entire transaction.

Avoiding Lemons

One way to avoid the sour taste of a lemon after you've bought your car is to protect yourself *before* you sign on the dotted line. These tips will help you avoid problems down the road.

1 **Avoid new models.** Any new car in its very first year of production usually turns out to have a lot of defects. Often, the manufacturer isn't able to remedy the defects until the second, third, or even fourth year of production. If the manufacturer has not worked out problems by the third model year, the car will likely be a lemon forever.

2 **Avoid the first cars off the line.** Most companies close down their assembly lines every year to make annual style changes. In addition to adding hundreds of dollars to the price of a new car, these changes can introduce new defects. It can take a few months to iron out these bugs. Ask the dealer when the vehicle you are interested in was manufactured; or look on the metal tag found on the inside of the driver-side door frame to find the date of manufacture.

3 **Avoid delicate options.** Delicate options have the highest frequency-of-repair records. Power seats, power windows, power antennas and special roofs are nice conveniences—until they break down. Of all the items on the vehicles, they tend to be the most expensive to repair.

4 **Inspect the dealer's checklist.** Request a copy of the dealer's pre-delivery service and adjustment checklist (also called a "make-ready list") at the time your new vehicle is delivered. Write the request directly on the new vehicle order. This request informs the dealer that you are aware of the dealer's responsibility to check your new car for defects.

5 **Examine the car on delivery.** Most of us are very excited when it comes time to take the vehicle home. This is the time where a few minutes of careful inspection can save hours of aggravation later. Carefully look over the body for any damage, check for the spare tire and jack equipment, make sure all electrical items work, make sure all the hubcaps and body molding are on. You may want to take a short test drive. Finally, make sure you have the owner's manual, warranty forms, and all the legal documents.

Getting the Best Price

One of the most difficult aspects of buying a new vehicle is getting the best price. Most of us are at a disadvantage negotiating because we don't know how much the car actually cost the dealer. The difference between what the dealer paid and the sticker price represents the negotiable amount.

Until recently, the key to getting the best price was finding out the dealer cost. Many shoppers now ask to see the factory invoice, so some dealers promote their vehicles by offering to sell at only $49 or $99 over invoice. This sounds like a good deal, but these vehicles often have options you may not want, and most invoice prices do not reveal the extra, hidden profit to the dealer.

Now that most savvy consumers know to check the so-called "dealer invoice," the industry has camouflaged this number. Special incentives, rebates and kickbacks can account for $500 to $2,000 worth of extra profit to a dealer selling a vehicle at "dealer invoice." The non-profit Center for the Study of Services recently discovered that in 37% of cases when dealers are forced to bid against each other for the sale, they offered the buyer a price below the "dealer invoice"—an unlikely event if the dealer was actually losing money. The bottom line is that dealer invoice doesn't mean anything anymore.

Because the rules have changed, we believe that most consumers are ill-advised to try and negotiate with a dealer. Introducing competition is the best way to get the lowest price on a new vehicle. What this means is that you have to convince 3-4 dealers that you are in fact prepared to buy a vehicle; that you have decided on the make, model and features;

and that your decision now rests solely on which dealer will give you the best price. You can try to do this by phone, but often dealers will not give you the best price, or worse, quote you a price over the phone that later they will not honor. Instead, you should try to do this in person. As anyone who has ventured into an auto showroom simply to get the best price knows, the process can be lengthy and arduous. Nevertheless, if you can convice the dealer that you are serious and are willing to take the time to go to a number of dealers, it will pay off. Otherwise, we suggest you use the CarBargains service listed on the next page.

If you find a big savings at a dealer far from your home, call a local dealer with the price. They may very well match it. If not, pick up the vehicle from the distant dealer, knowing your trip has saved you hundreds. You can still bring it to your local dealer for warranty work and repairs. Here are some other showroom strategies:

Beware of misleading advertising. New vehicle ads are meant to get you into the showroom. They usually promise low prices, big rebates, high trade-in, and spotless integrity—don't be dazzled. Advertised prices are rarely the true selling price. They usually exclude

transportation charges, service fees, or document fees. And always look out for the asterisk, both in advertisements and on invoices. It can be a signal that the advertiser has something to hide.

Don't talk price until you're ready to buy. On your first trips to the showroom, simply look over the vehicles, decide what options you want, and do your test driving.

Shop the corporate twins. Page 16 contains a list of corporate twins—nearly identical vehicles that carry different name plates. Check the price and options of the twins of the vehicle you like. A higher priced twin may have more options, so it may be a better deal than the lower priced vehicle without the options you want.

Watch out for dealer preparation overcharges. Before paying the dealer to clean your vehicle, make sure that preparation is not included in the basic price. The price sticker will state: "Manufacturer's suggested retail price of this model includes dealer preparation."

If you must negotiate . . . Negotiate from the "invoice" price. Rather than see how much you can get off the sticker price, simply make an offer close to or at the "invoice" price. If the sales person says that your offer is too low to make a profit, ask to see the factory invoice.

TIP

The 180 Degree Turn

If you try to negotiate a car purchase, remember that you have the most important weapon in the bargaining process: *the 180-degree turn.* Be prepared to walk away from a deal, even at the risk of losing the "very best deal" your salesperson has ever offered, and you will be in the best position to get a genuine "best deal." Remember: dealerships need you, the buyer, to survive.

Price Shopping Service

Even with the information that we provide you in this chapter of *The Truck, Van & 4x4 Book*, most of us will *not* be well prepared to negotiate a good price for the vehicles we are considering. In fact, as we indicated on the previous page, we don't believe that you can negotiate the best price with *a* dealer. The key to getting the best price is to get the dealers to compete with each other. This page describes a new and easy way to find the best price by actually getting the dealers to compete.

CarBargains is a service of the non-profit Center for the Study of Services, a Washington, D.C., consumer group, set up to provide comparative price information for many products and services.

CarBargains will "shop" the dealerships in your area and obtain at least five price quotes for the make and model of the vehicle that you want to buy. The dealers who submit quotes know that they are competing with other area dealerships and have agreed to honor the prices that they submit. It is important to note that CarBargains is not an auto broker or "car buying" service; they have no affiliation with dealers.

Here's how the service works:

1. You provide CarBargains with the make, model, and style of vehicle you wish to buy (Ford Taurus GL, for example) by phone or mail.

2. Within two weeks, CarBargains will send you dealer quote sheets from at least 5 local dealers who have bid against one another to sell you that vehicle. The offer is actually a commitment to a dollar amount above (or below) "factory invoice cost" for that model.

You will also receive a printout with the exact dealer cost for the vehicle and each available option. Included in the information will be the name of the sales manager responsible for honoring the quote.

3. Use the factory invoice cost printout to add up the invoice cost for the base vehicle and the options you want and then determine which dealer offers the best price using the dealer quote sheets. Contact the sales manager of that dealership and arrange to purchase the vehicle.

If a vehicle with the options you want is not available on the dealer's lot, you can have the dealer order the vehicle from the factory or, in some cases, from another dealer at the agreed price.

When you receive your quotes, you will also get some suggestions on low-cost sources of financing and a valuation of your used car (trade-in).

The price for this service may seem expensive, but when you consider the savings that will result by having dealers bid against each other as well as the time and effort of trying to get these bids yourself, we believe it's a great value. First of all, the dealers know they have a bona fide buyer (you've paid $135 for the service) and they know they are bidding against 5-7 of their competitors.

To obtain CarBargains' competitive price quotes, send a check for $135 to CarBargains, 733 15th St., NW, Suite 820CB, Washington, DC 20005. Include your complete mailing address, phone number (in case of questions), and the exact make, model, and year of the vehicle you want to buy. You should receive your bids within 2-3 weeks. For faster service, call them at 800-475-7283. They will accept Visa or Mastercard on phone orders.

Auto Brokers

While CarBargains is a non-profit organization created to help you find the best price for the car you want to purchase, auto brokers are typically in the business to make money. As such, what ever price you end up paying for the car will include additional profit for the broker. While many brokers are legitimately trying to get their customers the best price, others have developed special relationships with certain dealers and may not do much shopping for you. As a consumer, it is difficult to tell which are which. If you use a broker, make sure the contract to purchase the car is with the dealer, not the broker. In addition, it is best to pay the broker *after* the services is rendered, not before. There have been cases where the auto broker makes certain promises, takes your money, and you never hear from him or her again. If CarBargains is not for you, then we suggest you consider using a buying service associated with your credit union or auto club, which can arrange for the purchase of a car at some fixed price over "dealer invoice."

Depreciation

Over the past 15 years, new vehicle depreciation costs have steadily increased. A recent study conducted by the Runzheimer International management consulting firm shows that depreciation and interest now account for almost 50 percent of the costs of owning and operating a vehicle. This number is up from 41 percent in 1976. On the other hand, the relative cost of gasoline has dropped by half, from 35 cents to 17 cents of every dollar spent on the average vehicle. Other costs, including insurance, maintenance, and tires, have remained at relatively steady shares of the automotive dollar.

The high cost of depreciation is due in part to skyrocketing new vehicle prices, as well as a relatively soft used vehicle market. While there is no reliable method of predicting retained value, your best bet is to purchase a popular new vehicle. Chances are that it will also be popular as a used vehicle. Vehicles are generally poor investments in terms of retaining their value. There are some exceptions, however, and the following table indicates the current resale values for some 1990 vehicles. The highest-priced vehicles are not necessarily the best quality. Supply and demand, as well as appearance, are extremely important factors in determining used vehicle prices.

Vehicle	1990 Price	1994 Price	% of Cost	Vehicle	1990 Price	1994 Price	% of Cost
Chevrolet Astro	12,095	7,850	64%	GMC Safari	12,157	7,950	65%
Chevrolet Blazer	16,485	12,500	75%	GMC Suburban	15,808	14,025	88%
Chev. Chevy Van/Sport Van	12,650	8,850	69%	GMC Vandura/Rally	12,712	8,825	69%
Chev. CK Series Pickup*	10,445	9,475	90%	Isuzu Amigo	8,999	7,175	79%
Chevrolet Lumina APV■	12,895	7,375	57%	Isuzu Pickup	7,649	5,175	67%
Chevrolet S10	7,975	6,100	76%	Isuzu Trooper/Trooper II	13,499	10,350	76%
Chevrolet S10 Blazer	12,930	9,625	74%	Jeep Cherokee/Wagoneer	13,295	8,425	63%
Chevrolet Suburban*	15,615	13,925	89%	Jeep Comanche	8,095	6,475	79%
Chrys. Town And Country■	25,000	13,750	55%	Jeep Grand Wagoneer■	22,795	11,675	51%
Daihatsu Rocky	10,897	7,275	66%	Jeep Wrangler	12,029	10,375	86%
Dodge Caravan	11,125	6,750	60%	Mazda B Series Pickup	7,949	6,100	76%
Dodge Dakota	7,995	6,375	79%	Mazda MPV	11,699	9,550	81%
Dodge Ram Van/Ram Wgn	12,345	8,650	70%	Mitsubishi Mighty Max	7,689	5,275	68%
Dodge Ramcharger■	14,275	8,325	58%	Mitsubishi Montero	13,949	10,450	74%
Ford Aerostar	11,841	7,225	61%	Mitsubishi Van/Wagon	11,229	6,975	62%
Ford Bronco	16,795	12,525	74%	Nissan Pathfinder*	15,720	14,250	90%
Ford Bronco II	13,001	8,400	64%	Nissan Pickup	8,149	6,025	73%
Ford Econline/Club Wgn	12,740	8,775	68%	Oldsmobile Silhouette	17,195	11,125	64%
Ford F Series Pickup	10,249	9,050	88%	Range Rover■	38,025	22,500	59%
Ford Ranger	7,856	6,375	81%	Suzuki Samurai	7,999	5,250	65%
Geo Tracker	11,035	7,525	68%	Suzuki Sidekick	9,999	6,700	67%
GMC CK Series Pickup*	10,445	9,525	91%	Toyota 4 Runner*	16,718	14,950	89%
GMC Jimmy	16,547	12,450	75%	Toyota Land Cruiser	20,898	17,175	82%
GMC Jimmy S15	13,133	9,600	73%	Toyota Pickup	7,998	5,800	72%
GMC S15	8,057	6,125	76%	Volkswagen Vanagon	14,080	9,200	65%

* Top five in retained value.
■ Bottom five in retained value.

Leasing vs. Buying

As vehicle prices continue to rise and dealer ads scream out the virtues of leasing, many buyers are wondering whether they should lease rather than buy. Here is some information to help you make the right decision.

With a lease, you pay a monthly fee for a predetermined length of time in exchange for the use of a vehicle. Usually, however, you pay for maintenance, insurance, and repairs as if the vehicle were your own. There are two types of leases—*closed-* and *open-ended*. Most consumer leases are closed-ended, and you simply return the vehicle at the lease's end. Your monthly payment depends on the original cost of the vehicle and what the company thinks the vehicle can sell for after the lease is up. An open-ended lease is riskier because you pay the difference between the vehicle's expected value and its actual resale value when the lease ends. If the lessor underestimated the resale value of your payments, you'll pay a lump sum at the end.

While these terms describe general types of leases, within these categories the details may vary considerably. Some companies combine these concepts with a vehicle purchase option. They guarantee to sell you the vehicle at the end of the lease for a pre-determined amount, called the residual value. If, at the end, the vehicle is worth more than the pre-determined price, you may want to buy it. If it's worth less, simply turn it in.

Generally speaking, leasing costs more than buying outright or financing. In fact, when you lease a vehicle, you have all the headaches and responsibilities of ownership with none of the benefits. In addition, leased vehicles are often not covered by the Lemon Laws. However, if the benefit of the lower monthly payments outweighs the overall added costs, consider the following when shopping for a lease:

Know the make and model of the vehicle you want. Tell the agent exactly how you want the vehicle equipped. You don't have to pay for options you don't request. Decide in advance how long you will keep the vehicle.

Find out the price of the options on which the lease is based. Typically, it will be full retail price. The price can be negotiated (albeit with some difficultly)—before you settle on the monthly payment.

Find out how much you are required to pay at delivery. Most leases require at least the first month's payment. Others have a security deposit, registration fees, or other "hidden" costs. When shopping around, make sure price quotes include taxes—sales tax, monthly use tax, or gross receipt tax. Ask how the length of the lease affects your monthly cost.

Find out the annual mileage limit. Don't accept a contract with a lower limit than you need. Most standard contracts allow 15,000 to 18,000 miles per year. If you go under the allowance one year, you can go over it the next.

Avoid "capitalized cost reduction" or "equity leases." Here the lessor offers to lower the monthly payment by asking you for more money up front. This defeats the principal benefit of a lease. By paying more initially, you lose the opportunity to use or earn interest on this money. These opportunity costs are based on the interest rate that you would otherwise earn.

Ask about early termination. If you terminate the lease before it is up, what are the financial penalties? Ask the dealer *exactly* what you would owe at the end of each year if you wanted out of the lease. Remember, if your vehicle is stolen, the lease will typically be terminated. While your insurance should cover the value of the vehicle, you still may owe additional amounts per your lease contract.

Avoid maintenance contracts. Getting work done privately is cheaper in the long run—and don't forget, this is a new vehicle with a standard warranty.

Arrange for your own insurance. You can generally find less expensive insurance than the programs offered by the lessor.

Ask how quickly you can expect delivery. If your agent can't deliver in a reasonable time, maybe he or she can't meet the price quoted.

Find out the service charges at the end of the lease. Usually around $100, they can go up to $250.

Retain your option to buy the vehicle at the end of the lease at a predetermined price. The price should equal the residual value; if it is more, then the lessor is trying to make an additional profit. Regardless of how the end-of-lease value is determined, if you want the vehicle make an offer based on the current "Blue Book" value at the end of the lease.

Find out how the lease price was figured. Lease prices are generally based on the manu-facturer's suggested retail price, less the predetermined residual value. The best values are vehicles with a high expected residual value. To protect themselves, lessors tend to underestimate residual value, but you can do little about this estimate.

Here's what First National Lease Systems Automotive Lease Guide estimates the residual values for a few 1995 vehicles will be after four years:

Chevy Blazer 2WD 45%
Ford Windstar XL 41%
Ford Club Wagon XL 42%
Ford Ranger Splash 38%
GMC Sonoma SLE 41%
Jeep Wrangler 46%
Mitsubishi Montero LS 43%
Nissan Path. XE 4WD 51%
Plymouth Voy. SE AWD 42%
Range Rover 46%
Suzuki Samurai JL 36%
Toyota Pickup 2WD 36%

The following table compares the typical costs of leasing vs. buying the same vehicle. Your actual costs will vary slightly, but you can use this format to compare the vehicles you are considering. Our example assumes that the residual value of a purchased vehicle is 60 percent after two years and 45 percent after four.

A note about taxes: There has been a lot of talk about the effect of the new tax laws on leasing. Tax reform did not make leasing more attractive; it simply made buying a vehicle somewhat less attractive. Remember, you cannot deduct interest on car loans and the sales tax is also no longer deductible.

Finally, keep in mind that at the end of a lease period you have nothing—but at the end of your finance period you will own a vehicle.

Financing vs. Leasing

| | 2 Years | | 4 Years | |
	Lease	Finance*	Lease	Finance*
Number of Months	24	24	48	48
Manu. Suggested Price	$15,000	$15,000	$15,000	$15,000
Cash Down Payment		$1,500		$1,500
Monthly Payment	$425	$678	$300	$366
Total Amt. of Payments**	$10,200	$16,272	$14,400	$17,568
Less Vehicle Value at End	$0	$9,000	$0	$6,750
Actual Cost	$10,200	$8,772	$14,400	$12,318

*Based on an annual percentage rate of 8%
**In a lease, this is the total amount paid for the use of the vehicle. When financing, this is the total amount paid to become the owner.

Don't Buy Rustproofing

For years, we've recommended *against* spending the hundreds of dollars dealers charge for rustproofing. Some manufacturers (GM, Nissan, Saturn, Subaru, Suzuki, Toyota, and Volkswagen) now also recommend against aftermarket rustproofing. General Motors' warranty presents one of the clearest arguments against buying this expensive item: *Some after-manufacture rustproofing may create a potential environment which reduces the corrosion resistance designed and built into your vehicle. Depending upon application technique, some after-manufacture rustproofing could result in damage or failure of some electrical or mechanical systems of your vehicle. Repairs to correct damage or malfunctions caused by after-manufacture rustproofing are not covered under any of your GM new vehicle warranties.* Other manufacturers who suggest that rustproofing may void your corrosion warranty include Nissan, Saturn, and Volkswagen.

Options

You may want to consider the following options for your new vehicle:

Childproof Locks: Many vehicles come with a simple lever that disconnects the inside rear door handles, so the doors can only be opened from the outside. This device is especially important in family vans, yet only about half of the vans and sport utility vehicles on the market offer this valuable safety feature.

Cruise Control: A properly functioning cruise control system can be convenient and can even contribute to improved fuel efficiency on long trips. Unfortunately, in investigating the growing problem of sudden acceleration (when the vehicle suddenly lurches out of control), the Center for Auto Safety has related this problem to a failure in the cruise control system. If you do not regularly use cruise control, consider deleting it from the options on your new vehicle.

E-4WD: This electronically controlled system allows the 4WD clutch to engage and disengage whenever it is needed, without the driver having to switch it manually. E-4WD was introduced by Ford in 1991.

High-Tech Safety Belts: A few models have seat-belt tensioners on the front belts. In the event of a frontal crash, these devices take up any slack in the safety belt and reduce forward movement. Find out if the vehicles you are considering have these devices; they are an important advance in safety-belt technology.

Reinforced Door Beams: Injuries from side crashes or roll-overs can be greatly reduced by building reinforcing beams into the vehicle's doors. This feature is especially important in sport utility vehicles because of their high tendency to roll over—yet few of the current models offer this added important protection.

Head Restraints: Head restraints help prevent whiplash injuries. They have only recently become uniformly available, since the safety requirement for head restraints went into effect in 1992 for trucks, vans, and 4x4s.

Anti-lock Braking System: Many manufacturers offer a safety feature called anti-lock braking or ABS. ABS shortens stopping distance on dry, wet, and even icy roads. By preventing brake lockup, ABS ensures steering control even in severe emergency braking. Beware—ABS that only operates on rear wheels is of marginal value. Look for all-wheel ABS. (See page 23 for a list of which vehicles have ABS.)

Future Options

Here are some options you can expect in the future:

Radar Brakes: Using radar to detect objects in front of you, radar provides a warning for the need to brake. It can also be used to apply the brakes to reduce the chances of crashing—for a driver who falls asleep, for example.

Side Air Bags: Air bags that come out of the doors, and out of the back of the front seat would be triggered by "crash anticipation" sensors. Together with frontal air bags, the omni-directional air bag system would protect in crashes in all directions and in rollover crashes. Volvo has sent other manufacturers scrambling by offering this feature in the 850 Turbo in 1995.

Air Pads: Air pads are double layers of plastic with multiple compartments which look like ordinary trim in the uninflated condition. When the crash sensors for the air bags detect a crash, the air pads inflate out a few inches over all hard surfaces such as the window sills and the header over the windshield.

Night Vision Enhancement: Being developed by GM, this system uses cameras that detect the infrared light and projects a visible image of what's ahead on a screen located on the vehicle's instrument panel. The system could also detect, through a heat-seeking infrared system, someone lurking in a darkened parking lot. This would be most useful at night or in heavy fog or rain. This device will see through fog, rain and darkness and provide an image of any obstacles or problems in the road.

RATINGS

This chapter provides an overview of the most important features of the new 1995 cars. In this all-new section of *The Truck, Van & 4x4 Book* you can see on each "car page" all the ingredients you need to make a smart choice. In addition to some descriptive text and a photo, the page contains seven important information boxes:

THE DESCRIPTION

The vast majority of the information in *The Truck, Van & 4x4 Book* is purely objective—we research and present the facts so that you can make an informed choice among the models that fit your taste and pocketbook. For the second year we are adding, among other new features, some background details. Specifically, for every vehicle we include some general information to help you round out the hard facts. Much of the information in this section is subjective and you may not share our opinion. Nevertheless, like the photo, which will give you a general idea of what the vehicle looks like, the description will give you a snapshot of some of the features that we think are worth noting which may not show up in the statistics.

GENERAL INFORMATION

This is additional information you may want to consider when buying a new vehicle.

Fuel Economy: This is the EPA-rated fuel economy for city and highway driving measured in miles per gallon. Most models have a number of fuel economy ratings because of different engine and transmission options. We indicate the figure for what we expect to be the most popular model. For more individual ratings, see "The Fuel Economy Chapter".

Driving Range: Given the vehicle's expected fuel economy and gas tank size, this gives an idea of how far you can go on a full tank.

Parking Index: Using the vehicle's length, wheelbase and turning circle, we have calculated how easy it will be to maneuver this vehicle in tight spots. This rating of *very easy* to *very hard* is an indicator of how much difficulty you may have parking. If you regularly parallel park, or find yourself maneuvering in and out of tight spaces, this can be an important factor in your choice.

Theft Rating: This rating is given by the Insurance Institute for Highway Safety. It predicts the likelihood of the vehicle being stolen or broken into based on it's past history. If no information appears, it means that the vehicle is too new to have a rating.

Corporate Twins: Often a company will make numerous models on the same platform. This is a list of this vehicle's twins.

Where made: Here we tell you where the vehicle was assembled.

Year of Production: We generally don't recommend buying a vehicle during it's first model year of production. In addition, we believe that the longer a company makes the same vehicle, the less likely the vehicle is to have manufacturing and design defects. Usually, each year the model is made, the production process is improved and there are fewer minor design defects. Therefore, the longer a vehicle has been made, the less likely you are to be plagued with defects. On the other hand, the newer a vehicle is, the more likely it is to have the latest in engineering.

PRICES

This box contains sample price information. When available, we list the base and the most luxurious version of the vehicle. The difference is often substantial. Usually the more expensive versions have fancy trim, larger engines and lots of automatic equipment. The least expensive versions usually have manual transmission and few extra features. In addition, some manufacturers try to sell popular options as part of a package. For example, to get air conditioning you may have to buy power steering and deluxe seats.

This information provides an idea of the price range and the expected dealer markup. Be prepared for higher retail prices when you get to the showroom. Manufacturers like to load their vehicles with factory options, and dealers like to add their own items such as fabric protection and paint sealant. Remember, prices and dealer costs can change during the year. Use these figures for general reference and comparisons, not as a precise indication of exactly how much the vehicle you are interested in will cost. See page 92 for a new buying service designed to ensure that you get the very best price.

THE RATINGS

These are ratings in six important categories, as well as an overall rating. We have adopted the Olympic rating system with "10" being the best.

Overall Rating: This is the "bottom line." Using a combination of all of the ratings, this tells how this vehicle stacks up against the other '95s on a scale of 1 to 10. Due to the importance of crash tests, vehicles with no crash test results as of our publication date cannot be given an overall rating. More recent results may be available from the Auto Safety Hotline at 1-800-424-9393 (see page 73).

Crash Test Performance: This rating compares the 1994 models against all of the crash test results to date. We give the best performers a 10 and the worst a 1. Remember, it is important to compare crash test results relative to other vehicles in the same size class. For complete details see "The Safety Chapter".

Safety Features: This is an evaluation of how much extra safety is built into the vehicle. We give credit for air bags, ABS, rollover propensity, built-in child restraints and belt height adjustors.

Fuel Economy: Here we compare the EPA mileage ratings of each vehicle. The gas misers get a 10 and the guzzlers get a 1. For more information see "The Fuel Economy Chapter".

PM Cost: Each manufacturer suggests a preventive maintenance schedule designed to keep the vehicle in good shape and to protect your rights under the warranty. The cost of these schedules varies substantially from vehicle to vehicle—ranging from $0 to $1500 for the first 50,000 miles of driving. Those with the lowest PM costs get a 10 and the highest, a 1. See "The Maintenance Chapter" for the actual costs.

Repair Cost: It is virtually impossible to predict exactly what any new vehicle will cost you in repairs. As such, we take nine typical repairs that you are likely to experience *after* your warranty expires and compare those costs among this year's models. Those with the lowest cost get a 10 and the highest, a 1. For the details see "The Maintenance Chapter."

Warranty: There are good warranties and not so good warranties. This is an overall assessment of the vehicle's warranty when compared to all 1994 warranties. The rating considers the important features of each warranty, with emphasis on the length of the basic and powertrain warranties. We give the highest rated warranties a 10 and the lowest a 1. See "The Warranty Chapter" for details.

Complaints: This is where you'll find how your vehicle stacks up against hundreds of others on the road, based on the U.S. government complaint data. We can only rate vehicles which have enough on-the-road complaint history, so if no information is listed, the vehicle has not been around long enough to have developed a complaint history—good or bad. The least complained about vehicles get a 10 and the most problematic, a 1.

Insurance Cost: Insurance companies have rated most of the vehicles on the road to determine how they plan to charge for insurance. Here, you'll find whether you can expect to pay a *discount* or a *surcharge*. If the vehicle is likely to receive neither, we label it *regular*. Those receiving a discount get a 10, while those with a surcharge get a 1. Unrated vehicles get a 5.

SAFETY

For most of us, safety is a critical consideration in buying a new vehicle. This box will tell you, at a glance, whether or not the vehicle has the safety features you care about.

Crash Test: Here's where we tell you if its crash test was *very good, good, average, poor* or *very poor*, compared to all tests ever performed by the government.

Rollover: The higher the center of gravity and the narrower the track width, the more likely the vehicle is to roll over. *Very high, high, moderate,* and *low* ratings compare the potential likelihood of these vehicles to roll over.

Air Bag: Here's where you'll find out which occupants benefit from this invaluable safety feature and who is left unprotected.

Anti-lock Brakes: This safety feature comes in two or four wheelversions. Two wheel ABS is of marginal value. An asterisk indicates if you have to pay extra to get ABS.

Belt Adjustors: This tells if the car maker offers a safety belt height/comfort adjustor. People often don't wear safety belts because they are uncomfortable. In fact, a belt's effectiveness is due, in part, to how well it fits your body. In order to make sure shoulder belts fit properly (squarely across the front of your chest) some manufacturers have installed devices that let you adjust the height of the belt. This allows for proper fit among drivers and passengers of various heights. In addition to allowing a safer fit, it helps prevent such problems as the belt scraping across the neck of a shorter driver. Availability is indicated for both front seat occupants, unless otherwise noted.

Child Safety Seats: Some manufacturers are offering "built-in" child safety seats which reduces the chances that your child rides unprotected.

Occupant Injury: This is the expected injury rating, as presented by the Insurance Institute for Highway Safety, based on actual experience. If the model or style is all new this year, it has no rating. A vehicle may have a good crash test rating, but a poor injury rating. This could be due to the way the vehicle is driven. For example, a sporty car may have a good crash test result, but a poor injury rating. This may be due to the fact that the car is typically driven by young males who are in accidents more frequently than others.

SPECIFICATIONS

Here are the "nuts and bolts." In this box we have listed seven key specifications which enable you to evaluate how best that vehicle meets your particular needs.

Length: This is the overall length of the vehicle from bumper to bumper.

Head/Leg Room: This tells how roomy the front seat is.

Cargo Space: This gives you the cubic feet available for cargo. For vans, it is the back of the two front seats to the rear of the vehicle. It is difficult to give a specific volume for the cargo space of pickups since you can pile stuff to the sky. Check the length and width of the bed when selecting a pickup.

Payload: This is the amount of weight that is safe for the vehicle to carry, including passengers and cargo. Where variations are indicated, different models of the vehicle have different capacities. In such cases, we tried to choose a median value.

Tow Rating: Ratings of *very low, low, average, high* and *very high* indicate the vehicle's relative ability to tow trailers or other loads. The towing weight at which the vehicle is rated is also given.

Seating: This figure represents the maximum number of seating positions equipped with safety belts. When more than one number is listed (for example, 5/6/7) it means that different models have different seat configurations.

Wheel Size: See what your choices are for wheel diameters. Remember—larger wheels raise the center of gravity of the vehicle and increase your risk of rolling over.

COMPETITION

Here we tell you how the vehicle stacks up with what is expected to be its competition. Use this information to compare the overall rating of similar vehicles and as a stepping off point to broaden your choice of new vehicle possibilities. This may help you select a more economical or better performing vehicle than the one you were originally considering. We've added page references so you can easily check out the details on the competition. In cases where a competing vehicle was not crash tested, we could not give it an overall rating—but check it out on the referenced page for further details. This list is meant as a guideline, not as an all inclusive list of every possible competitive choice.

Using the Ratings Pages

When using the ratings pages remember:

1. Blanks mean data unavailable.

2. Crash tests are not available for all vehicles—when crash rating is missing, we cannot give an overall rating.

3. Use the competition table as a guide to other possible choices.

4. For various specifications, we have chosen the numbers for the model expected to be the most popular. However, other models may be available.

5. The price information is meant as a guideline. See page 92 for a great way to get the very best price.

These GM minivans lag behind the more modern GM minivans (the Chevy Lumina, Olds Silhouette and Pontiac Trans Sport) in styling, performance and safety. A 1995 facelift makes them more contemporary, but it is their only significant alteration since being introduced in 1985. A driver air bag is standard, but occupant protection, as measured by the government's crash test program, is still the worst on the road.

The standard 4.3-liter V6 and automatic overdrive provide ample power, but gas mileage is poor, even for a minivan. Handling is sloppy, although the optional touring suspension will help. Ride is unsettling once you get off the highway. Getting in and out of the front seats is tricky. The seats are reasonably comfortable, but make sure you have enough leg room in the front. This vehicle is greatly outclassed by its rivals.

The Ratings

(Scale: POOR ← → GOOD)

COMPARATIVE RATING*	Average
CRASH TEST	Poor
SAFETY FEATURES	Poor
FUEL ECONOMY	Poor
PM COST	Good
REPAIR COST	Very Good
WARRANTY	Below Average
COMPLAINTS	Good
INSURANCE COST	Very Good

Safety

CRASH TEST	Very Poor
ROLLOVER	High
AIR BAG	Driver
ANTI-LOCK BRAKES	4-wheel
BELT ADJUSTORS	Standard
BUILT-IN CHILD SEAT	None
OCCUPANT INJURY	Good (AWD=Very Good)

General Information

FUEL ECONOMY	16/21	POOR
DRIVING RANGE	486	VERY LONG
PARKING INDEX	Average	
THEFT RATING	Average (Cargo=Vry. Pr.)	
CORPORATE TWINS		
WHERE MADE	U.S.	
YEAR OF PRODUCTION	Eleventh	

Specifications

LENGTH (in.)	189.8	AVERAGE
HEAD/LEG ROOM (in.)	39.2/41.6	AVERAGE
CARGO SPACE (cu. ft.)	170	VERY LARGE
PAYLOAD	1950	LOW
TOW RATING (lbs.)	5500	HIGH
SEATING	5/8	
WHEEL SIZE (in.)	15	

Specifications may vary.

Prices

Model	Retail	Mkup
Astro Cargo	18,340	10%
Astro RWD	18,843	10%
Astro RWD w/A-C	19,366	10%
Astro AWD	21,043	10%
Astro AWD w/A-C	21,566	10%

Competition

(Scale: POOR ← → GOOD)

Model	Rating	Pg.
Astro/Safari	Average	99
Dodge Caravan	Very Good	108
Ford Aerostar	Below Average	112
Mercury Villager	Below Average	141
Toyota Previa	Average	155

* Due to the importance of crash tests, vehicles with no results as of publication date cannot be given an overall rating.

Chevrolet Blazer

The redesign of this aging sport utility vehicle for 1995 will enable Chevy customers to benefit from the addition of a driver's air bag, as well as by the more simple nomenclature—what used to be the S-10 Blazer is now just the Blazer, not to be confused with the larger sport utility that used to be the Blazer and is now called the Tahoe. ABS is standard.

Chevrolet hopes the more contemporary styling which will enable the Blazer to better compete with the Ford Explorer and Jeep Grand Cherokee. The 4.3-liter V6 provides plenty of power. With two body styles (2- or 4-door), three trim levels (base, LS or LST), two drive types (2- or 4-wheel) and five suspension packages (from smooth riding to off-roading) the Blazer offers many options. Shop carefully, as you'll be required to buy options you don't want to get the ones you do want.

The Ratings

	POOR ... GOOD
COMPARATIVE RATING*	
CRASH TEST	
SAFETY FEATURES	
FUEL ECONOMY	
PM COST	
REPAIR COST	
WARRANTY	
COMPLAINTS	
INSURANCE COST	

Safety

CRASH TEST	No government results
ROLLOVER	Very High
AIR BAG	Driver
ANTI-LOCK BRAKES	4-wheel
BELT ADJUSTORS	None
BUILT-IN CHILD SEAT	None
OCCUPANT INJURY	

General Information

FUEL ECONOMY	17/22	POOR
DRIVING RANGE	380	AVERAGE
PARKING INDEX	Easy	
THEFT RATING		
CORPORATE TWINS	GMC Jimmy	
WHERE MADE	U.S.	
YEAR OF PRODUCTION	First	

Specifications

LENGTH (in.)	174.7	SHORT
HEAD/LEG ROOM (in.)	39.6/42.5	ROOMY
CARGO SPACE (cu. ft.)	67	SMALL
PAYLOAD	1000	VERY LOW
TOW RATING (lbs.)	5000	AVERAGE
SEATING	2/6	
WHEEL SIZE (in.)	15	

Specifications may vary.

Prices

Model	Retail	Mkup
Blazer S10 2-dr.	18,630	
Blazer S10 4-dr.	20,336	
Blazer T10 2-dr.	20,390	
Blazer T10 4-dr.	22,438	

Competition

	POOR ... GOOD	Pg.
Chevrolet Blazer		100
Isuzu Rodeo		130
Jeep Gr. Cherokee		133
Mits. Montero		143
Nissan Pathfinder		144

* Due to the importance of crash tests, vehicles with no results as of publication date cannot be given an overall rating.

Although the styling changes little, the C/K pickups have several additions that will keep it popular in the standard-size pickup market in 1995. A driver air bag comes on 1500s and 2500s, and 4-wheel ABS is finally standard.

There are several engines to choose from: a V6, three gasoline V8s, and two diesel V8s, which can be teamed with 5-speed manual or 4-speed automatic transmissions. The "C" indicates 2-wheel drive, while the "K" stands for 4-wheel drive. There are three cab sizes, regular, extended or crew, and two box sizes, Fleetside or Sportside pickup box. The option list is long, and there are dozens of option packages. Ride and handling depend on the suspension choice. A strong choice, if you can wade through the options list.

The Ratings

	POOR ... GOOD
COMPARATIVE RATING*	
CRASH TEST	
SAFETY FEATURES	
FUEL ECONOMY	
PM COST	
REPAIR COST	
WARRANTY	
COMPLAINTS	
INSURANCE COST	

Safety

CRASH TEST	Very Good
ROLLOVER	High
AIR BAG	Driver (optional)
ANTI-LOCK BRAKES	4-wheel
BELT ADJUSTORS	None
BUILT-IN CHILD SEAT	None
OCCUPANT INJURY	Very Good

General Information

FUEL ECONOMY	15/18	VERY POOR
DRIVING RANGE	400	AVERAGE
PARKING INDEX	Hard	
THEFT RATING	Very Poor (K2500=Avg.)	
CORPORATE TWINS	GMC Sierra	
WHERE MADE	Canada/U.S.	
YEAR OF PRODUCTION	Eighth	

Specifications

LENGTH (in.)	194.4	LONG
HEAD/LEG ROOM (in.)	39.9/41.7	ROOMY
CARGO SPACE (cu. ft.)		
PAYLOAD	2000	LOW
TOW RATING (lbs.)	7500	VERY HIGH
SEATING	2/3/5/6	
WHEEL SIZE (in.)	15/16	

Specifications may vary.

Prices

Model	Retail	Mkup
C1500 SpSide Sh. Box	16,220	14%
C1500 FlSide Ext. Lg. Box	18,310	
K2500 FlSide Lg. Box	18,598	14%
K1500 FlSide Ext. Sh. Box	19,792	
K3500 FlSide Crew Lg. Box	23,717	

Competition

	POOR ... GOOD	Pg.
Chevy CK Series		101
Dodge Ram		110
Ford F-Series		116
GMC Sierra		120
Toyota T100		156

* Due to the importance of crash tests, vehicles with no results as of publication date cannot be given an overall rating.

Chevrolet Lumina Minivan

The Lumina Minivan and its twins, the Pontiac Trans Sport and Olds Silhouette, get few changes for 1995. Traction control is optional, and ABS and a driver air bag are standard.

The standard 3.1-liter V6 delivers inferior acceleration and average gas mileage. The optional 3.8-liter V6 offers acceptable power and increases highway fuel economy, but city fuel economy suffers. Rear child seats are an excellent option—you have your choice of either one seat or two—but you'll have to buy expensive options you may not want before you can buy the child seats. Ride is smooth on good roads, but handling is a bit sluggish. Driving position and visibility take some getting used to. Center and rear seats are easy to remove or install, but there isn't as much cargo room as other minivans.

The Ratings

	POOR ··· GOOD
COMPARATIVE RATING*	good
CRASH TEST	average
SAFETY FEATURES	average
FUEL ECONOMY	poor
PM COST	average
REPAIR COST	above average
WARRANTY	poor
COMPLAINTS	above average
INSURANCE COST	below average

Safety

CRASH TEST	Good
ROLLOVER	Moderate
AIR BAG	Driver
ANTI-LOCK BRAKES	4-wheel
BELT ADJUSTORS	None
BUILT-IN CHILD SEAT	Optional (two)
OCCUPANT INJURY	Average

General Information

FUEL ECONOMY	19/23	POOR
DRIVING RANGE	400	AVERAGE
PARKING INDEX	Hard	
THEFT RATING	Average	
CORPORATE TWINS	Silhouette, Trans Sport	
WHERE MADE	U.S.	
YEAR OF PRODUCTION	Sixth	

Specifications

LENGTH (in.)	191.5	AVERAGE
HEAD/LEG ROOM (in.)	39.2/40.0	CRAMPED
CARGO SPACE (cu. ft.)	113	LARGE
PAYLOAD	1900	LOW
TOW RATING (lbs.)	3000	LOW
SEATING	2/5/7	
WHEEL SIZE (in.)	15	

Specifications may vary.

Prices

Model	Retail	Mkup
Lumina Minivan Cargo	16,775	10%
Lumina Minivan Base	18,135	10%
Lumina Minivan w/3.8L	18,954	10%
Lumina Minivan w/A-C	18,965	10%
Lumina Minivan w/3.8L and A-C	19,784	10%

Competition

	POOR ··· GOOD	Pg.
Lumina Minivan	good	**102**
Dodge Caravan	above average	108
Ford Aerostar	average	112
Mercury Villager	poor	141
Toyota Previa	below average	155

* Due to the importance of crash tests, vehicles with no results as of publication date cannot be given an overall rating.

Chevrolet S-Series Pickup

After undergoing a successful redesign last year, the S-Series pickup adds some major finishing touches for 1995. A driver air bag is finally standard, and daytime running lights, which increase other drivers' visibility of your vehicle, have also been added. Rear-wheel ABS is standard on 4-cylinder models, so go for the optional V6 which comes with 4-wheel ABS.

The standard 2.2-liter 4-cylinder is adequate, but the optional 4.3-liter V6 is much more powerful and comes with the better ABS. You'll have the choice of 2- or 4-wheel drive, regular or extended cab, base or LS trim level, and seven suspension packages, so do your homework. With its redesign last year and the appearance of a driver air bag this year, the S-Series is a better choice than its predecessor.

The Ratings

	POOR — GOOD
COMPARATIVE RATING*	(no rating)
CRASH TEST	(no rating)
SAFETY FEATURES	poor
FUEL ECONOMY	poor
PM COST	average
REPAIR COST	good
WARRANTY	poor
COMPLAINTS	(no rating)
INSURANCE COST	poor

Safety

CRASH TEST	No government results
ROLLOVER	High
AIR BAG	Driver
ANTI-LOCK BRAKES	2-whl. (4-whl. optional)
BELT ADJUSTORS	None
BUILT-IN CHILD SEAT	None
OCCUPANT INJURY	

General Information

FUEL ECONOMY	17/21	POOR
DRIVING RANGE	360	SHORT
PARKING INDEX	Easy	
THEFT RATING		
CORPORATE TWINS	GMC Sonoma	
WHERE MADE	U.S.	
YEAR OF PRODUCTION	Second	

Specifications

LENGTH (in.)	189.0	AVERAGE
HEAD/LEG ROOM (in.)	39.6/42.4	ROOMY
CARGO SPACE (cu. ft.)		
PAYLOAD	1650	LOW
TOW RATING (lbs.)	5500	HIGH
SEATING	2/3/4/5	
WHEEL SIZE (in.)	15	

Specifications may vary.

Prices

Model	Retail	Mkup
S10 Base Short Box	10,875	6%
S10 LS Long Box	12,185	6%
S10 LS Ext. Cab Short Box	12,990	11%
T10 Base Long Box	15,820	6%
T10 LS Ext. Cab Short Box	17,350	11%

Competition

	POOR — GOOD	Pg.
Chevy S-Series	(no rating)	103
Dodge Dakota	average	109
Ford Ranger	average	117
Nissan Pickup	poor	145
Toyota Pickup	poor	154

* Due to the importance of crash tests, vehicles with no results as of publication date cannot be given an overall rating.

Chevrolet Suburban

The Suburban is a 4-door station wagon version of a Chevrolet C/K pickup, and no other manufacturer offers anything quite like it. ABS is standard, and a driver air bag has finally been added.

Since even an unloaded Suburban weighs close to 5,000 pounds, the standard 5.7-liter V8 has a lot of work to do. Optional engines include a 7.4-liter V8 and a 6.5-liter turbo-diesel V8; all engines come with 4-speed automatic overdrive. Gas mileage is dreary with the 5.7-liter, abysmal with the 7.4-liter. 4-wheel drive is available. The interior is spacious and can be quite comfortable, if you choose one of the interior upgrades. A variety of seating options are available. You can tow up to five tons. Handling is sluggish, but you don't buy a Suburban for its handling—you buy it for its sheer size.

The Ratings

	POOR — GOOD
COMPARATIVE RATING*	▓ (poor end)
CRASH TEST	▓ (good end)
SAFETY FEATURES	▓ (mid)
FUEL ECONOMY	▓ (poor end)
PM COST	▓ (mid)
REPAIR COST	▓ (good)
WARRANTY	▓ (poor)
COMPLAINTS	▓ (poor)
INSURANCE COST	▓ (good end)

Safety

CRASH TEST	Very Good
ROLLOVER	High
AIR BAG	Driver
ANTI-LOCK BRAKES	4-wheel
BELT ADJUSTORS	Standard
BUILT-IN CHILD SEAT	None
OCCUPANT INJURY	Very Good

General Information

FUEL ECONOMY	13/15	VERY POOR
DRIVING RANGE	546	VERY LONG
PARKING INDEX	Very Hard	
THEFT RATING	Very Poor	
CORPORATE TWINS	GMC Suburban	
WHERE MADE	U.S.	
YEAR OF PRODUCTION	Fourth	

Specifications

LENGTH (in.)	220.0	VERY LONG
HEAD/LEG ROOM (in.)	39.9/41.3	AVERAGE
CARGO SPACE (cu. ft.)	150	VERY LARGE
PAYLOAD	2200	AVERAGE
TOW RATING (lbs.)	6000	HIGH
SEATING	3/6/9	
WHEEL SIZE (in.)	15/16	

Specifications may vary.

Prices

Model	Retail	Mkup
Suburban C1500	22,237	14%
Suburban C2500	23,470	14%
Suburban K1500	24,547	14%
Suburban K2500	25,689	14%
Suburban K2500 w/6.5L dsl.	27,549	14%

Competition

	POOR — GOOD	Pg.
Chevy Suburban	▓ (poor)	104
Ford Bronco	▓ (mid)	113
Isuzu Rodeo	▓ (poor end)	130
Jeep Gr. Cherokee	▓ (poor)	133
Mits. Montero	▓ (poor)	143

* Due to the importance of crash tests, vehicles with no results as of publication date cannot be given an overall rating.

Chevrolet Tahoe

Formerly called the Blazer, the Tahoe is Chevrolet's large sport utility vehicle and has little in common with this year's smaller Blazer. Despite the new name, the Tahoe is essentially unchanged, with the exception of a standard driver air bag. The Tahoe has only been available as a 2-door vehicle, but a 4-door model should be in showrooms by this spring. ABS is standard.

Though the Tahoe shares its chassis with the C/K pickups, its engines choices and option list are quite limited. The 2-door model is only available in 4-wheel drive, though the 4-door model will offer 2- or 4-wheel drive. Your only engine choices are a 5.7-liter V8 and a weaker 6.5-liter turbo-diesel. Fuel economy is quite bad. Room is good in front, but it may be a squeeze in the back. In the back, you'll have the choice of van-type panel doors and a pickup-like liftgate.

The Ratings

	POOR	GOOD
COMPARATIVE RATING*		
CRASH TEST		
SAFETY FEATURES		
FUEL ECONOMY		
PM COST		
REPAIR COST		
WARRANTY		
COMPLAINTS		
INSURANCE COST		

Safety

CRASH TEST	No government results
ROLLOVER	High
AIR BAG	Driver
ANTI-LOCK BRAKES	4-wheel
BELT ADJUSTORS	None
BUILT-IN CHILD SEAT	None
OCCUPANT INJURY	Very Good

General Information

FUEL ECONOMY	12/16	VERY POOR
DRIVING RANGE	420	LONG
PARKING INDEX	Average	
THEFT RATING		
CORPORATE TWINS	GMC Yukon	
WHERE MADE	U.S.	
YEAR OF PRODUCTION	Fourth	

Specifications

LENGTH (in.)	188.5	AVERAGE
HEAD/LEG ROOM (in.)	39.9/41.9	ROOMY
CARGO SPACE (cu. ft.)	99	AVERAGE
PAYLOAD	1600	LOW
TOW RATING (lbs.)	7000	HIGH
SEATING	5/6	
WHEEL SIZE (in.)	16	

Specifications may vary.

Prices

Model	Retail	Mkup
Tahoe Base	22,440	
Tahoe w/Towing Pkg.	22,835	
Tahoe w/6.5L	25,300	
Tahoe w/6.5L and Towing Pkg.	25,464	

Competition

	POOR	GOOD	Pg.
Chevrolet Tahoe			105
Ford Bronco			113
Honda Passport			127
Jeep Gr. Cherokee			133
Mits. Montero			143

* Due to the importance of crash tests, vehicles with no results as of publication date cannot be given an overall rating.

Though the big Chevy van has received some facelifts over the years, it hasn't undergone a major overhaul since its introduction back in 1971. The Chevy Van is for cargo, while the Sport Van is for people. All Sport Vans added a driver air bag last year which improved its government crash test score dramatically. ABS is standard on all four wheels.

Each of the six engine choices is matched to an automatic overdrive transmission. With the standard V8, performance is adequate, but don't expect good gas mileage on this heavy vehicle which is not aerodynamic in the least. You don't get any suspension choices; the mid-length wheelbase, the most popular choice of the three, gives a decent ride. Tow up to five tons and haul up to 15 people. Rather sloppy handling gives away the Chevy van's age, as do the controls and dashboard layout.

The Ratings

	POOR — GOOD
COMPARATIVE RATING*	
CRASH TEST	
SAFETY FEATURES	
FUEL ECONOMY	
PM COST	
REPAIR COST	
WARRANTY	
COMPLAINTS	
INSURANCE COST	

Safety

CRASH TEST	Poor
ROLLOVER	High
AIR BAG	Driver (optional)
ANTI-LOCK BRAKES	4-wheel
BELT ADJUSTORS	None
BUILT-IN CHILD SEAT	None
OCCUPANT INJURY	Very Good

General Information

FUEL ECONOMY	14/16	VERY POOR
DRIVING RANGE	495	VERY LONG
PARKING INDEX	Hard	
THEFT RATING	Very Poor	
CORPORATE TWINS	GMC Vandura/Rally	
WHERE MADE	Canada	
YEAR OF PRODUCTION	Twenty-fifth	

Specifications

LENGTH (in.)	204.1	VERY LONG
HEAD/LEG ROOM (in.)	40.9/39.5	AVERAGE
CARGO SPACE (cu. ft.)	260	VERY LARGE
PAYLOAD	2150	AVERAGE
TOW RATING (lbs.)	7000	HIGH
SEATING	5/8/12/15	
WHEEL SIZE (in.)	15/16	

Specifications may vary.

Prices

Model	Retail	Mkup
Sport Van 8-pass.	20,226	14%
Sport Van 12-pass.	21,620	14%
Sport Van 8-pass. Ext.	22,776	14%
Sport Van 8-pass. w/6.5L	23,096	14%
Sport Van 12-pass. w/6.5L	23,275	14%

Competition

	POOR — GOOD	Pg.
Chevy Van/Sprt. Van		106
Dodge Caravan		108
Dodge Ram Van		111
Ford Club Wagon		114
GMC Vandura		123

* Due to the importance of crash tests, vehicles with no results as of publication date cannot be given an overall rating.

The Town & Country, due for replacement this spring, is a luxury version of the Dodge and Plymouth Grand minivans. For the extra money, you get lots of power equipment and the option of leather upholstery. The Town & Country seats seven, all but the rear three in captain's chairs. Dual air bags and ABS are standard.

The Town & Country offers a 3.8-liter V6 to go with the standard automatic overdrive, and gas mileage is about as poor as you'll find anywhere. All-wheel drive is optional. You can't get the "sport handling" package that's optional on the Grand Voyager, but if you want a firmer suspension, check out the trailer-towing package. Ride is comfortable on smooth roads. The built-in child restraints are an excellent option.

The Ratings

	POOR — GOOD
COMPARATIVE RATING*	▮ (near good)
CRASH TEST	▮
SAFETY FEATURES	▮
FUEL ECONOMY	▮ (poor)
PM COST	▮
REPAIR COST	▮
WARRANTY	▮
COMPLAINTS	▮ (poor)
INSURANCE COST	▮ (good)

Safety

CRASH TEST	Good
ROLLOVER	Moderate
AIR BAG	Dual
ANTI-LOCK BRAKES	4-wheel
BELT ADJUSTORS	Standard
BUILT-IN CHILD SEAT	Optional (two)
OCCUPANT INJURY	Very Good

General Information

FUEL ECONOMY	17/23	POOR
DRIVING RANGE	380	AVERAGE
PARKING INDEX	Hard	
THEFT RATING	Very Poor	
CORPORATE TWINS	Gr. Caravan, Gr. Voyager	
WHERE MADE	U.S.	
YEAR OF PRODUCTION	Sixth	

Specifications

LENGTH (in.)	192.8	LONG
HEAD/LEG ROOM (in.)	39.1/38.3	VERY CRAMPED
CARGO SPACE (cu. ft.)	141	VERY LARGE
PAYLOAD	2000	LOW
TOW RATING (lbs.)	2000	VERY LOW
SEATING	7	
WHEEL SIZE (in.)	15	

Specifications may vary.

Prices

Model	Retail	Mkup
Town and Country Base	28,240	10%
Town and Country AWD	30,335	11%

Competition

	POOR — GOOD	Pg.
Chrysler T&C	▮ (near good)	107
Ford Windstar	▮ (good)	118
Nissan Quest	▮	146
Olds Silhouette	▮	147
Toyota Previa	▮	155

* Due to the importance of crash tests, vehicles with no results as of publication date cannot be given an overall rating.

The Caravan, which along with the Plymouth Voyager was the original minivan, is due to be replaced this spring. For now, consumers can choose between four trim levels (base, SE, LE and ES), two transmissions (a three- and a four-speed automatic) and four engines (a 2.4-liter four-cylinder, a 3-liter V6, a 3.3-liter V6 and a 3.8-liter V6). The Caravan has dual air bags and meets 1997 government side impact standards for passenger cars.

The longer wheelbase and length of the Grand Caravan translates into more cargo room. The 4-cylinder engine is really not adequate—get the 3-liter V6. On the Grand Caravan, the optional 3.3-V6 is a good starting point. Order the heavy duty suspension or "sport handling group" for improved cornering ability. The built-in child restraints are a great option.

The Ratings

	POOR → GOOD
COMPARATIVE RATING*	Good
CRASH TEST	Above average
SAFETY FEATURES	Above average
FUEL ECONOMY	Poor
PM COST	Above average
REPAIR COST	Above average
WARRANTY	Poor
COMPLAINTS	Poor
INSURANCE COST	Good

Safety

CRASH TEST	Good
ROLLOVER	Moderate
AIR BAG	Dual
ANTI-LOCK BRAKES	4-wheel (optional)
BELT ADJUSTORS	Standard
BUILT-IN CHILD SEAT	Optional (two)
OCCUPANT INJURY	Good (4WD=Very Good)

General Information

FUEL ECONOMY	20/24	POOR
DRIVING RANGE	440	LONG
PARKING INDEX	Average	
THEFT RATING	Good (4WD=Average)	
CORPORATE TWINS	Voy., Town & Country	
WHERE MADE	Canada/U.S.	
YEAR OF PRODUCTION	Fifth	

Specifications

LENGTH (in.)	178.1	SHORT
HEAD/LEG ROOM (in.)	39.1/38.3	VERY CRAMPED
CARGO SPACE (cu. ft.)	117	LARGE
PAYLOAD	1200	VERY LOW
TOW RATING (lbs.)	2000	VERY LOW
SEATING	2/5/7	
WHEEL SIZE (in.)	14/15	

Specifications may vary.

Prices

Model	Retail	Mkup
Caravan Base	16,720	9%
Caravan SE	19,415	10%
Caravan Grand LE	24,240	11%
Caravan ES	24,450	10%
Caravan Grand ES AWD	26,825	11%

Competition

	POOR → GOOD	Pg.
Dodge Caravan	Good	108
Chevy Lumina	Above average	102
Ford Aerostar	Poor	112
Nissan Quest	Above average	146
Toyota Previa	Poor	155

* Due to the importance of crash tests, vehicles with no results as of publication date cannot be given an overall rating.

The mid-size Dakota, which changes very little for 1995, bridges the gap between compact pickups like the Chevrolet S-10 and traditional large pickups like the Ford F-series. A driver air bag was added last year, dramatically improving driver protection. The standard ABS still operates only on the rear wheels.

A weak 2.5-liter 4-cylinder is the standard engine. For heavier work, you'll be happier with the optional 3.9-liter V6 or Chrysler's 5.2-liter V8. You'll have to choose between two- or four-wheel drive, short or long bed, manual or automatic transmission, regular or club cab and several option packages. Ride is smoother than compact trucks, and handling is more responsive than larger pickups. Pay the extra money for 4-wheel ABS.

The Ratings

	POOR → GOOD
COMPARATIVE RATING*	▮ (above average)
CRASH TEST	▮ (good)
SAFETY FEATURES	▮ (below average)
FUEL ECONOMY	▮ (poor)
PM COST	▮ (above average)
REPAIR COST	▮ (good)
WARRANTY	▮ (poor)
COMPLAINTS	▮ (good)
INSURANCE COST	▮ (below average)

Safety

CRASH TEST	Very Good
ROLLOVER	High
AIR BAG	Driver
ANTI-LOCK BRAKES	2-whl. (4-whl. optional)
BELT ADJUSTORS	None
BUILT-IN CHILD SEAT	None
OCCUPANT INJURY	Average (4x4=Very Gd.)

General Information

FUEL ECONOMY	15/19	VERY POOR
DRIVING RANGE	240	VERY SHORT
PARKING INDEX	Average	
THEFT RATING	Very Good (4WD=Good)	
CORPORATE TWINS		
WHERE MADE	U.S.	
YEAR OF PRODUCTION	Ninth	

Specifications

LENGTH (in.)	195.3	LONG
HEAD/LEG ROOM (in.)	39.5/41.8	ROOMY
CARGO SPACE (cu. ft.)		
PAYLOAD	1450	LOW
TOW RATING (lbs.)	4300	AVERAGE
SEATING	3/6	
WHEEL SIZE (in.)	15	

Specifications may vary.

Prices

Model	Retail	Mkup
Dakota 4x2 WS	10,781	4%
Dakota 4x2 Sport Short Box	11,489	7%
Dakota 4x2 Base Long Box	13,921	10%
Dakota 4x4 Sport Short Box	16,504	10%
Dakota 4x4 Base Club	19,545	11%

Competition

	POOR → GOOD	Pg.
Dodge Dakota	▮ (above average)	109
Ford Ranger	▮ (average)	117
Isuzu Pickup	▮ (average)	129
Mits. Mighty Max	▮ (poor)	142
Toyota Pickup	▮ (poor)	154

* Due to the importance of crash tests, vehicles with no results as of publication date cannot be given an overall rating.

Dodge Ram Pickup

Standard Pickup

The Ram pickup was completely overhauled last year, with a most-distinctive front end. A driver's air bag was added last year, greatly improving driver protection in the government's crash test. ABS is standard only on the rear wheels, optional on all four wheels.

Engines range from a 3.9-liter V6, two V8s and a turbo-diesel 6, up to a thirsty 8.0-liter V-10, a heavier version of the Dodge Viper's engine; all get poor gas mileage. The biggest change for 1995 is the appearance of an extended cab version, with seating for six. Other choices to make include two other cab configurations, three trim levels, manual or automatic transmission and two- or four-wheel drive. Sit down before you scan the option list—it's expensive.

The Ratings

	POOR ... GOOD
COMPARATIVE RATING*	(no rating)
CRASH TEST	(no rating)
SAFETY FEATURES	▮
FUEL ECONOMY	▮
PM COST	▮
REPAIR COST	▮
WARRANTY	▮
COMPLAINTS	(no rating)
INSURANCE COST	▮

Safety

CRASH TEST	No government results
ROLLOVER	Moderate
AIR BAG	Driver
ANTI-LOCK BRAKES	2-whl. (4-whl. opt.)
BELT ADJUSTORS	None
BUILT-IN CHILD SEAT	None
OCCUPANT INJURY	

General Information

FUEL ECONOMY	12/16	VERY POOR
DRIVING RANGE	338	SHORT
PARKING INDEX	Hard	
THEFT RATING		
CORPORATE TWINS		
WHERE MADE	U.S.	
YEAR OF PRODUCTION	Second	

Specifications

LENGTH (in.)	204.1	VERY LONG
HEAD/LEG ROOM (in.)	40.2/41.0	AVERAGE
CARGO SPACE (cu. ft.)		
PAYLOAD	1850	LOW
TOW RATING (lbs.)	4800	AVERAGE
SEATING	3/6	
WHEEL SIZE (in.)	16	

Specifications may vary.

Prices

Model	Retail	Mkup
1500 4x2 WS Short Box	13,538	9%
1500 4x2 Base Long Box	15,567	13%
1500 4x4 Base Long Box	18,709	14%
2500 4x2 Club Cab	20,322	14%
1500 4x4 Club Cab Short Box	20,794	14%

Competition

	POOR ... GOOD	Pg.
Dodge Ram Pickup	(no rating)	110
Chevy C/K	▮	101
Ford F-Series	▮	116
GMC Sierra	▮	120
Toyota T100	▮	156

* Due to the importance of crash tests, vehicles with no results as of publication date cannot be given an overall rating.

Though its body has not changed significantly since its introduction in 1971, the Ram Van and Ram Wagon get a significant change for 1995 in the form of a driver air bag. Dodge is hoping it will help the Van/Wagon's previously poor showing in the government crash test. Rear-wheel ABS is standard on Vans; 4-wheel ABS is standard on Wagons and optional on Vans.

You select from three payload options, six engines, and manual or automatic transmissions. Even on the highway, gas mileage will be poor; the 4-speed automatic is a little more efficient than the 3-speed. Ride on the shortest-wheelbase models tends to be bouncy and uncomfortable. Chrysler has improved the van's instrument panel and controls over the years, but they're not up to the best international designs.

The Ratings

	POOR	GOOD
COMPARATIVE RATING*		
CRASH TEST		
SAFETY FEATURES	▪	
FUEL ECONOMY	▪	
PM COST	▪	
REPAIR COST		▪
WARRANTY	▪	
COMPLAINTS		▪
INSURANCE COST		▪

Safety

CRASH TEST	No government results
ROLLOVER	Very High
AIR BAG	Driver
ANTI-LOCK BRAKES	2-whl. (4-whl. opt.)
BELT ADJUSTORS	None
BUILT-IN CHILD SEAT	None
OCCUPANT INJURY	Very Good

General Information

FUEL ECONOMY	15/17	VERY POOR
DRIVING RANGE	352	SHORT
PARKING INDEX	Hard	
THEFT RATING	Average	
CORPORATE TWINS		
WHERE MADE	Canada	
YEAR OF PRODUCTION	Twenty-fifth	

Specifications

LENGTH (in.)	205.2	VERY LONG
HEAD/LEG ROOM (in.)	40.5/39.0	CRAMPED
CARGO SPACE (cu. ft.)	247	VERY LARGE
PAYLOAD	1800	LOW
TOW RATING (lbs.)	8500	VERY HIGH
SEATING	8/12/15	
WHEEL SIZE (in.)	15/16	

Specifications may vary.

Prices

Model	Retail	Mkup
B150 Van SWB	14,879	9%
B150 Wagon	16,052	9%
B250 Wagon	19,728	14%
B350 Maxi Van	20,682	14%
B350 Wagon	21,315	14%

Competition

	POOR	GOOD	Pg.
Ram Van/Wagon			111
Chevy Sport Van	▪		106
Dodge Caravan		▪	108
Ford Club Wagon	▪		114
GMC Vandura	▪		123

* Due to the importance of crash tests, vehicles with no results as of publication date cannot be given an overall rating.

Ford Aerostar

The Ratings

	POOR	GOOD
COMPARATIVE RATING*		
CRASH TEST		
SAFETY FEATURES		
FUEL ECONOMY		
PM COST		
REPAIR COST		
WARRANTY		
COMPLAINTS		
INSURANCE COST		

The Aerostar was scheduled to cease production in 1994, with the introduction of the Windstar, but it has been carried over into 1995 buoyed by continued steady sales. The Aerostar only comes with a driver air bag and rear-wheel ABS, two huge strikes against it.

The passenger van is actually called a wagon, while the cargo van is called a van. The wagon is available in rear-wheel drive regular- and extended-length, or 4WD extended-length. The 3-liter V6, standard on the rear-wheel drive models, is adequate. The 4-liter V6, standard on 4WD models and available on the rear-wheel drive extended-length model, is slightly more powerful. Handling improves with 4WD, and ride is fairly good. Built-in child restraints are a noteworthy option. Watch out for the brakes, especially on wet roads.

Safety

CRASH TEST	Moderate
ROLLOVER	Very High
AIR BAG	Driver
ANTI-LOCK BRAKES	2-wheel
BELT ADJUSTORS	None
BUILT-IN CHILD SEAT	Optional
OCCUPANT INJURY	Average (4WD=Good)

General Information

FUEL ECONOMY	17/23	POOR
DRIVING RANGE	399	AVERAGE
PARKING INDEX	Hard	
THEFT RATING	Very Good	
CORPORATE TWINS		
WHERE MADE	U.S.	
YEAR OF PRODUCTION	Eleventh	

Specifications

LENGTH (in.)	174.9	SHORT
HEAD/LEG ROOM (in.)	39.5/41.4	AVERAGE
CARGO SPACE (cu. ft.)	140	VERY LARGE
PAYLOAD	1950	LOW
TOW RATING (lbs.)	4400	AVERAGE
SEATING	2/7	
WHEEL SIZE (in.)	14	

Specifications may vary.

Prices

Model	Retail	Mkup
Aerostar Cargo 2WD Reg.	17,265	12%
Aerostar XLT 2WD Reg.	17,895	12%
Aerostar XLT 2WD Ext.	21,195	12%
Aerostar XLT 4WD Ext.	23,520	13%

Competition

	POOR	GOOD	Pg.
Ford Aerostar			**112**
Chevy Astro			99
Chevy Lumina			102
Mercury Villager			141
Plymouth Voyager			148

* Due to the importance of crash tests, vehicles with no results as of publication date cannot be given an overall rating.

Ford Bronco

The Bronco hasn't changed much since its last revision in 1980. A driver air bag was added last year, improving the Bronco's already good driver protection in the government crash test program.

Ford offers a 5-liter V8 and an optional 5.8-liter V8, both with plenty of power. The standard 5-liter offers a choice of manual or automatic transmissions, but if you opt for the more powerful 5.8-liter you'll be stuck with an automatic transmission. Acceleration is peppier with the big engine; gas mileage with either V8 on this heavy vehicle is very poor. Handling, like the big Ford pickup's, is cumbersome, and the Bronco's relatively short wheelbase gives it a choppy ride. Comfort is pretty good in front, but adults will suffer a bit in the back. The Bronco only comes as a 2-door vehicle.

The Ratings

	POOR ... GOOD
COMPARATIVE RATING*	
CRASH TEST	
SAFETY FEATURES	
FUEL ECONOMY	
PM COST	
REPAIR COST	
WARRANTY	
COMPLAINTS	
INSURANCE COST	

Safety

CRASH TEST	Very Good
ROLLOVER	High
AIR BAG	Driver
ANTI-LOCK BRAKES	4-wheel
BELT ADJUSTORS	None
BUILT-IN CHILD SEAT	None
OCCUPANT INJURY	Very Good

General Information

FUEL ECONOMY	14/19	VERY POOR
DRIVING RANGE	512	VERY LONG
PARKING INDEX	Easy	
THEFT RATING	Poor	
CORPORATE TWINS		
WHERE MADE	U.S.	
YEAR OF PRODUCTION	Sixteenth	

Specifications

LENGTH (in.)	183.6	SHORT
HEAD/LEG ROOM (in.)	41.2/41.1	ROOMY
CARGO SPACE (cu. ft.)	50	VERY SMALL
PAYLOAD	1050	VERY LOW
TOW RATING (lbs.)	7000	HIGH
SEATING	5/6	
WHEEL SIZE (in.)	15	

Specifications may vary.

Prices

Model	Retail	Mkup
Bronco XL	21,785	16%
Bronco XLT	24,540	16%
Bronco Eddie Bauer	27,610	17%

Competition

	POOR ... GOOD	Pg.
Ford Bronco		**113**
Chevy Suburban		104
Isuzu Rodeo		130
Jeep Gr. Cherokee		133
Mits. Montero		143

* Due to the importance of crash tests, vehicles with no results as of publication date cannot be given an overall rating.

Although Ford restyled the Econoline and Club Wagon several years ago, the vehicles have not changed much since their introduction in 1974. The Econoline is for hauling cargo, and the Club Wagon is for carrying people. Ford led all van-makers with the addition of a driver air bag in 1993. The optional ABS operates on all four wheels.

Ford offers three payload options and four engines. The standard 6-cylinder has enough power for average use, but for heavier duty, you may want one of the optional V8s. All come with automatic transmission. Though a bit more aero-dynamic than its competitors, the Ford van is on the heavy side and thus not very fuel efficient. The Regular van seats 8, the Heavy Duty seats 12, and the Super seats 15. Ride is decent, but handling is cumbersome, though the optional handling package may help.

The Ratings

	POOR ◻◻◻ GOOD
COMPARATIVE RATING*	◻◻◻■◻◻◻◻◻◻
CRASH TEST	◻◻◻◻◻■◻◻◻◻
SAFETY FEATURES	◻◻■◻◻◻◻◻◻◻
FUEL ECONOMY	■◻◻◻◻◻◻◻◻◻
PM COST	◻◻◻◻◻◻◻■◻◻
REPAIR COST	◻◻◻◻◻◻◻◻■◻
WARRANTY	◻■◻◻◻◻◻◻◻◻
COMPLAINTS	◻◻◻◻◻◻◻■◻◻
INSURANCE COST	◻◻◻◻◻◻◻◻■◻

Safety

CRASH TEST	Moderate
ROLLOVER	
AIR BAG	Driver
ANTI-LOCK BRAKES	2-wheel
BELT ADJUSTORS	None
BUILT-IN CHILD SEAT	None
OCCUPANT INJURY	Very Good

General Information

FUEL ECONOMY	13/17	VERY POOR
DRIVING RANGE	490	VERY LONG
PARKING INDEX	Very Hard	
THEFT RATING	Average	
CORPORATE TWINS		
WHERE MADE	U.S.	
YEAR OF PRODUCTION	Twenty-first	

Specifications

LENGTH (in.)	211.8	VERY LONG
HEAD/LEG ROOM (in.)	42.3/40.3	VERY ROOMY
CARGO SPACE (cu. ft.)	255	VERY LARGE
PAYLOAD	2000	LOW
TOW RATING (lbs.)	6400	HIGH
SEATING	7/8/12/15	
WHEEL SIZE (in.)	15/16	

Specifications may vary.

Prices

Model	Retail	Mkup
Econoline E-150	16,985	16%
Club Wagon Reg. XL	19,022	16%
Club Wagon Reg. XLT	21,930	17%
Club Wagon Super XLT	24,195	17%
Club Wagon Reg. Chateau	25,215	17%

Competition

	POOR ◻◻◻ GOOD	Pg.
Econ./Club Wagon	◻◻◻■◻◻◻◻◻◻	**114**
Chevy Sport Van	◻◻◻■◻◻◻◻◻◻	106
Dodge Caravan	◻◻◻◻◻◻◻◻◻■	108
Dodge Ram Van	◻◻■◻◻◻◻◻◻◻	111
GMC Vandura	◻◻◻■◻◻◻◻◻◻	123

* Due to the importance of crash tests, vehicles with no results as of publication date cannot be given an overall rating.

Ford Explorer

Just as other manufacturers' products were beginning to catch up with the Ford Explorer's popularity, Ford is upping the ante with an all-new Explorer. If consumers liked its predecessor, they'll love this Explorer. It has a more contemporary front end, similar to the F-Series pickups. Most importantly, dual air bags and 4-wheel ABS are standard equipment. The Explorer's engine is a 4-liter V6, with 5-speed manual or automatic overdrive, and 2- or part-time 4-wheel drive. Gas mileage is better than larger utility vehicles and was rumored at press time to have been improved over 1994 models; however, it's still worse than on many full-size cars. There are two body styles, 2- or 4-door; the 4-door has more room for adults in back. One can only hope Ford has done something to help the unresponsive handling and poorly-designed dashboard. If so, the Explorer will have few drawbacks.

The Ratings

	POOR – GOOD
COMPARATIVE RATING*	
CRASH TEST	
SAFETY FEATURES	
FUEL ECONOMY	
PM COST	
REPAIR COST	
WARRANTY	
COMPLAINTS	
INSURANCE COST	

Safety

CRASH TEST	No government results
ROLLOVER	High
AIR BAG	Dual
ANTI-LOCK BRAKES	4-wheel
BELT ADJUSTORS	Standard
BUILT-IN CHILD SEAT	Optional
OCCUPANT INJURY	

General Information

FUEL ECONOMY**	15/20	VERY POOR
DRIVING RANGE**	357	SHORT
PARKING INDEX	Average	
THEFT RATING		
CORPORATE TWINS		
WHERE MADE	U.S.	
YEAR OF PRODUCTION	First	

**Based on 1994 data.

Specifications

LENGTH (in.)	188.5	AVERAGE
HEAD/LEG ROOM (in.)	39.8/42.4	ROOMY
CARGO SPACE (cu. ft.)	82	AVERAGE
PAYLOAD	NOT AVAILABLE	
TOW RATING (lbs.)	5300	HIGH
SEATING	5	
WHEEL SIZE (in.)	15/16	

Specifications may vary.

Prices

Model	Retail	Mkup
Prices unavailable at press time.		
Expected range: $18-30,000.		

Competition

	POOR – GOOD	Pg.
Ford Explorer		**115**
Isuzu Rodeo		130
Jeep Gr. Cherokee		133
Mits. Montero		143
Nissan Pathfinder		144

* Due to the importance of crash tests, vehicles with no results as of publication date cannot be given an overall rating.

The F-Series pickup has not changed much since 1980. A driver air bag was added last year, dramatically improving driver protection in the government crash test. ABS is inexplicably not available.

Ford offers a 4.9-liter 6-cylinder, 3 gasoline V8s, and a beefed-up diesel V8, all of which can be coupled with automatic or manual transmissions. The standard 6-cylinder is fairly powerful, and the electronic automatic is a good choice with any engine. Two- or four-wheel drive is available, as is a stretched "super cab" and a 4-door "crew cab" (F-350 only). Handling is typical for a large pickup: sluggish, and cumbersome. Ride isn't bad on the F-150. The dashboard and controls are worse than on GM's trucks—they're illogical and old-fashioned. Otherwise, a strong choice.

The Ratings

	POOR — GOOD
COMPARATIVE RATING*	■ (middle)
CRASH TEST **	■ (good/right)
SAFETY FEATURES	■ (poor/left)
FUEL ECONOMY	■ (poor/left)
PM COST	■ (good/right)
REPAIR COST	■ (good/right)
WARRANTY	■ (poor/far left)
COMPLAINTS	■ (good/right)
INSURANCE COST	■ (left-middle)

Safety

CRASH TEST **	Good
ROLLOVER	
AIR BAG	Driver (optional)
ANTI-LOCK BRAKES	2-wheel
BELT ADJUSTORS	None
BUILT-IN CHILD SEAT	None
OCCUPANT INJURY	Very Good

General Information

FUEL ECONOMY	15/19	VERY POOR
DRIVING RANGE	291	VERY SHORT
PARKING INDEX	Average	
THEFT RATING	Average	
CORPORATE TWINS		
WHERE MADE	U.S./Canada	
YEAR OF PRODUCTION	Sixteenth	

Specifications

LENGTH (in.)	197.1	LONG
HEAD/LEG ROOM (in.)	40.3/41.0	ROOMY
CARGO SPACE (cu. ft.)		
PAYLOAD	2050	AVERAGE
TOW RATING (lbs.)	1900	VERY LOW
SEATING	3/6	
WHEEL SIZE (in.)	15	

Specifications may vary.

Prices

Model	Retail	Mkup
F150 4x2 SWB	13,001	12%
F150 4x4 LWB XL	17,091	16%
F150 Sup. Cab 4x4 SWB Fl.	19,144	16%
F250 Hvy Dty Reg Cab 4x4	19,146	16%
F150 4x2 Lightning	20,070	16%

Competition

	POOR — GOOD	Pg.
Ford F-Series	■ (middle)	**116**
Chevy C/K	■ (middle-right)	101
Dodge Ram	■ (left)	110
GMC Sierra	■ (middle-right)	120
Toyota T100	■ (middle-right)	156

**Data given for model with air bag. See Safety Chapter for crash test results for model without air bag.

* Due to the importance of crash tests, vehicles with no results as of publication date cannot be given an overall rating.

The Ford Ranger enters its third year with some significant changes, the most important of which is a standard driver air bag. The grille, interior and already well-designed instrument panel have been improved. 4-wheel ABS is finally available and is standard on 4x2 models with the optional 4-liter engine and on all 4x4 models.

The Ranger comes with a relatively weak 2.3-liter 4-cylinder engine. The available 3- or 4-liter V6s are better for serious load carrying. To save some money, get the options you want in a complete package. The Splash has a "step-side" pickup box, but nothing useful you can't order on cheaper Rangers. The Super Cab is a longer version of the Ranger. Handling is typical of small pickups, but you can order a handling package to get better response.

The Ratings

	POOR	GOOD
COMPARATIVE RATING*		
CRASH TEST		
SAFETY FEATURES		
FUEL ECONOMY		
PM COST		
REPAIR COST		
WARRANTY		
COMPLAINTS		
INSURANCE COST		

Safety

CRASH TEST	Good
ROLLOVER	Moderate
AIR BAG	Driver
ANTI-LOCK BRAKES	2-whl. (4-whl. optional)
BELT ADJUSTORS	Standard
BUILT-IN CHILD SEAT	None
OCCUPANT INJURY	Average (4x4=Good)

General Information

FUEL ECONOMY	21/24	POOR
DRIVING RANGE	359	SHORT
PARKING INDEX	Easy	
THEFT RATING	Very Good	
CORPORATE TWINS	Mazda B-Series	
WHERE MADE	U.S.	
YEAR OF PRODUCTION	Third	

Specifications

LENGTH (in.)	184.3	AVERAGE
HEAD/LEG ROOM (in.)	39.1/42.4	ROOMY
CARGO SPACE (cu. ft.)		
PAYLOAD	1550	LOW
TOW RATING (lbs.)	1850	VERY LOW
SEATING	3	
WHEEL SIZE (in.)	14/15	

Specifications may vary.

Prices

Model	Retail	Mkup
Prices unavailable at press time.		
Expected range: $14-18,000.		

Competition

	POOR	GOOD	Pg.
Ford Ranger			117
Dodge Dakota			109
Isuzu Pickup			129
Mits. Mighty Max			143
Nissan Pickup			145

* Due to the importance of crash tests, vehicles with no results as of publication date cannot be given an overall rating.

Ford Windstar

With their latest entry into the minivan fray, Ford has finally caught up to Chrysler. Unfortunately for Ford, Chrysler will be unveiling a new minivan this Spring. The Windstar offers optional built-in child restraints, standard dual air bags and standard 4-wheel ABS.

The base GL comes standard with the same 3-liter V6 as is available on the Aerostar and Ranger. A 3.8-liter V6 is optional on the GL and standard on the LX, though it provides only slightly more power. At over 200 inches, the Windstar is the longest minivan you can buy, and it has more interior room than even a Grand Caravan, but not quite as much as a Toyota Previa. Most of that room is given to rear seat passengers. With its contemporary styling and decent handling, the Windstar provides the first good alternative to the current generation of Chrysler minivans.

The Ratings

	POOR → GOOD
COMPARATIVE RATING*	
CRASH TEST	
SAFETY FEATURES	
FUEL ECONOMY	
PM COST	
REPAIR COST	
WARRANTY	
COMPLAINTS	
INSURANCE COST	

Safety

CRASH TEST	Very Good
ROLLOVER	Moderate
AIR BAG	Dual
ANTI-LOCK BRAKES	4-wheel
BELT ADJUSTORS	Standard
BUILT-IN CHILD SEAT	Optional
OCCUPANT INJURY	

General Information

FUEL ECONOMY	17/24	POOR
DRIVING RANGE	400	AVERAGE
PARKING INDEX	Hard	
THEFT RATING		
CORPORATE TWINS		
WHERE MADE	U.S.	
YEAR OF PRODUCTION	First	

Specifications

LENGTH (in.)	201.2	LONG
HEAD/LEG ROOM (in.)	39.3/41.8	AVERAGE
CARGO SPACE (cu. ft.)	144	VERY LARGE
PAYLOAD	1800	LOW
TOW RATING (lbs.)	3500	LOW
SEATING	7	
WHEEL SIZE (in.)	15	

Specifications may vary.

Prices

Model	Retail	Mkup
Windstar Cargo	18,285	12%
Windstar GL	20,130	12%
Windstar LX	24,300	12%

Competition

	POOR → GOOD	Pg.
Ford Windstar		118
Dodge Caravan		108
Nissan Quest		146
Olds Silhouette		147
Toyota Previa		155

* Due to the importance of crash tests, vehicles with no results as of publication date cannot be given an overall rating.

GMC Jimmy

The Jimmy, like its twin the Chevrolet Blazer, is all-new for 1995. Its similarity to the industry-leading Ford Explorer is no coincidence, although GMC considers the Jimmy to be a cleaner, more modern version of the Explorer. ABS is standard, and a driver air bag is finally available.

The Jimmy's 4.3-liter V6 is powerful enough. You'll have to choose between 2- and 4-door models, four different suspensions and 2- or 4-wheel drive. The suspension packages go a long way towards tailoring the ride and handling to the customer's preference, one shortcoming of the previous Jimmy. The 1995 Jimmy is lower, wider and longer, increasing interior room, another previous shortcoming. It seats four comfortably, and you can squeeze up to six with the optional bench seat in front.

The Ratings

	POOR					GOOD
COMPARATIVE RATING*						
CRASH TEST						
SAFETY FEATURES	■					
FUEL ECONOMY	■					
PM COST					■	
REPAIR COST					■	
WARRANTY	■					
COMPLAINTS						
INSURANCE COST	■					

Safety

CRASH TEST	No government results
ROLLOVER	Very High
AIR BAG	Driver
ANTI-LOCK BRAKES	4-wheel
BELT ADJUSTORS	None
BUILT-IN CHILD SEAT	None
OCCUPANT INJURY	

General Information

FUEL ECONOMY	16/21	POOR
DRIVING RANGE	360	SHORT
PARKING INDEX	Easy	
THEFT RATING		
CORPORATE TWINS	Chevrolet Blazer	
WHERE MADE	U.S.	
YEAR OF PRODUCTION	First	

Specifications

LENGTH (in.)	175.1	SHORT
HEAD/LEG ROOM (in.)	39.6/42.5	ROOMY
CARGO SPACE (cu. ft.)	67	SMALL
PAYLOAD	1000	VERY LOW
TOW RATING (lbs.)	5500	HIGH
SEATING	4/6	
WHEEL SIZE (in.)	15	

Specifications may vary.

Prices

Model	Retail	Mkup
Jimmy 2-dr. 4X2	18,274	11%
Jimmy 2-dr. 4X4	20,157	11%
Jimmy 4-dr. 4X2	19,980	11%
Jimmy 4-dr. 4X4	22,205	11%

Competition

	POOR			GOOD		Pg.
GMC Jimmy						119
Isuzu Rodeo	■					130
Jeep Gr. Cherokee	■					133
Mits. Montero	■					143
Nissan Pathfinder	■					144

* Due to the importance of crash tests, vehicles with no results as of publication date cannot be given an overall rating.

The Sierra gets some significant changes for 1995 that will make it a much more competitive vehicle. A driver air bag is standard, and the standard ABS is now on all four wheels.

An all-new, more contemporary, interior alleviates one of the Sierra's previous shortcomings. You'll have plenty of choices when buying a Sierra. You'll have to choose between eight engines (a V6, three gasoline V8s and four diesel V8s), manual or automatic transmission, 2-or 4-wheel drive, three cab sizes, two box lengths, three trim levels and five stereos. Ride and handling are going to vary with the suspension choice. Choose between five radios, including one that has a CD- and cassette-player. If you have the patience to wade carefully through the options list to personalize your Sierra, you should find something that meets your needs well.

The Ratings

	POOR	GOOD
COMPARATIVE RATING*		
CRASH TEST		
SAFETY FEATURES		
FUEL ECONOMY		
PM COST		
REPAIR COST		
WARRANTY		
COMPLAINTS		
INSURANCE COST		

Safety

CRASH TEST	Very Good
ROLLOVER	High
AIR BAG	Driver (optional)
ANTI-LOCK BRAKES	4-wheel
BELT ADJUSTORS	None
BUILT-IN CHILD SEAT	None
OCCUPANT INJURY	Very Good

General Information

FUEL ECONOMY	15/19	VERY POOR
DRIVING RANGE	425	LONG
PARKING INDEX	Hard	
THEFT RATING	2WD=Vry. Pr., 4WD=Poor	
CORPORATE TWINS	Chevrolet C/K Pickup	
WHERE MADE	U.S./Canada	
YEAR OF PRODUCTION	Eighth	

Specifications

LENGTH (in.)	194.5	LONG
HEAD/LEG ROOM (in.)	39.9/41.7	ROOMY
CARGO SPACE (cu. ft.)		
PAYLOAD	2000	LOW
TOW RATING (lbs.)	7500	VERY HIGH
SEATING	3/5/6	
WHEEL SIZE (in.)	15/16	

Specifications may vary.

Prices

Model	Retail	Mkup
Sierra C Reg Cab Sh. Box 4X2	14,867	14%
Sierra C Reg Cab Sh. Box 4X4	17,459	14%
Sierra Club Cab Sh. Box 4X2	16,827	14%
Sierra Club Cab Sh. Box 4X4	19,248	14%
Sierra Crew Cab Lg. Box 4X4	23,172	14%

Competition

	POOR	GOOD	Pg.
GMC Sierra			120
Chevy C/K			101
Dodge Ram			110
Ford F-Series			116
Toyota T100			156

* Due to the importance of crash tests, vehicles with no results as of publication date cannot be given an overall rating.

One year after its redesign, the Sonoma brings only one major change into 1995—the availability of a driver air bag. ABS is standard on the rear wheels only.

The Sonoma's 2.2-liter 4-cylinder engine, which is only available on 2-wheel drive models, may be OK for some buyers. You should consider one of two 4.3-liter V6 engine options if you anticipate doing much hauling. You'll have to choose between manual or automatic transmission, two cab sizes, two box sizes, three wheelbases, 2- or 4-wheel drive and seven suspension packages. Many of the option packages offer significant discounts. The Highrider package incorporates a stronger body and suspension and much larger tires.

The Ratings

	POOR — GOOD
COMPARATIVE RATING*	(no rating)
CRASH TEST	(no rating)
SAFETY FEATURES	◼ (low)
FUEL ECONOMY	◼ (low)
PM COST	◼ (mid)
REPAIR COST	◼ (good)
WARRANTY	◼ (poor)
COMPLAINTS	(no rating)
INSURANCE COST	◼ (mid)

Safety

CRASH TEST	No government results
ROLLOVER	High
AIR BAG	Driver
ANTI-LOCK BRAKES	2-whl. (4-whl. Opt.)
BELT ADJUSTORS	None
BUILT-IN CHILD SEAT	None
OCCUPANT INJURY	Average (4x4=Good)

General Information

FUEL ECONOMY	16/22	POOR
DRIVING RANGE	360	SHORT
PARKING INDEX	Easy	
THEFT RATING	Average (4WD=Vry. Pr.)	
CORPORATE TWINS	Chevrolet S-10 Pickup	
WHERE MADE	U.S.	
YEAR OF PRODUCTION	Fifth	

Specifications

LENGTH (in.)	188.8	AVERAGE
HEAD/LEG ROOM (in.)	39.5/43.2	VY. ROOMY
CARGO SPACE (cu. ft.)		
PAYLOAD	1650	LOW
TOW RATING (lbs.)	5500	HIGH
SEATING	3/5	
WHEEL SIZE (in.)	15	

Specifications may vary.

Prices

Model	Retail	Mkup
Sonoma Reg. Cab 4X2 S10	11,768	6%
Sonoma Reg. Cab 4X4 T10	16,128	6%
Sonoma Club Cab 4X2 S10	12,848	11%
Sonoma Club Cab 4X4 T10	17,183	11%

Competition

	POOR — GOOD	Pg.
GMC Sonoma	(no rating)	**121**
Dodge Dakota	◼ (mid)	109
Ford Ranger	◼ (mid)	117
Isuzu Pickup	◼ (mid)	129
Mits. Mighty Max	◼ (poor)	142

* Due to the importance of crash tests, vehicles with no results as of publication date cannot be given an overall rating.

GMC Suburban

GM doesn't even change the name for this twin of the Chevrolet Suburban, which is alright, since there really isn't any competition from other manufacturers. A driver air bag is a welcome addition in 1995. ABS is standard and operates on all four wheels.

The 5.7-liter V8 has its work cut out for it, given that an unloaded Suburban weighs close to 5,000 pounds and you can tow up to five tons. 7.4-liter V8 or 6.5-liter turbo-diesel V8 options are available for towing or carrying heavy loads. Both engines come with automatic overdrive; 4-wheel-drive is extra. Gas mileage is about as bad as it gets. The interior, which is huge, has been updated to be more car-like. Thanks to its huge size, Suburban's handling is awkward, but you don't buy a Suburban for its agility.

The Ratings

	POOR	GOOD
COMPARATIVE RATING*		
CRASH TEST		
SAFETY FEATURES		
FUEL ECONOMY		
PM COST		
REPAIR COST		
WARRANTY		
COMPLAINTS		
INSURANCE COST		

Safety

CRASH TEST	Very Good
ROLLOVER	High
AIR BAG	Driver
ANTI-LOCK BRAKES	4-wheel
BELT ADJUSTORS	Standard
BUILT-IN CHILD SEAT	None
OCCUPANT INJURY	Very Good

General Information

FUEL ECONOMY	12/15	VERY POOR
DRIVING RANGE	546	VERY LONG
PARKING INDEX	Very Hard	
THEFT RATING		
CORPORATE TWINS	Chevrolet Suburban	
WHERE MADE	U.S.	
YEAR OF PRODUCTION	Fourth	

Specifications

LENGTH (in.)	220.0	VERY LONG
HEAD/LEG ROOM (in.)	39.9/41.3	AVERAGE
CARGO SPACE (cu. ft.)	146	VERY LARGE
PAYLOAD	2200	AVERAGE
TOW RATING (lbs.)	6500	HIGH
SEATING	3/6/9	
WHEEL SIZE (in.)	15/16	

Specifications may vary.

Prices

Model	Retail	Mkup
Suburban 1/2 Ton 4X2	21,657	14%
Suburban 1/2 Ton 4X4	23,963	14%
Suburban 3/4 Ton 4X2	22,885	14%
Suburban 3/4 Ton 4X4	25,104	14%

Competition

	POOR	GOOD	Pg.
GMC Suburban			122
Ford Bronco			113
Isuzu Rodeo			130
Jeep Gr. Cherokee			133
Mits. Montero			143

* Due to the importance of crash tests, vehicles with no results as of publication date cannot be given an overall rating.

The Rally/Vandura, like its van twin from Chevrolet, has not changed drastically since its introduction in 1971, although a replacement may arrive next year. The Vandura is a cargo mover, while the Rally is a people hauler. A driver air bag and 4-wheel ABS are standard.

There are four engine options to choose from, all matched to an automatic overdrive transmission. With the standard 4.3-liter V6, performance is adequate, but you'll want more for those times when the van is full. Since this heavy vehicle has to move a lot of air out of the way as it goes down the road, don't expect good fuel economy. Ride is OK, better with the longer wheelbases. The generally sloppy handling and ancient dashboard give away the GMC van's age. You'll have to choose between several sizes and trim levels, but taking a good look at discount option packages can save some money.

The Ratings

	POOR	GOOD
COMPARATIVE RATING*		
CRASH TEST		
SAFETY FEATURES		
FUEL ECONOMY		
PM COST		
REPAIR COST		
WARRANTY		
COMPLAINTS		
INSURANCE COST		

Safety

CRASH TEST	Poor
ROLLOVER	High
AIR BAG	Driver (optional)
ANTI-LOCK BRAKES	2-wheel
BELT ADJUSTORS	None
BUILT-IN CHILD SEAT	None
OCCUPANT INJURY	Very Good

General Information

FUEL ECONOMY	14/16	VERY POOR
DRIVING RANGE	495	VERY LONG
PARKING INDEX	Hard	
THEFT RATING	Very Poor	
CORPORATE TWINS	Chevrolet Van/Sport Van	
WHERE MADE	Canada/U.S.	
YEAR OF PRODUCTION	Fifteenth	

Specifications

LENGTH (in.)	204.1	VERY LONG
HEAD/LEG ROOM (in.)	40.8/39.5	AVERAGE
CARGO SPACE (cu. ft.)	207	VERY LARGE
PAYLOAD	2150	AVERAGE
TOW RATING (lbs.)	10000	VERY HIGH
SEATING	5/8/12/15	
WHEEL SIZE (in.)	15/16	

Specifications may vary.

Prices

Model	Retail	Mkup
Vandura SWB 4X2	19,706	14%
Vandura LWB 4X2	21,100	14%

Competition

	POOR	GOOD	Pg.
GMC Vandura/Rally			123
Chevy Sport Van			106
Dodge Caravan			108
Dodge Ram Van			111
Ford Club Wagon			114

* Due to the importance of crash tests, vehicles with no results as of publication date cannot be given an overall rating.

This upscale twin of the full-size Chevrolet Tahoe brings a standard driver air bag and a redesigned interior with a more contemporary feel into 1995. 4-wheel ABS is standard.

   Like the Tahoe, the Yukon has a shorter list of engines and options than the full-size pickups with which they share a chassis. Choose between a 5.7-liter V8 and a 6.5-liter turbo-diesel V8, a manual or automatic transmission and five stereos. A 4-door model should be in showrooms by this spring. Ride is rough on anything but smooth roads. Handling is more stable than many smaller utility vehicles, but it's certainly no sports car. You'll have your choice of five stereos, including one with both a CD- and cassette-player. Comfort in front is OK, but any adults in back will likely complain.

The Ratings

	POOR	GOOD
COMPARATIVE RATING*		
CRASH TEST		
SAFETY FEATURES		
FUEL ECONOMY		
PM COST		
REPAIR COST		
WARRANTY		
COMPLAINTS		
INSURANCE COST		

Safety

CRASH TEST	No government results
ROLLOVER	High
AIR BAG	Driver
ANTI-LOCK BRAKES	4-wheel
BELT ADJUSTORS	None
BUILT-IN CHILD SEAT	None
OCCUPANT INJURY	

General Information

FUEL ECONOMY	12/15	VERY POOR
DRIVING RANGE	390	AVERAGE
PARKING INDEX	Average	
THEFT RATING		
CORPORATE TWINS	Chevrolet Tahoe	
WHERE MADE	U.S.	
YEAR OF PRODUCTION	Fourth	

Specifications

LENGTH (in.)	188.5	AVERAGE
HEAD/LEG ROOM (in.)	39.9/41.9	ROOMY
CARGO SPACE (cu. ft.)	99	AVERAGE
PAYLOAD	1600	LOW
TOW RATING (lbs.)	6500	HIGH
SEATING	6	
WHEEL SIZE (in.)	16	

Specifications may vary.

Prices

Model	Retail	Mkup
Yukon 4X4	21,896	14%

Competition

	POOR	GOOD	Pg.
GMC Yukon			124
Ford Bronco			113
Isuzu Rodeo			130
Jeep Gr. Cherokee			133
Mits. Montero			143

* Due to the importance of crash tests, vehicles with no results as of publication date cannot be given an overall rating.

The Tracker, only available as a 2-door, is almost identical to the Suzuki Sidekick. Unlike the Sidekick, which only comes with a soft top, the Tracker is available either as a hardtop or a convertible. Air bags are still not available, and the ABS operates only on the rear wheels.

The only two-wheel drive model is a base convertible; four-wheel drive models are available as convertibles or hardtops. All Trackers get a 1.6-liter, 4-cylinder engine, although there is a peppier version on four-wheel drive models and on two-wheel drive models in states with relaxed emissions standards. Ride is on the stiff side, but tolerable on smooth roads. Accommodations are OK up front, but it's a tight squeeze for two in back. Don't take turns too tightly in this vehicle—it's too narrow and high off the ground to handle sudden movements.

The Ratings

	POOR ... GOOD
COMPARATIVE RATING*	(no rating)
CRASH TEST	(no rating)
SAFETY FEATURES	■ (1)
FUEL ECONOMY	■ (6)
PM COST	■ (9)
REPAIR COST	■ (3)
WARRANTY	■ (4)
COMPLAINTS	■ (9)
INSURANCE COST	■ (1)

Safety

CRASH TEST	No government results
ROLLOVER	High
AIR BAG	None
ANTI-LOCK BRAKES	2-wheel
BELT ADJUSTORS	None
BUILT-IN CHILD SEAT	None
OCCUPANT INJURY	Very Poor

General Information

FUEL ECONOMY	24/26	AVERAGE
DRIVING RANGE	278	VERY SHORT
PARKING INDEX	Very Easy	
THEFT RATING	Poor	
CORPORATE TWINS	Suzuki Sidekick	
WHERE MADE	Canada	
YEAR OF PRODUCTION	Seventh	

Specifications

LENGTH (in.)	142.5	VERY SHORT
HEAD/LEG ROOM (in.)	39.5/42.1	ROOMY
CARGO SPACE (cu. ft.)	33	VERY SMALL
PAYLOAD	850	VERY LOW
TOW RATING (lbs.)	1000	VERY LOW
SEATING	2/4	
WHEEL SIZE (in.)	15	

Specifications may vary.

Prices

Model	Retail	Mkup
Tracker 4x2 Conv.	11,980	5%
Tracker 4x4 Conv.	13,245	5%
Tracker 4x4 Hard Top	13,325	5%
Tracker 4x4 LSi Conv.	14,615	5%
Tracker 4x4 LSi Hard Top	14,795	5%

Competition

	POOR ... GOOD	Pg.
Geo Tracker	(no rating)	**125**
Isuzu Amigo	■ (2)	128
Jeep Wrangler	■ (1)	134
Nissan Pathfinder	■ (2)	144
Suzuki Samurai	■ (5)	150

* Due to the importance of crash tests, vehicles with no results as of publication date cannot be given an overall rating.

The Odyssey is Honda's first entry into the minivan market. This front-wheel drive vehicle is lower than, but not as wide as, other minivans, making it easier to maneuver. The most striking feature about the Odyssey is that it has two sedan-type doors that access the rear seats, while most minivans have only one cumbersome sliding door. Dual air bags and ABS are standard, and the Odyssey meets 1997 passenger car side impact standards. Honda may introduce a V6 for the Odyssey in the spring. For now, it gets the same 2.2-liter 4-cylinder engine found on the Accord. The middle bench seat doesn't come out, but easily lifts forward to rest against the front seats; the rear seat folds into the floor. The middle and rear seat backs fold down to make a big daybed. With removable captain's chairs in the middle row, the Odyssey has more cargo space than the Chrysler Grands and almost as much as the Toyota Previa.

The Ratings

	POOR	GOOD
COMPARATIVE RATING*		
CRASH TEST		
SAFETY FEATURES		
FUEL ECONOMY		
PM COST		
REPAIR COST		
WARRANTY		
COMPLAINTS		
INSURANCE COST		

Safety

CRASH TEST	No government results
ROLLOVER	Moderate
AIR BAG	Dual
ANTI-LOCK BRAKES	4-wheel
BELT ADJUSTORS	None
BUILT-IN CHILD SEAT	None
OCCUPANT INJURY	

General Information

FUEL ECONOMY	19/23	POOR
DRIVING RANGE	344	SHORT
PARKING INDEX	Easy	
THEFT RATING		
CORPORATE TWINS		
WHERE MADE	Japan	
YEAR OF PRODUCTION	First	

Specifications

LENGTH (in.)	186.7	AVERAGE
HEAD/LEG ROOM (in.)	NOT AVAILABLE	
CARGO SPACE (cu. ft.)	151	VERY LARGE
PAYLOAD	NOT AVAILABLE	
TOW RATING (lbs.)	NOT AVAILABLE	
SEATING	6/7	
WHEEL SIZE (in.)	15	

Specifications may vary.

Prices

Model	Retail	Mkup
Prices unavailable at press time.		
Expected range: $22-25,000.		

Competition

	POOR	GOOD	Pg.
Honda Odyssey			**126**
Dodge Caravan			108
Mercury Villager			141
Olds Silhouette			147
Toyota Previa			155

* Due to the importance of crash tests, vehicles with no results as of publication date cannot be given an overall rating.

Honda Passport

The all-new Passport, which is basically an Isuzu Rodeo with the Honda name, represents Honda's first attempt at testing the light truck waters in this country. Honda will be offering a minivan later this year and plans to offer a smaller sport utility, which it will build itself, in the near future. Air bags are not available, which is unfortunate as the Rodeo has done poorly in the government crash test program. ABS only operates on the rear wheels. The base DX is only available with two-wheel drive, a manual transmission, and a weak 2.6-liter 4-cylinder engine. The mid-level LX comes with a more powerful 3.2-liter V6 and offers two- or four-wheel drive and manual or automatic transmission. The up-level EX comes with the larger engine, but only with four-wheel drive. One would hope that Honda will pick a better vehicle to market, or build a better one themselves, next time.

The Ratings

	POOR		GOOD
COMPARATIVE RATING*			
CRASH TEST **			
SAFETY FEATURES			
FUEL ECONOMY			
PM COST			
REPAIR COST			
WARRANTY			
COMPLAINTS			
INSURANCE COST			

Safety

CRASH TEST **	Poor
ROLLOVER	High
AIR BAG	None
ANTI-LOCK BRAKES	2-wheel
BELT ADJUSTORS	None
BUILT-IN CHILD SEAT	None
OCCUPANT INJURY	

General Information

FUEL ECONOMY	16/19	VERY POOR
DRIVING RANGE	372	AVERAGE
PARKING INDEX	Easy	
THEFT RATING		
CORPORATE TWINS	Isuzu Rodeo	
WHERE MADE	U.S.	
YEAR OF PRODUCTION	Second	

Specifications

LENGTH (in.)	176.5	SHORT
HEAD/LEG ROOM (in.)	38.0/42.5	AVERAGE
CARGO SPACE (cu. ft.)	75	SMALL
PAYLOAD	900	VERY LOW
TOW RATING (lbs.)	4500	AVERAGE
SEATING	5/6	
WHEEL SIZE (in.)	15/16	

Specifications may vary.

Prices

Model	Retail	Mkup
Passport DX 4x2	16,610	15%
Passport LX 4x2	20,015	15%
Passport LX 4x4	22,680	15%
Passport LX 4x4 w/16 tires	23,280	15%
Passport EX 4x4	25,780	15%

Competition

	POOR		GOOD	Pg.
Honda Passport				127
Ford Bronco				113
Isuzu Rodeo				130
Jeep Gr. Cherokee				133
Mits. Montero				143

** Data given for 4x2 model. See Safety Chapter for crash test results of 4x4 model.   * Due to the importance of crash tests, vehicles with no results as of publication date cannot be given an overall rating.

Isuzu Amigo

The Amigo, a 2-door utility vehicle based on the Isuzu pickup body and chassis, has not changed at all for the past several years. Isuzu will be dropping production of the Amigo in 1995, though it will be available through the spring. Standard ABS operates only on the rear wheels. Air bags are nowhere to be found. Isuzu's 2.6-liter 4-cylinder engine is not very powerful, so you'll burn a lot of gas in the Amigo. You'll have to choose manual or automatic transmission and two- or four-wheel drive. Because of the Amigo's short wheelbase, ride is rough, even worse than the Rodeo's. Handling is a bit better than the Rodeo's, but nothing special. Be sure to get power steering. The instrument panel has too many pods and buttons. Air bags would make the Amigo as safe as better vehicles. That, along with four-wheel ABS, would make the Amigo's evenual replacement a solid competitor.

The Ratings

	POOR	GOOD
COMPARATIVE RATING*		
CRASH TEST		
SAFETY FEATURES		
FUEL ECONOMY		
PM COST		
REPAIR COST		
WARRANTY		
COMPLAINTS		
INSURANCE COST		

Safety

CRASH TEST	Poor
ROLLOVER	Very High
AIR BAG	None
ANTI-LOCK BRAKES	2-wheel
BELT ADJUSTORS	None
BUILT-IN CHILD SEAT	None
OCCUPANT INJURY	Very Poor

General Information

FUEL ECONOMY	16/20	POOR
DRIVING RANGE	394	AVERAGE
PARKING INDEX	Very Easy	
THEFT RATING	Very Poor	
CORPORATE TWINS		
WHERE MADE	Japan	
YEAR OF PRODUCTION	Seventh	

Specifications

LENGTH (in.)	168.1	VERY SHORT
HEAD/LEG ROOM (in.)	38.0/42.5	AVERAGE
CARGO SPACE (cu. ft.)	51	VERY SMALL
PAYLOAD	900	VERY LOW
TOW RATING (lbs.)	2000	VERY LOW
SEATING	4	
WHEEL SIZE (in.)	16	

Specifications may vary.

Prices

Model	Retail	Mkup
Amigo S 2WD	15,399	14%
Amigo XS 2WD	16,049	14%
Amigo S 4WD	17,349	14%
Amigo XS 4WD	17,749	14%
Amigo XS 4WD w/A-C	18,579	14%

Competition

	POOR	GOOD	Pg.
Isuzu Amigo			**128**
Jeep Wrangler			134
Kia Sportage			135
Nissan Pathfinder			144
Suzuki Samurai			150

* Due to the importance of crash tests, vehicles with no results as of publication date cannot be given an overall rating.

Isuzu Pickup

The Isuzu Pickup has not changed much in the past few years, and is not scheduled for a redesign any time soon. However, Isuzu will add another pickup to the lineup next year. Because of poor sales, Isuzu has dropped production of automobiles in order to focus on pickups and utility vehicles. Air bags are nowhere to be found.

Neither the two-wheel drive's 2.3-liter 4-cylinder engine nor the four-wheel drive's 2.6-liter 4-cylinder offer much power, though they will give you better fuel economy than most other pickups' engines. You have the choice of automatic or manual transmission and standard or long bed. Ride, comfort and handling is generally adequate, but not great. Options are minimal; power steering is a desirable choice. A solid choice, but it could use an air bag or two to outdistance the Ranger and Dakota.

The Ratings

	POOR → GOOD
COMPARATIVE RATING*	▪ middle
CRASH TEST	▪ low-middle
SAFETY FEATURES	▪ very poor
FUEL ECONOMY	▪ poor
PM COST	▪ middle
REPAIR COST	▪ good
WARRANTY	▪ good
COMPLAINTS	▪ very good
INSURANCE COST	▪ poor

Safety

CRASH TEST	Moderate
ROLLOVER	Very High
AIR BAG	None
ANTI-LOCK BRAKES	2-wheel
BELT ADJUSTORS	None
BUILT-IN CHILD SEAT	None
OCCUPANT INJURY	Average

General Information

FUEL ECONOMY	17/20	POOR
DRIVING RANGE	252	VERY SHORT
PARKING INDEX	Easy	
THEFT RATING	Average	
CORPORATE TWINS		
WHERE MADE	Japan/U.S.	
YEAR OF PRODUCTION	Eighth	

Specifications

LENGTH (in.)	177.3	SHORT
HEAD/LEG ROOM (in.)	38.2/42.5	AVERAGE
CARGO SPACE (cu. ft.)		
PAYLOAD	1350	VERY LOW
TOW RATING (lbs.)	2000	VERY LOW
SEATING	2	
WHEEL SIZE (in.)	15	

Specifications may vary.

Prices

Model	Retail	Mkup
Pickup 2WD Std. Bed 2.3L	10,399	11%
Pickup 2WD Long Bed 2.3L	11,809	12%
Pickup 2WD Space Cab 2.6L	13,709	21%
Pickup 4WD Std. Bed 2.6L	14,519	12%
Pickup 4WD Std. Bed 3.1L	15,379	14%

Competition

	POOR → GOOD	Pg.
Isuzu Pickup	▪ middle	129
Dodge Dakota	▪ middle	109
Ford Ranger	▪ low-middle	117
Mits. Mighty Max	▪ very poor	142
Toyota Pickup	▪ poor	154

* Due to the importance of crash tests, vehicles with no results as of publication date cannot be given an overall rating.

The Rodeo, built on the Isuzu pickup's body and chassis, is basically a four-door Amigo station wagon. Like the Amigo, the Rodeo has no air bags, which is unfortunate as the Rodeo has not protected its occupants very well in the government crash test program. The standard ABS operates only on the rear wheels. The 2.6-liter, 120-hp 4-cylinder engine, available only on manual transmission two-wheel drive Rodeos, is completely inadequate. The optional 3.2-liter, 175-hp V6 is more powerful. Fuel economy with both engines is poor. Ride is miserable, and there's a lot of racket inside. Handling is poor. If you need to carry four people, you'll find more room inside the Rodeo than in the Amigo. The sloping roof cuts rear cargo space. The instrument panel has some weird buttons for the lights and wipers. The Rodeo could really use air bags, 4-wheel ABS, and a stronger, yet more efficient, engine.

The Ratings

	POOR ··· GOOD
COMPARATIVE RATING*	▮□□□□□□□□□
CRASH TEST **	□□▮□□□□□□□
SAFETY FEATURES	▮□□□□□□□□□
FUEL ECONOMY	□▮□□□□□□□□
PM COST	□□□□▮□□□□□
REPAIR COST	□□□□□□□□▮□
WARRANTY	□□□□□□□□▮□
COMPLAINTS	□□□□□▮□□□□
INSURANCE COST	▮□□□□□□□□□

Safety

CRASH TEST **	Poor
ROLLOVER	High
AIR BAG	None
ANTI-LOCK BRAKES	2-wheel
BELT ADJUSTORS	None
BUILT-IN CHILD SEAT	None
OCCUPANT INJURY	Average

General Information

FUEL ECONOMY	15/18	VERY POOR
DRIVING RANGE	372	AVERAGE
PARKING INDEX	Easy	
THEFT RATING	Average (4WD=Poor)	
CORPORATE TWINS	Honda Passport	
WHERE MADE	U.S.	
YEAR OF PRODUCTION	Fifth	

Specifications

LENGTH (in.)	176.5	SHORT
HEAD/LEG ROOM (in.)	38.2/42.5	AVERAGE
CARGO SPACE (cu. ft.)	75	SMALL
PAYLOAD	900	VERY LOW
TOW RATING (lbs.)	4500	AVERAGE
SEATING	5	
WHEEL SIZE (in.)	15/16	

Specifications may vary.

Prices

Model	Retail	Mkup
Rodeo S 2WD 2.6L Man.	16,250	11%
Rodeo S 2WD 3.2L Auto.	19,830	14%
Rodeo S 4WD 3.2L Man.	20,750	14%
Rodeo LS 2WD 3.2L Auto.	24,400	15%
Rodeo LS 4WD 3.2L Auto.	26,670	15%

Competition

	POOR ··· GOOD	Pg.
Isuzu Rodeo	▮□□□□□□□□□	130
Ford Bronco	□□□□□□□▮□□	113
Honda Passport	□▮□□□□□□□□	127
Jeep Gr. Cherokee	□▮□□□□□□□□	133
Mits. Montero	□▮□□□□□□□□	143

** Data given for 4x2 model. See Safety Chapter for crash test results on 4x4 model.

* Due to the importance of crash tests, vehicles with no results as of publication date cannot be given an overall rating.

The Trooper, which comes as a two- or four-door, four-wheel drive model, is the only Isuzu product that isn't based on the Isuzu pickup's chassis and body. 1995 model have dual air bags which will help improve up previously abysmal occupant protection. Rear brakes have ABS; a 4-wheel system is optional on S and RS models, standard on LS.

The 3.2-liter V6 comes in single or twin-cam form, but even the twin-cam has barely enough power for this two-ton vehicle. The Trooper's gas mileage is almost as bad as it comes. Ride is poor, but at least it's not as noisy as the Rodeo. Handling is inferior to most other utility vehicles. It's roomy and comfortable with a nicely shaped cargo area. The dashboard is better than on other Isuzu models. The Trooper will benefit from its dual air bags, but it could use a bigger, more economical engine.

The Ratings

	POOR → GOOD
COMPARATIVE RATING*	(no rating)
CRASH TEST	(no rating)
SAFETY FEATURES	below average
FUEL ECONOMY	poor
PM COST	average
REPAIR COST	above average
WARRANTY	above average
COMPLAINTS	above average
INSURANCE COST	below average

Safety

CRASH TEST	No government results
ROLLOVER	Very High
AIR BAG	Dual
ANTI-LOCK BRAKES	2-whl. (4-whl. optional)
BELT ADJUSTORS	None
BUILT-IN CHILD SEAT	None
OCCUPANT INJURY	Good

General Information

FUEL ECONOMY	15/18	VERY POOR
DRIVING RANGE	360	SHORT
PARKING INDEX	Very Easy	
THEFT RATING	Good	
CORPORATE TWINS		
WHERE MADE	Japan	
YEAR OF PRODUCTION	Fourth	

Specifications

LENGTH (in.)	166.5	VERY SHORT
HEAD/LEG ROOM (in.)	39.8/40.8	AVERAGE
CARGO SPACE (cu. ft.)	90	AVERAGE
PAYLOAD	1300	VERY LOW
TOW RATING (lbs.)	5000	AVERAGE
SEATING	5	
WHEEL SIZE (in.)	16	

Specifications may vary.

Prices

Model	Retail	Mkup
S 4-dr. 4WD Auto. w/ABS	24,350	16%
RS 2-dr. 4WD Man. w/ABS	25,950	14%
LS 4-dr. 4WD Man.	27,700	18%
LS 4-dr. 4WD Auto.	28,850	18%
SE 4-dr. 4WD Auto.	33,450	18%

Competition

	POOR → GOOD	Pg.
Isuzu Trooper	(poor)	131
Ford Bronco	above average	113
Jeep Gr. Cherokee	below average	133
Mits. Montero	below average	143
Nissan Pathfinder	poor	144

* Due to the importance of crash tests, vehicles with no results as of publication date cannot be given an overall rating.

Jeep Cherokee

The Cherokee, pioneer of the four-door sport utility market, adds a driver air bag to its standard list of offerings for 1995 and comes in two- or four-door models. To get ABS, you must pay extra and buy a model with a 4-liter engine. The standard engine on the base SE is an anemic 2.5-liter 4-cylinder. A 4-liter V6 with automatic overdrive is optional on the SE and standard on the Sport and Country models. You have the choice of two-wheel drive or one of two four-wheel drive systems. Handling is among the best of utility vehicles. Ride is poor except on smooth roads. The new front seat, which is shared with the Grand Cherokee, is roomy and comfortable, but the rear seat is cramped for adults. Dashboard has a dated look and feel. One virtue is low price, but fancy Cherokees approach the price of a Grand Cherokee, a better vehicle.

The Ratings

	POOR	GOOD
COMPARATIVE RATING*		
CRASH TEST		
SAFETY FEATURES		
FUEL ECONOMY		
PM COST		
REPAIR COST		
WARRANTY		
COMPLAINTS		
INSURANCE COST		

Safety

CRASH TEST	No government results
ROLLOVER	Moderate
AIR BAG	Driver
ANTI-LOCK BRAKES	4-wheel (optional)
BELT ADJUSTORS	None
BUILT-IN CHILD SEAT	None
OCCUPANT INJURY	Avg. (4-dr. 4x4=Good)

General Information

FUEL ECONOMY	17/19	VERY POOR
DRIVING RANGE	343	SHORT
PARKING INDEX	Easy	
THEFT RATING	Poor (4-dr.=Very Poor)	
CORPORATE TWINS		
WHERE MADE	U.S.	
YEAR OF PRODUCTION	Twelfth	

Specifications

LENGTH (in.)	166.9	VERY SHORT
HEAD/LEG ROOM (in.)	38.3/41.4	CRAMPED
CARGO SPACE (cu. ft.)	72	SMALL
PAYLOAD	1150	VERY LOW
TOW RATING (lbs.)	5000	AVERAGE
SEATING	5	
WHEEL SIZE (in.)	15	

Specifications may vary.

Prices

Model	Retail	Mkup
Cherokee SE 2WD 2-dr.	14,134	6%
Cherokee SE 4WD 4-dr.	16,683	6%
Cherokee Sport 4WD 4-dr.	19,101	10%
Cherokee Country 2WD 4-dr.	19,151	10%
Cherokee Country 4WD 4-dr.	20,665	11%

Competition

	POOR	GOOD	Pg.
Jeep Cherokee			132
Ford Explorer			115
Isuzu Rodeo			130
Mits. Montero			143
Nissan Pathfinder			144

* Due to the importance of crash tests, vehicles with no results as of publication date cannot be given an overall rating.

Jeep Grand Cherokee

The Ratings

	POOR	GOOD
COMPARATIVE RATING*		
CRASH TEST		
SAFETY FEATURES		
FUEL ECONOMY		
PM COST		
REPAIR COST		
WARRANTY		
COMPLAINTS		
INSURANCE COST		

The Grand Cherokee is the best of what sport utilities can be, though its driver protection could be improved. However, it is entering its fourth year without a major change and is feeling the consequences. It is due for a redesign next year and will hopefully get a second air bag. A driver air bag and ABS are now standard. The Grand Cherokee comes with a powerful 4-liter V6 or a more powerful 5.2-liter V8. You can choose two-wheel drive, or one of three four-wheel drive systems; "Quadra-Trac" is the easiest to use. A built-in foldout child safety seat is a great new option. Handling is quite good for a sport-utility vehicle, and it improves with the optional Up Country suspension. Ride is average for this class, but inferior to most passenger cars. The Grand Cherokee has only a little more room inside than the Cherokee. Front seats are comfortable, but the rear seat isn't as pleasant or spacious. Cargo room is adequate.

Safety

CRASH TEST	Moderate
ROLLOVER	High
AIR BAG	Driver
ANTI-LOCK BRAKES	4-wheel
BELT ADJUSTORS	None
BUILT-IN CHILD SEAT	Optional
OCCUPANT INJURY	Very Good

General Information

FUEL ECONOMY	15/20	VERY POOR
DRIVING RANGE	391	AVERAGE
PARKING INDEX	Easy	
THEFT RATING	Very Poor	
CORPORATE TWINS		
WHERE MADE	U.S.	
YEAR OF PRODUCTION	Third	

Specifications

LENGTH (in.)	179.0	SHORT
HEAD/LEG ROOM (in.)	38.9/40.9	CRAMPED
CARGO SPACE (cu. ft.)	81	AVERAGE
PAYLOAD	1150	VERY LOW
TOW RATING (lbs.)	5000	AVERAGE
SEATING	5	
WHEEL SIZE (in.)	15	

Specifications may vary.

Prices

Model	Retail	Mkup
Grand Cherokee SE 2WD	23,138	10%
Grand Cherokee SE 4WD	25,075	10%
Grand Cherokee Limited 2WD	28,755	10%
Grand Cherokee Limited 4WD	31,182	10%

Competition

	POOR	GOOD	Pg.
Jeep Gr. Cherokee			133
Ford Bronco			113
GMC Suburban			122
Honda Passport			127
Mits. Montero			143

* Due to the importance of crash tests, vehicles with no results as of publication date cannot be given an overall rating.

The Wrangler changes little this year. In fact, with the exception of improved stability, its roots as a World War II-era vehicle are clearly visible. Air bags are not available, but ABS is now optional on all models.

The 2.5-liter 4-cylinder engine found on the S offers adequate power in the relatively light Wrangler; the 4-liter V6 found on the SE and Sahara models is much better, however. Transmission choices are 5-speed manual or 3-speed automatic, and all Wranglers come with part-time 4-wheel drive. Handling is about average for sport-utility vehicles, and notably worse than any car. The Wrangler's element is really off the road. Ride is harsh on any surface, and the rear seat is cramped and uncomfortable for adults. Comfort and weather sealing are minimal with the soft top, but the heater is powerful.

The Ratings

	POOR ... GOOD
COMPARATIVE RATING*	■ (1st — poor)
CRASH TEST	(3rd)
SAFETY FEATURES	■ (1st — poor)
FUEL ECONOMY	(3rd)
PM COST	(6th)
REPAIR COST	(9th — good)
WARRANTY	(3rd)
COMPLAINTS	(5th)
INSURANCE COST	(5th)

Safety

CRASH TEST	Poor
ROLLOVER	Very High
AIR BAG	None
ANTI-LOCK BRAKES	4-wheel (optional)
BELT ADJUSTORS	None
BUILT-IN CHILD SEAT	None
OCCUPANT INJURY	Average

General Information

FUEL ECONOMY	19/20	POOR
DRIVING RANGE	285	VERY SHORT
PARKING INDEX	Very Easy	
THEFT RATING	Very Poor	
CORPORATE TWINS		
WHERE MADE	U.S.	
YEAR OF PRODUCTION	Ninth	

Specifications

LENGTH (in.)	151.9	VERY SHORT
HEAD/LEG ROOM (in.)	41.4/39.4	AVERAGE
CARGO SPACE (cu. ft.)	22	VERY SMALL
PAYLOAD	2000	LOW
TOW RATING (lbs.)	2000	VERY LOW
SEATING	2/4	
WHEEL SIZE (in.)	15	

Specifications may vary.

Prices

Model	Retail	Mkup
Wrangler S	12,313	4%
Wrangler SE	15,932	10%

Competition

	POOR ... GOOD	Pg.
Jeep Wrangler	■ (1st)	**134**
Geo Tracker		125
Isuzu Amigo	(2nd)	128
LR Defender 90		136
Suzuki Samurai	(4th)	150

* Due to the importance of crash tests, vehicles with no results as of publication date cannot be given an overall rating.

Though Kia has been manufacturing vehicles for Ford since the mid-80s, the Sportage is only the second U.S. model Kia has offered under its own nameplate. The Sportage (pronounced SPOR-tedge), was designed for the growing U.S. sport utility market. Although it was just recently designed from the ground up, Kia did not include air bags and the standard ABS operates only on the rear wheels.

The 2-liter 4-cylinder engine is adequate, and fuel economy is average for this segment of vehicles. The model lineup is fairly simple, with only a base model and an optional EX package that comes with some luxury amenities. Four-wheel drive is standard, and only one body style (4-door) is available.

The Ratings

	POOR — GOOD
COMPARATIVE RATING*	
CRASH TEST	
SAFETY FEATURES	▮
FUEL ECONOMY	▮
PM COST	▮
REPAIR COST	▮
WARRANTY	▮
COMPLAINTS	
INSURANCE COST	▮

Safety

CRASH TEST	No government results
ROLLOVER	High
AIR BAG	None
ANTI-LOCK BRAKES	2-wheel
BELT ADJUSTORS	None
BUILT-IN CHILD SEAT	None
OCCUPANT INJURY	

General Information

FUEL ECONOMY	20/24	POOR
DRIVING RANGE	348	SHORT
PARKING INDEX	Very Easy	
THEFT RATING		
CORPORATE TWINS		
WHERE MADE	South Korea	
YEAR OF PRODUCTION	First	

Specifications

LENGTH (in.)	159.4	VERY SHORT
HEAD/LEG ROOM (in.)	39.6/44.5	VERY ROOMY
CARGO SPACE (cu. ft.)	NOT AVAILABLE	
PAYLOAD	950**	VERY LOW
TOW RATING (lbs.)	2000**	VERY LOW
SEATING	5	
WHEEL SIZE (in.)	15	

Specifications may vary. ** Preliminary.

Prices

Model	Retail	Mkup
Prices unavailable at press time.		
Expected range: $14-18,000		

Competition

	POOR — GOOD	Pg.
Kia Sportage		135
Isuzu Amigo	▮	128
Jeep Wrangler	▮	134
Nissan Pathfinder	▮	144
Suzuki Samurai	▮	150

* Due to the importance of crash tests, vehicles with no results as of publication date cannot be given an overall rating.

If you're looking for a sport utility vehicle that doesn't focus on luxury or sophistication, here it is. The Defender 90, a direct descendant of the Land Rovers used on African safaris, is probably the noisiest vehicle you can drive. Although its engine is smooth enough, its uninsulated floor panels, non-aerodynamic design and thin soft top combine to create quite a din on the highway. Air bags and ABS are not available.

The 3.9-liter V8 is quite powerful, though fuel economy is dismal. Four-wheel drive is standard, as you would expect, but the interior is oddly spaced and uncomfortable. Ride can be harsh, and the soft top provides little protection from the elements, especially in bad weather. You will not buy the Defender 90 for its comforts; you will buy it because it is the best vehicle at holding its own against off-road terrain.

The Ratings

	POOR	GOOD
COMPARATIVE RATING*		
CRASH TEST		
SAFETY FEATURES	▮	
FUEL ECONOMY	▮	
PM COST	▮	
REPAIR COST	▮	
WARRANTY	▮	
COMPLAINTS		
INSURANCE COST	▮	

Safety

CRASH TEST	No government results
ROLLOVER	Very High
AIR BAG	None
ANTI-LOCK BRAKES	None
BELT ADJUSTORS	Standard
BUILT-IN CHILD SEAT	None
OCCUPANT INJURY	

General Information

FUEL ECONOMY	12/16	VERY POOR
DRIVING RANGE	218	VERY SHORT
PARKING INDEX	Easy	
THEFT RATING		
CORPORATE TWINS		
WHERE MADE	England	
YEAR OF PRODUCTION	Second	

Specifications

LENGTH (in.)	160.5	VERY SHORT
HEAD/LEG ROOM (in.)	57.0/43.5	VERY ROOMY
CARGO SPACE (cu. ft.)		
PAYLOAD	1450	LOW
TOW RATING (lbs.)	7700	VERY HIGH
SEATING	4	
WHEEL SIZE (in.)	16	

Specifications may vary.

Prices **

Model	Retail	Mkup
Defender 90	28,495	

Competition

	POOR	GOOD	Pg.
Land Rvr. Defnd.90			**136**
Isuzu Amigo	▮		128
Jeep Wrangler	▮		134
Nissan Pathfinder	▮		144
Suzuki Samurai	▮		150

**Based on 1994 data.

* Due to the importance of crash tests, vehicles with no results as of publication date cannot be given an overall rating.

Land Rover Discovery

Land Rover has accomplished what no other sport utility manufacturer has been able to accomplish, providing standard dual air bags on the new Discovery, which is $20,000 cheaper than its sibling the Range Rover. Although it's slightly smaller, you should have no problem doing any necessary suburban hauling in comfort. 4-wheel ABS is standard.

The 3.9-liter V8 is powerful enough, but with the vehicle alone weighing over two tons, it may strain under heavy loads. Though it officially seats seven, the two seats in the rear are uncomfortable and only for children. Four-wheel drive is standard, as is most anything else you could possibly want. Options include fog lights and a CD-player. The new Land Rover Discovery will make you feel like you are on a safari, when all you are doing is the carpool and grocery shopping.

The Ratings

	POOR — GOOD
COMPARATIVE RATING*	
CRASH TEST	
SAFETY FEATURES	
FUEL ECONOMY	
PM COST	
REPAIR COST	
WARRANTY	
COMPLAINTS	
INSURANCE COST	

Safety

CRASH TEST	No government results
ROLLOVER	Very High
AIR BAG	Dual
ANTI-LOCK BRAKES	4-wheel
BELT ADJUSTORS	None
BUILT-IN CHILD SEAT	None
OCCUPANT INJURY	

General Information

FUEL ECONOMY	13/16	VERY POOR
DRIVING RANGE	328	VERY SHORT
PARKING INDEX	Average	
THEFT RATING		
CORPORATE TWINS		
WHERE MADE	England	
YEAR OF PRODUCTION	First	

Specifications

LENGTH (in.)	178.7	SHORT
HEAD/LEG ROOM (in.)	37.4/38.5	VERY CRAMPED
CARGO SPACE (cu. ft.)	70	SMALL
PAYLOAD	1650	LOW
TOW RATING (lbs.)	7700	VERY HIGH
SEATING	5/7	
WHEEL SIZE (in.)	16	

Specifications may vary.

Prices

Model	Retail	Mkup
Discovery	29,350	

Competition

	POOR — GOOD	Pg.
Lnd. Rvr. Discovery		**137**
Honda Passport		127
Jeep Cherokee		132
Jeep Gr. Cherokee		133
Nissan Pathfinder		144

* Due to the importance of crash tests, vehicles with no results as of publication date cannot be given an overall rating.

The most significant change to the Range Rover, whose design dates back to 1970, lies in the addition of air bags. While other manufacturers seem to be adding them one at a time, Land Rover added two at once to the 1995 Range Rover. 4-wheel ABS continues to be standard.

The short-wheelbase Range Rovers disappear this year, leaving only the long-wheelbase (LWB) models. Land Rover's Range Rover County LWB has a powerful 4.2-liter V8 that brings the County's towing capacity to almost four tons. Four-wheel drive and an automatic transmission are standard. A Range Rover weighs roughly 4,500 pounds, so acceleration is fairly slow and fuel economy is dismal. Typical of the class of vehicles, handling is on the sluggish side, though the ride is comfortable enough.

The Ratings

	POOR — GOOD
COMPARATIVE RATING*	
CRASH TEST	
SAFETY FEATURES	
FUEL ECONOMY	
PM COST	
REPAIR COST	
WARRANTY	
COMPLAINTS	
INSURANCE COST	

Safety

CRASH TEST	No government results
ROLLOVER	Very High
AIR BAG	Dual
ANTI-LOCK BRAKES	4-wheel
BELT ADJUSTORS	Standard
BUILT-IN CHILD SEAT	None
OCCUPANT INJURY	

General Information

FUEL ECONOMY	12/15	VERY POOR
DRIVING RANGE	304	VERY SHORT
PARKING INDEX	Hard	
THEFT RATING		
CORPORATE TWINS		
WHERE MADE	England	
YEAR OF PRODUCTION	Third	

Specifications

LENGTH (in.)	184.1	AVERAGE
HEAD/LEG ROOM (in.)	38.4/41.0	CRAMPED
CARGO SPACE (cu. ft.)	83	AVERAGE
PAYLOAD	1200	VERY LOW
TOW RATING (lbs.)	7700	VERY HIGH
SEATING	5	
WHEEL SIZE (in.)	16	

Specifications may vary.

Prices

Model	Retail	Mkup
Range Rover County	53,125	

Competition

	POOR — GOOD	Pg.
Land Rvr. Rng. Rvr.		**138**
Chevy Suburban		104
Ford Bronco		113
Jeep Gr. Cherokee		133
Mits. Montero		143

* Due to the importance of crash tests, vehicles with no results as of publication date cannot be given an overall rating.

The B-Series, which was all-new just last year, has as its main change for 1995 the addition of a driver air bag. The B-Series is a clone of the Ford Ranger, whose introduction preceded that of the B-Series by one year. The Ranger gets optional 4-wheel ABS this year; with luck, that option will appear on the B-Series also.

The standard 2.3-liter 4-cylinder engine (on the B2300) is OK for light duty use, but if you plan on carrying a significant load or simply want more power, consider the 3- or 4-liter V6 options (on the B3000 or B4000, respectively); the 4x4 version only comes with the 4-liter engine. Option choices aren't quite as extensive as they are for the Ranger; most are grouped in packages. An extended cab is available. The instrument panel features functional design and well-placed controls.

The Ratings

	POOR — GOOD
COMPARATIVE RATING*	▮ (poor side)
CRASH TEST	▮ (good side)
SAFETY FEATURES	▮ (poor side)
FUEL ECONOMY	▮ (poor side)
PM COST	▮ (poor side)
REPAIR COST	▮ (good end)
WARRANTY	▮ (middle)
COMPLAINTS	▮ (middle)
INSURANCE COST	▮ (poor end)

Safety

CRASH TEST	Good
ROLLOVER	High
AIR BAG	Driver
ANTI-LOCK BRAKES	2-wheel
BELT ADJUSTORS	Standard
BUILT-IN CHILD SEAT	None
OCCUPANT INJURY	

General Information

FUEL ECONOMY	16/21	POOR
DRIVING RANGE	293	VERY SHORT
PARKING INDEX	Easy	
THEFT RATING		
CORPORATE TWINS	Ford Ranger	
WHERE MADE	Japan	
YEAR OF PRODUCTION	Second	

Specifications

LENGTH (in.)	184.5	AVERAGE
HEAD/LEG ROOM (in.)	39.1/42.4	ROOMY
CARGO SPACE (cu. ft.)		
PAYLOAD	1550	LOW
TOW RATING (lbs.)	2000	VERY LOW
SEATING	2/3	
WHEEL SIZE (in.)	14/15	

Specifications may vary.

Prices**

Model	Retail	Mkup
B2300 4x2 Short Bed Man.	9,930	8%
B3000 4x2 SE Sh. Bed Auto	13,640	12%
B4000 4x2 SE Lg. Bed Man.	13,145	12%
B3000 4x4 Short Bed Man.	15,080	7%
B4000 4x4 SE Cab Plus Man	17,940	12%

Competition

	POOR — GOOD	Pg.
Mazda B-Series	▮ (poor side)	139
Dodge Dakota	▮ (good side)	109
Isuzu Pickup	▮ (good side)	129
Nissan Pickup	▮ (middle)	145
Toyota Pickup	▮ (poor end)	154

** Based on 1994 data.

* Due to the importance of crash tests, vehicles with no results as of publication date cannot be given an overall rating.

The Mazda MPV, or multipurpose passenger vehicle, has changed little in the past seven years, and it hangs on for one more year before a replacement arrives in 1996. The MPV shares its name with the government regulatory classification created in the '60s to exempt vans and light trucks from car safety standards. Only a driver air bag is offered, and the standard ABS operates only on the rear wheels.

Five-passenger seating and the 4-cylinder engine have been discontinued, leaving customers with seven-passenger seating and the more-powerful 3-liter V6 engine, which were the better options to begin with. Fuel economy is poor; it gets even worse with the optional 4-wheel drive, which is otherwise a fine choice. Brakes, handling and ride are inferior to most minivans. You'll probably be happier with another minivan, or else wait until 1996.

The Ratings

	POOR — GOOD
COMPARATIVE RATING*	(no result)
CRASH TEST	(no result)
SAFETY FEATURES	▮ (poor)
FUEL ECONOMY	▮ (poor)
PM COST	▮ (below average)
REPAIR COST	▮ (average)
WARRANTY	▮ (average)
COMPLAINTS	▮ (average)
INSURANCE COST	▮ (below average)

Safety

CRASH TEST	No government results
ROLLOVER	High
AIR BAG	Driver
ANTI-LOCK BRAKES	2-wheel
BELT ADJUSTORS	None
BUILT-IN CHILD SEAT	None
OCCUPANT INJURY	Average

General Information

FUEL ECONOMY	16/22	POOR
DRIVING RANGE	353	SHORT
PARKING INDEX	Easy	
THEFT RATING	Good (4WD=Average)	
CORPORATE TWINS		
WHERE MADE	Japan	
YEAR OF PRODUCTION	Seventh	

Specifications

LENGTH (in.)	175.8	SHORT
HEAD/LEG ROOM (in.)	40.0/40.6	AVERAGE
CARGO SPACE (cu. ft.)	38	VERY SMALL
PAYLOAD	1000	VERY LOW
TOW RATING (lbs.)	4500	AVERAGE
SEATING	7	
WHEEL SIZE (in.)	15	

Specifications may vary.

Prices

Model	Retail	Mkup
MPV L	21,135	11%
MPV LX	21,985	11%
MPV LXE	24,375	11%
MPV LX 4WD	25,380	11%
MPV LXE 4WD	27,670	11%

Competition

	POOR — GOOD	Pg.
Mazda MPV	(no result)	**140**
Chevy Lumina	(good)	102
Ford Aerostar	(below average)	112
Mercury Villager	(poor)	141
Plymouth Voyager	(good)	148

* Due to the importance of crash tests, vehicles with no results as of publication date cannot be given an overall rating.

The Villager minivan, a near-twin of the Nissan Quest, is available in three trim levels - base GS, luxury LS, and sport-luxury Nautica. The Villager's resemblance to the Dodge Caravan is no coincidence; Mercury is trying to emulate Chrysler's minivan success. ABS and a driver air bag are standard, but the Villager keeps awkward motorized shoulder belts and separate lap belts.

Ride is a bit soft, very much like a regular passenger car, with standard suspension. Handling is competent, but can be firmed up with the optional handling package. The 3-liter V6, with automatic overdrive, is acceptably responsive. Go for the towing package if you'll be hauling anything at all. The Villager needs a second air bag before it becomes decent competition among the better minivans.

The Ratings

	POOR → GOOD
COMPARATIVE RATING*	▮ (poor)
CRASH TEST	(above average)
SAFETY FEATURES	(below average)
FUEL ECONOMY	(poor)
PM COST	(good)
REPAIR COST	(average)
WARRANTY	(poor)
COMPLAINTS	(poor)
INSURANCE COST	(good)

Safety

CRASH TEST	Moderate
ROLLOVER	Moderate
AIR BAG	Driver
ANTI-LOCK BRAKES	4-wheel
BELT ADJUSTORS	None
BUILT-IN CHILD SEAT	None
OCCUPANT INJURY	Very Good

General Information

FUEL ECONOMY	17/23	POOR
DRIVING RANGE	400	AVERAGE
PARKING INDEX	Average	
THEFT RATING	Very Good	
CORPORATE TWINS	Nissan Quest	
WHERE MADE	U.S.	
YEAR OF PRODUCTION	Third	

Specifications

LENGTH (in.)	189.9	AVERAGE
HEAD/LEG ROOM (in.)	39.4/39.9	CRAMPED
CARGO SPACE (cu. ft.)	126	LARGE
PAYLOAD	1200	VERY LOW
TOW RATING (lbs.)	3500	LOW
SEATING	7	
WHEEL SIZE (in.)	15	

Specifications may vary.

Prices

Model	Retail	Mkup
Villager Cargo	18,455	12%
Villager GS	19,045	12%
Villager LS	23,825	13%
Villager Nautica	25,305	13%

Competition

	POOR → GOOD	Pg.
Mercury Villager	(poor)	141
Dodge Caravan	(good)	108
Ford Aerostar	(below average)	112
Pontiac Trans Sport	(good)	149
Toyota Previa	(below average)	155

* Due to the importance of crash tests, vehicles with no results as of publication date cannot be given an overall rating.

The Mighty Max has not changed much since the mid-80s, and is showing its age. For 1995, Mitsubishi has dropped the four-wheel drive model, losing its more-powerful engine and ABS. The styling on the available two-wheel drive model is outdated, and ABS and air bags are not available.

The 2.4-liter 4-cylinder engine will most likely not be powerful enough for carrying loads. The "Macro Cab" version has more room inside. Ride, handling, and accommodations are comparable to other small pickups. The option list is fairly short; one of the most desirable options is power steering. Basic controls and gauges are well laid out. The most significant changes for 1995 consist of an optional CD-player and two new colors. The Mighty Max is a holdover from the 80s, and unfortunately Mitsubishi has no immediate plans to give it an overhaul.

The Ratings

	POOR — GOOD
COMPARATIVE RATING*	▓ (poor)
CRASH TEST	(above average)
SAFETY FEATURES	▓ (poor)
FUEL ECONOMY	(poor)
PM COST	(poor)
REPAIR COST	(above average)
WARRANTY	(below average)
COMPLAINTS	(good)
INSURANCE COST	(poor)

Safety

CRASH TEST	Moderate
ROLLOVER	Moderate
AIR BAG	None
ANTI-LOCK BRAKES	None
BELT ADJUSTORS	None
BUILT-IN CHILD SEAT	None
OCCUPANT INJURY	Poor

General Information

FUEL ECONOMY	19/23	POOR
DRIVING RANGE	288	VERY SHORT
PARKING INDEX	Average	
THEFT RATING	Average	
CORPORATE TWINS		
WHERE MADE	Japan	
YEAR OF PRODUCTION	Ninth	

Specifications

LENGTH (in.)	177.2	SHORT
HEAD/LEG ROOM (in.)	38.8/41.9	AVERAGE
CARGO SPACE (cu. ft.)		
PAYLOAD	1600	LOW
TOW RATING (lbs.)	3500	LOW
SEATING	3	
WHEEL SIZE (in.)	14	

Specifications may vary.

Prices

Model	Retail	Mkup
Mighty Max 2WD Man.	10,359	11%
Mighty Max 2WD Man. w/CD	10,985	
Mighty Max 2WD Auto.	11,299	14%
Mighty Max 2WD Auto. w/CD	11,925	
Mighty Max 2WD Auto. W/A-C	12,104	

Competition

	POOR — GOOD	Pg.
Mits. Mighty Max	▓ (poor)	142
Ford Ranger	(average)	117
Isuzu Pickup	(average)	129
Nissan Pickup	(below average)	145
Nissan Pickup	(below average)	145

* Due to the importance of crash tests, vehicles with no results as of publication date cannot be given an overall rating.

The Montero receives slight refinements and a simplified lineup for 1995. Monteros now come in either LS or SR trim. The LS has a more powerful engine this year, and both trim levels have increased towing capability. A driver air bag was added last year. The ABS, optional on LS and standard on SR, operates on all four wheels.

The improved 3-liter V6 on the LS should do a better job at accelerating this 2-ton behemoth when empty, but with a load, you'll likely find it a bit lacking. The 3.5-liter V6 on the SR is much more powerful. Gas mileage with either engine is abysmal. Automatic overdrive is standard on the SR, optional on the LS. If you like real wood and leather, Mitsubishi will tack them on to the SR for about $2,200. Ride is smoother and quieter than most utility vehicles, but handling is very clumsy. Comfort inside is good, but cargo area is skimpy.

The Ratings

	POOR ← → GOOD
COMPARATIVE RATING*	▨ (poor end)
CRASH TEST	▨ (good end)
SAFETY FEATURES	▨ (left of center)
FUEL ECONOMY	▨ (poor end)
PM COST	▨ (poor end)
REPAIR COST	▨ (center)
WARRANTY	▨ (right of center)
COMPLAINTS	▨ (good end)
INSURANCE COST	▨ (poor end)

Safety

CRASH TEST	Good
ROLLOVER	Very High
AIR BAG	Driver
ANTI-LOCK BRAKES	4-wheel (optional)
BELT ADJUSTORS	Standard
BUILT-IN CHILD SEAT	None
OCCUPANT INJURY	

General Information

FUEL ECONOMY	15/18	VERY POOR
DRIVING RANGE	389	AVERAGE
PARKING INDEX	Average	
THEFT RATING		
CORPORATE TWINS		
WHERE MADE	Japan	
YEAR OF PRODUCTION	Fourth	

Specifications

LENGTH (in.)	185.2	AVERAGE
HEAD/LEG ROOM (in.)	40.9/40.3	AVERAGE
CARGO SPACE (cu. ft.)	45	VERY SMALL
PAYLOAD	NOT AVAILABLE	
TOW RATING (lbs.)	5000	AVERAGE
SEATING	7	
WHEEL SIZE (in.)	15	

Specifications may vary.

Prices

Model	Retail	Mkup
Montero LS Man.	27,625	17%
Montero LS Auto.	28,475	17%
Montero LS Auto. w/ABS	29,900	17%
Montero SR	34,625	20%
Montero SR w/leather, wood	36,788	20%

Competition

	POOR ← → GOOD	Pg.
Mitsubishi Montero	▨ (poor end)	**143**
Ford Bronco	▨ (good end)	113
GMC Suburban	▨ (left of center)	122
Isuzu Rodeo	▨ (poor end)	130
Jeep Gr. Cherokee	▨ (poor end)	133

* Due to the importance of crash tests, vehicles with no results as of publication date cannot be given an overall rating.

143

The Nissan Pathfinder is a wagon version of the Nissan Pickup. Neither vehicle has changed much since the mid-80s. The Pathfinder is due for a much-needed redesign next year. For the time being, air bags are not available, which is unfortunate, as the Pathfinder has not protected its occupants well in the government's crash test program. The standard ABS operates on the rear wheels only. A 3-liter V6 is the only engine choice on the Pathfinder. Base XE and mid-level SE Pathfinders come with either manual or automatic transmission; up-level LE models come only with automatic. Handling, like the Jeep Cherokee's, is about as good as it gets for a utility vehicle, but short of the mark set by the better cars. Ride is forgiving, better than most utility vehicles. It's a bit tight inside, and not too comfortable in back. Like the Pickup, the major controls and gauges are good.

The Ratings

	POOR	GOOD
COMPARATIVE RATING*	■	
CRASH TEST	■	
SAFETY FEATURES	■	
FUEL ECONOMY	■	
PM COST	■	
REPAIR COST		■
WARRANTY		■
COMPLAINTS		■
INSURANCE COST	■	

Safety

CRASH TEST	Poor
ROLLOVER	High
AIR BAG	None
ANTI-LOCK BRAKES	2-wheel (optional)
BELT ADJUSTORS	None
BUILT-IN CHILD SEAT	None
OCCUPANT INJURY	Average

General Information

FUEL ECONOMY	15/18	VERY POOR
DRIVING RANGE	326	VERY SHORT
PARKING INDEX	Average	
THEFT RATING	Very Poor	
CORPORATE TWINS		
WHERE MADE	Japan	
YEAR OF PRODUCTION	Ninth	

Specifications

LENGTH (in.)	171.9	VERY SHORT
HEAD/LEG ROOM (in.)	39.3/42.6	ROOMY
CARGO SPACE (cu. ft.)	80	SMALL
PAYLOAD	NOT AVAILABLE	
TOW RATING (lbs.)	NOT AVAILABLE	
SEATING	5	
WHEEL SIZE (in.)	15	

Specifications may vary.

Prices

Model	Retail	Mkup
Pathfinder XE 4x2 Man.	20,589	13%
Pathfinder XE 4x4 Auto.	23,599	13%
Pathfinder SE 4x4 Man.	26,539	13%
Pathfinder SE 4x4 Auto.	27,639	13%
Pathfinder LE 4x4 Auto.	30,359	13%

Competition

	POOR	GOOD	Pg.
Nissan Pathfinder	■		144
Honda Passport	■		127
Jeep Gr. Cherokee	■		133
Mits. Montero	■		143
Toyota 4Runner			152

* Due to the importance of crash tests, vehicles with no results as of publication date cannot be given an overall rating.

The Nissan pickup has not changed much since the mid-80s, although the lineup does get shuffled a little for 1995. You'll have several models to choose from: Regular or King Cab, standard or long bed, 4x2 or 4x4. You won't find air bags, and the new standard ABS operates only on the rear wheels.

The 2.4-liter 4-cylinder engine provides adequate power for most uses; a more powerful 3-liter V6 better suited for any heavier hauling is available on both 4x2 and 4x4 models. Either engine can be combined with a 5-speed manual or automatic overdrive. The King Cab has extra interior room. If you're familiar with Japanese pickups, the Nissan won't surprise you in ride, handling, or interior comfort; all are worse than on typical cars, but that's expected. Options are minimal; power steering makes handling more enjoyable. Basic controls and gauges are easy to use.

The Ratings

	POOR		GOOD
COMPARATIVE RATING*			
CRASH TEST			
SAFETY FEATURES			
FUEL ECONOMY			
PM COST			
REPAIR COST			
WARRANTY			
COMPLAINTS			
INSURANCE COST			

Safety

CRASH TEST	Moderate
ROLLOVER	Very High
AIR BAG	None
ANTI-LOCK BRAKES	2-wheel
BELT ADJUSTORS	None
BUILT-IN CHILD SEAT	None
OCCUPANT INJURY	Average

General Information

FUEL ECONOMY	18/20	POOR
DRIVING RANGE	302	VERY SHORT
PARKING INDEX	Easy	
THEFT RATING	Average	
CORPORATE TWINS		
WHERE MADE	Japan/U.S.	
YEAR OF PRODUCTION	Tenth	

Specifications

LENGTH (in.)	174.6	SHORT
HEAD/LEG ROOM (in.)	39.3/42.2	ROOMY
CARGO SPACE (cu. ft.)		
PAYLOAD	1400	LOW
TOW RATING (lbs.)	3500	LOW
SEATING	2/4	
WHEEL SIZE (in.)	14/15	

Specifications may vary.

Prices

Model	Retail	Mkup
Pickup Standard 4x2	9,929	6%
Pickup Standard Longbed 4x2	12,089	8%
Pickup XE V6 King Cab 4x2	13,919	12%
Pickup XE Reg. Cab 4x4	15,129	10%
Pickup SE King Cab 4x4	20,599	13%

Competition

	POOR		GOOD	Pg.
Nissan Pickup				145
Dodge Dakota				109
Ford Ranger				117
Mits. Mighty Max				142
Toyota Pickup				154

* Due to the importance of crash tests, vehicles with no results as of publication date cannot be given an overall rating.

With the Quest and its look-alike twin the Villager, Nissan and Mercury have tried to catch up with Chrysler's successful minivans. On many fronts, they've been successful, however, only a driver air bag is standard, and both front seat occupants must deal with a motorized shoulder belt with a separate lap belt. Four-wheel ABS is optional on the base XE and standard on the deluxe GXE. The only available engine is a 3-liter V6. Acceleration is OK, though the engine may strain trying to carry this two-ton vehicle up hills. Fuel economy is poor. Ride and handling are good by minivan standards. The extra performance package, adds a firmer suspension, ABS, and other useful features at a tempting price. With better instrumentation and a passenger air bag, not due until 1996, the Quest would be a good alternative to the current generation of Chrysler minivans—but the Chryslers are due to be replaced this spring.

The Ratings

	POOR — GOOD
COMPARATIVE RATING*	
CRASH TEST	
SAFETY FEATURES	
FUEL ECONOMY	
PM COST	
REPAIR COST	
WARRANTY	
COMPLAINTS	
INSURANCE COST	

Safety

CRASH TEST	Moderate
ROLLOVER	Low
AIR BAG	Driver
ANTI-LOCK BRAKES	4-wheel (optional)
BELT ADJUSTORS	None
BUILT-IN CHILD SEAT	None
OCCUPANT INJURY	Very Good

General Information

FUEL ECONOMY	17/23	POOR
DRIVING RANGE	380	AVERAGE
PARKING INDEX	Average	
THEFT RATING	Very Good	
CORPORATE TWINS	Mercury Villager	
WHERE MADE	U.S.	
YEAR OF PRODUCTION	Third	

Specifications

LENGTH (in.)	189.9	AVERAGE
HEAD/LEG ROOM (in.)	39.5/39.9	CRAMPED
CARGO SPACE (cu. ft.)	125	LARGE
PAYLOAD	1600	LOW
TOW RATING (lbs.)	3500	LOW
SEATING	4/7	
WHEEL SIZE (in.)	15	

Specifications may vary.

Prices

Model	Retail	Mkup
Quest XE	19,839	14%
Quest XE w/ABS package	22,308	15%
Quest GXE	24,609	14%
Quest GXE w/handling pkg.	25,088	14%
Quest GXE w/leather	27,088	14%

Competition

	POOR — GOOD	Pg.
Nissan Quest		146
Dodge Caravan		108
Ford Aerostar		112
Pontiac Trans Sport		149
Toyota Previa		155

* Due to the importance of crash tests, vehicles with no results as of publication date cannot be given an overall rating.

Oldsmobile Silhouette

The Oldsmobile Silhouette, along with its twins the Pontiac Trans Sport and the Chevy Lumina Minivan, have been good competition for the Chrysler minivans. Although the Silhouette performs well in the government's frontal impact crash test, a second air bag is sorely missed in this family vehicle.

The 3.8-liter V6, the only engine choice this year, has fuel economy that is improved on the highway, but worse in the city, than last year's 3.1-liter. You have your choice of one or two built-in child restraints, an excellent option. Ride is competent on good roads, but handling is unresponsive at highway speeds. The optional touring suspension and traction control, which you have to buy together, improve handling. You'll need some time to get used to the driving position and visibility. Though cargo space is lacking, the seats are easily installed and removed.

The Ratings

	POOR — GOOD
COMPARATIVE RATING*	▮ near good
CRASH TEST	▮ above middle
SAFETY FEATURES	▮ middle
FUEL ECONOMY	▮ poor
PM COST	▮ good
REPAIR COST	▮ above middle
WARRANTY	▮ poor
COMPLAINTS	▮ middle
INSURANCE COST	▮ good

Safety

CRASH TEST	Good
ROLLOVER	Moderate
AIR BAG	Driver
ANTI-LOCK BRAKES	4-wheel
BELT ADJUSTORS	None
BUILT-IN CHILD SEAT	Optional (two)
OCCUPANT INJURY	Good

General Information

FUEL ECONOMY	17/25	POOR
DRIVING RANGE	400	AVERAGE
PARKING INDEX	Hard	
THEFT RATING	Average	
CORPORATE TWINS	Lum. Minivan, Trans Sprt.	
WHERE MADE	U.S.	
YEAR OF PRODUCTION	Sixth	

Specifications

LENGTH (in.)	194.7	LONG
HEAD/LEG ROOM (in.)	39.2/40.0	CRAMPED
CARGO SPACE (cu. ft.)	113	LARGE
PAYLOAD	1400	LOW
TOW RATING (lbs.)	2000	VERY LOW
SEATING	7	
WHEEL SIZE (in.)	15	

Specifications may vary.

Prices

Model	Retail	Mkup
Silhouette I	20,795	11%
Silhouette I w/one child seat	20,920	11%
Silhouette I w/two child seats	21,020	
Silhouette II	22,295	
Silhouette II w/two child seat	22,520	

Competition

	POOR — GOOD	Pg.
Olds Silhouette	▮ near good	147
Dodge Caravan	▮ above middle	108
Nissan Quest	▮ middle	146
Plymouth Voyager	▮ above middle	148
Pontiac Trans Sport	▮ near good	149

* Due to the importance of crash tests, vehicles with no results as of publication date cannot be given an overall rating.

Plymouth Voyager

The Voyager, along with the other Chrysler minivans, are due for a redesign this spring. In the meantime, these industry leaders carry on with standard dual air bags and a structure that Chrysler claims meets 1997 government side impact standards for passenger cars. ABS is available, and recommended.

You'll have to choose between four engines (an inadequate 2.5-liter 4-cylinder, an adequate 3-liter V6, or the more powerful 3.3-liter or 3.8-liter V6s), and all except the 3.8-liter are equally efficient. Since Grand Voyagers have a longer wheelbase and body with more room inside, the 3.3-liter is worth the extra money. Four-wheel drive is available on Grand Voyagers. Handling improves with the heavy duty suspension or the sport handling group (only available on the LE), yet ride remains good. The built-in child restraints are an excellent option.

The Ratings

	POOR — GOOD
COMPARATIVE RATING*	
CRASH TEST	
SAFETY FEATURES	
FUEL ECONOMY	
PM COST	
REPAIR COST	
WARRANTY	
COMPLAINTS	
INSURANCE COST	

Safety

CRASH TEST	Good
ROLLOVER	Moderate
AIR BAG	Dual
ANTI-LOCK BRAKES	4-wheel (optional)
BELT ADJUSTORS	Standard
BUILT-IN CHILD SEAT	Optional (two)
OCCUPANT INJURY	Very Good

General Information

FUEL ECONOMY	20/24	POOR
DRIVING RANGE	440	LONG
PARKING INDEX	Average	
THEFT RATING	Average	
CORPORATE TWINS	Caravan, Town & Country	
WHERE MADE	Canada/U.S.	
YEAR OF PRODUCTION	Fifth	

Specifications

LENGTH (in.)	178.1	SHORT
HEAD/LEG ROOM (in.)	39.1/38.3	VERY CRAMPED
CARGO SPACE (cu. ft.)	117	LARGE
PAYLOAD	1200	VERY LOW
TOW RATING (lbs.)	2000	VERY LOW
SEATING	5 /7	
WHEEL SIZE (in.)	14/15	

Specifications may vary.

Prices

Model	Retail	Mkup
Voyager Base	16,720	9%
Voyager SE	19,415	10%
Voyager Grand SE	20,155	10%
Voyager LE	23,940	11%
Voyager Grand LE AWD	26,315	11%

Competition

	POOR — GOOD	Pg.
Plymouth Voyager		**148**
Chevy Lumina		102
Ford Aerostar		112
Nissan Quest		146
Toyota Previa		155

* Due to the importance of crash tests, vehicles with no results as of publication date cannot be given an overall rating.

The Trans Sport was slightly redesigned last year and brings few changes into 1995. Traction control is now optional, and a driver's air bag and ABS remain standard.

The optional 3.8-liter V6 with automatic overdrive provides more power and about the same gas mileage as the standard engine - even better on the highway. You have the choice of one or two optional fold-out child safety restraints. Ride is generally smooth, but handling is sluggish on the open road. The windshield posts are distracting. The Trans Sport, like its twins the Olds Silhouette and Chevy Lumina Minivan, has much less cargo space than other minivans. One fancy option is the new power sliding door, designed to overcome the inability of children to close those heavy side doors.

The Ratings

	POOR · · · GOOD
COMPARATIVE RATING*	
CRASH TEST	
SAFETY FEATURES	
FUEL ECONOMY	
PM COST	
REPAIR COST	
WARRANTY	
COMPLAINTS	
INSURANCE COST	

Safety

CRASH TEST	Good
ROLLOVER	Moderate
AIR BAG	Driver
ANTI-LOCK BRAKES	4-wheel
BELT ADJUSTORS	None
BUILT-IN CHILD SEAT	Optional (two)
OCCUPANT INJURY	Good

General Information

FUEL ECONOMY	19/23	POOR
DRIVING RANGE	400	AVERAGE
PARKING INDEX	Hard	
THEFT RATING	Average	
CORPORATE TWINS	Lum. Minivan, Silh.	
WHERE MADE	U.S.	
YEAR OF PRODUCTION	Sixth	

Specifications

LENGTH (in.)	192.2	AVERAGE
HEAD/LEG ROOM (in.)	39.2/40.0	CRAMPED
CARGO SPACE (cu. ft.)	113	LARGE
PAYLOAD	1400	LOW
TOW RATING (lbs.)	2000	VERY LOW
SEATING	2/5/7	
WHEEL SIZE (in.)	15	

Specifications may vary.

Prices

Model	Retail	Mkup
Trans Sport SE	18,429	10%

Competition

	POOR · · · GOOD	Pg.
Pontiac Trans Sport		**149**
Dodge Caravan		108
Ford Aerostar		112
Nissan Quest		146
Toyota Previa		155

* Due to the importance of crash tests, vehicles with no results as of publication date cannot be given an overall rating.

The Samurai, in spite of bad publicity, hangs on for another year, now with only one trim level and few options. Air bags and ABS are nowhere to be found.

The Samurai's 1.3-liter 4 cylinder engine provides minimal acceleration and requires a lot of shifting of the 5-speed transmission; automatic isn't offered. Though fuel efficiency is not bad, you won't be able to buy this vehicle in Massachusetts or California where emissions requirements are tougher. Ride is very rough, even worse than the Jeep Wrangler's. When accelerating or at highway speeds, it's extremely noisy inside. Accommodations and comfort are sparse for two; any luggage or cargo might adversely affect handling and acceleration. Take your corners slowly in this vehicle.

The Ratings

	POOR ... GOOD
COMPARATIVE RATING*	▨
CRASH TEST	▨
SAFETY FEATURES	▨
FUEL ECONOMY	▨
PM COST	▨
REPAIR COST	▨
WARRANTY	▨
COMPLAINTS	▨
INSURANCE COST	▨

Safety

CRASH TEST	Moderate
ROLLOVER	Very High
AIR BAG	None
ANTI-LOCK BRAKES	None
BELT ADJUSTORS	None
BUILT-IN CHILD SEAT	None
OCCUPANT INJURY	

General Information

FUEL ECONOMY	28/29	AVERAGE
DRIVING RANGE	297	VERY SHORT
PARKING INDEX	Very Easy	
THEFT RATING	Very Poor	
CORPORATE TWINS		
WHERE MADE	Japan	
YEAR OF PRODUCTION	Tenth	

Specifications

LENGTH (in.)	135.0	VERY SHORT
HEAD/LEG ROOM (in.)	40.2/38.3	VERY CRAMPED
CARGO SPACE (cu. ft.)	28	VERY SMALL
PAYLOAD	850	VERY LOW
TOW RATING (lbs.)	1000	VERY LOW
SEATING	2	
WHEEL SIZE (in.)	15	

Specifications may vary.

Prices

Model	Retail	Mkup
Samurai JL 4WD	9,889	9%

Competition

	POOR ... GOOD	Pg.
Suzuki Samurai	▨	**150**
Isuzu Amigo	▨	128
Jeep Wrangler	▨	134
Kia Sportage	▨	135
Nissan Pathfinder	▨	144

* Due to the importance of crash tests, vehicles with no results as of publication date cannot be given an overall rating.

The Sidekick, available in 2- and 4-door versions, has not changed for 1995. This is unfortunate, as the Sidekick has been an abysmal performer in the government's crash test program. You still can't get any air bags, and the standard ABS operates only on the rear wheels. The base, or JS, 2-door Sidekicks get a 1.6-liter, 8-valve, 4-cylinder engine; the 4-doors, up-level JX 2-doors, and California and Massachusetts JS 2-doors get a 16-valve version of that engine, which produces a little more power with little loss in fuel economy. All Sidekicks have a standard 5-speed manual transmission, or optional automatic. Acceleration, noise, and fuel economy are much better with the 5-speed. The longer-wheelbase 4-doors ride better. You might choose the number of doors by the roof type - 2-doors come only in canvas-top, and 4-doors come only in hardtop. Don't take turns too quickly.

The Ratings

	POOR → GOOD
COMPARATIVE RATING*	(not rated)
CRASH TEST	(not rated)
SAFETY FEATURES	■ (poor, position 1)
FUEL ECONOMY	position 3
PM COST	position 8
REPAIR COST	position 2
WARRANTY	■ (poor, position 1)
COMPLAINTS	position 8
INSURANCE COST	position 3

Safety

CRASH TEST	No government results
ROLLOVER	High
AIR BAG	None
ANTI-LOCK BRAKES	2-wheel (optional)
BELT ADJUSTORS	None
BUILT-IN CHILD SEAT	None
OCCUPANT INJURY	Average

General Information

FUEL ECONOMY	23/26	POOR
DRIVING RANGE	266	VERY SHORT
PARKING INDEX	Very Easy	
THEFT RATING	Very Poor (4-dr.=Avg.)	
CORPORATE TWINS	Geo Tracker (2-dr. only)	
WHERE MADE	Japan/Canada	
YEAR OF PRODUCTION	Seventh	

Specifications

LENGTH (in.)	142.5	VERY SHORT
HEAD/LEG ROOM (in.)	39.5/42.1	ROOMY
CARGO SPACE (cu. ft.)	45	VERY SMALL
PAYLOAD	850	VERY LOW
TOW RATING (lbs.)	1000	VERY LOW
SEATING	4	
WHEEL SIZE (in.)	15	

Specifications may vary.

Prices

Model	Retail	Mkup
Sidekick JS 2WD 2-dr. Conv.	11,699	6%
Sidekick JS 2WD 4-dr. Hardtop	13,499	6%
Sidekick JX 4WD 2-dr. Conv.	14,099	9%
Sidekick JX 4WD 4-dr. Hardtop	14,809	9%
Sidekick JLX 4WD 4-dr. Hardtop	17,269	12%

Competition

	POOR → GOOD	Pg.
Suzuki Sidekick	(not rated)	151
Geo Tracker	(not rated)	125
Isuzu Amigo	position 2	128
Jeep Wrangler	position 1	134
Suzuki Samurai	position 2	150

* Due to the importance of crash tests, vehicles with no results as of publication date cannot be given an overall rating.

The Toyota 4Runner is basically a wagon version of last year's compact Toyota Pickup. The 4Runner will be redesigned next year. On safety features, the 4Runner trails the pack: No air bags are available, and ABS (standard with the V6, optional with the 4) works only on the rear wheels, though four-wheel ABS is an option on the V6 this year.

Engine choices are an adequate 2.4-liter 4-cylinder, or a more powerful and much less fuel efficient 3-liter V6. Optional 4-wheel drive destroys fuel economy on the V6. The 4Runner shares both engines with the Toyota Pickup; however, since the 4Runner is roughly 700 pounds heavier, it's a lot slower. For towing, you'll want the V6. Ride, handling, rear-seat room and comfort, are inferior to other sport utility vehicles, but the dashboard is better.

The Ratings

	POOR GOOD
COMPARATIVE RATING*	□□□□□□□□□□
CRASH TEST	□□□□□□□□□□
SAFETY FEATURES	■□□□□□□□□□
FUEL ECONOMY	□□□■□□□□□□
PM COST	□□□□■□□□□□
REPAIR COST	□□□□□□■□□□
WARRANTY	□□□■□□□□□□
COMPLAINTS	□□□□□□□■□□
INSURANCE COST	■□□□□□□□□□

Safety

CRASH TEST	No government results
ROLLOVER	High
AIR BAG	None
ANTI-LOCK BRAKES	2-wheel (optional)
BELT ADJUSTORS	None
BUILT-IN CHILD SEAT	None
OCCUPANT INJURY	Average

General Information

FUEL ECONOMY	19/21	POOR
DRIVING RANGE	344	SHORT
PARKING INDEX	Easy	
THEFT RATING	Very Poor	
CORPORATE TWINS		
WHERE MADE	Japan	
YEAR OF PRODUCTION	Sixth	

Specifications

LENGTH (in.)	176.0	SHORT
HEAD/LEG ROOM (in.)	38.7/41.5	AVERAGE
CARGO SPACE (cu. ft.)	78	SMALL
PAYLOAD	300	VERY LOW
TOW RATING (lbs.)	3500	LOW
SEATING	5	
WHEEL SIZE (in.)	15	

Specifications may vary.

Prices

Model	Retail	Mkup
4Runner SR5 4WD	21,495	18%
4Runner SR5 V6 2WD	22,145	18%
4Runner SR5 V6 4WD	23,545	18%

Competition

	POOR GOOD	Pg.
Toyota 4Runner	□□□□□□□□□□	152
Honda Passport	■□□□□□□□□□	127
Jeep Gr. Cherokee	■■□□□□□□□□	133
Mits. Montero	■□□□□□□□□□	143
Nissan Pathfinder	■□□□□□□□□□	144

* Due to the importance of crash tests, vehicles with no results as of publication date cannot be given an overall rating.

Toyota Land Cruiser

The Land Cruiser has been around in various forms since the 1960's; the latest version does battle with the Jeep Grand Cherokee. Those models both have standard ABS and at least one air bag. Despite the Land Cruiser's high price, you can't get air bags, and you have to spend a lot of extra money to get ABS.

The engine is a hefty gas-guzzling 4.5-liter 6-cylinder, with automatic transmission and all-wheel-drive. Because the Land Cruiser tips the scales at 4,700 pounds, don't expect stunning acceleration. Ride is fairly comfortable, but handling is sluggish. Seats are roomy, as is the cargo area. Controls are competent, in the Toyota tradition. The differential-locks package, which includes ABS, may be useful for foul-weather driving.

The Ratings

	POOR — GOOD
COMPARATIVE RATING*	(no rating)
CRASH TEST	(no rating)
SAFETY FEATURES	Poor
FUEL ECONOMY	Poor
PM COST	Below average
REPAIR COST	Average
WARRANTY	Below average
COMPLAINTS	Average
INSURANCE COST	Poor

Safety

CRASH TEST	No government results
ROLLOVER	High
AIR BAG	None
ANTI-LOCK BRAKES	4-wheel (optional)
BELT ADJUSTORS	Standard
BUILT-IN CHILD SEAT	None
OCCUPANT INJURY	Very Good

General Information

FUEL ECONOMY	12/15	VERY POOR
DRIVING RANGE	326	VERY SHORT
PARKING INDEX	Average	
THEFT RATING	Very Poor	
CORPORATE TWINS		
WHERE MADE	Japan	
YEAR OF PRODUCTION	Fifth	

Specifications

LENGTH (in.)	188.2	AVERAGE
HEAD/LEG ROOM (in.)	40.7/42.2	VERY ROOMY
CARGO SPACE (cu. ft.)	91	AVERAGE
PAYLOAD	1750	LOW
TOW RATING (lbs.)	5000	AVERAGE
SEATING	5/7	
WHEEL SIZE (in.)	16	

Specifications may vary.

Prices

Model	Retail	Mkup
Land Cruiser Base	37,105	20%

Competition

	POOR — GOOD	Pg.
Toyota Land Cruiser	(no rating)	153
Ford Bronco	Good	113
Honda Passport	Poor	127
Jeep Gr. Cherokee	Poor	133
Mits. Montero	Poor	143

* Due to the importance of crash tests, vehicles with no results as of publication date cannot be given an overall rating.

Toyota Pickup

Although they were rumored to be all-new some-time this year, the compact pickups from Toyota enter the 1995 model year with few changes. You still can't get air bags, and the available ABS operates only on the rear wheels.

Engines are a 2.4-liter 4-cylinder and a 3.0-liter V6, with automatic overdrive or 5-speed manual, and two- or four-wheel-drive. Output of the 2.4-liter engine is adequate for light duty, but it'll be strained if you carry much cargo. Fuel economy suffers with the 3-liter. Ride and handling, as well as room and comfort inside, present no surprises. Like most Toyotas, the Pickup has a nicely laid-out dashboard and controls. Power steering, an option on several of the cheaper models, improves handling and parking. Trim levels and option packages present a confusing array of choices.

The Ratings

	POOR	GOOD
COMPARATIVE RATING*	■	
CRASH TEST **		■
SAFETY FEATURES	■	
FUEL ECONOMY	■	
PM COST		■
REPAIR COST		■
WARRANTY	■	
COMPLAINTS		■
INSURANCE COST	■	

Safety

CRASH TEST **	Average
ROLLOVER	High
AIR BAG	None
ANTI-LOCK BRAKES	2-wheel (optional)
BELT ADJUSTORS	None
BUILT-IN CHILD SEAT	None
OCCUPANT INJURY	

General Information

FUEL ECONOMY	19/22	POOR
DRIVING RANGE	344	SHORT
PARKING INDEX	Easy	
THEFT RATING		
CORPORATE TWINS		
WHERE MADE	U.S./Japan	
YEAR OF PRODUCTION	First	

Specifications

LENGTH (in.)	174.4	SHORT
HEAD/LEG ROOM (in.)	38.3/41.5	CRAMPED
CARGO SPACE (cu. ft.)		
PAYLOAD	2050	AVERAGE
TOW RATING (lbs.)	3500	LOW
SEATING	3/5	
WHEEL SIZE (in.)	14/15	

Specifications may vary.

Prices

Model	Retail	Mkup
Pickup Standard 4x2	10,745	
Pickup Deluxe 4x2	11,645	13%
Pickup Deluxe 4x4	15,485	14%
Pickup Deluxe V6 4x4	16,795	
Pickup Xtracab SR5 V6 4x4	20,395	

Competition

	POOR	GOOD	Pg.
Toyota Pickup	■		154
Dodge Dakota		■	109
Ford Ranger		■	117
Isuzu Pickup		■	129
Mits. Mighty Max	■		142

**Data given for 4x2 model. See Safety Chapter for crash test results for 4x4 model.   * Due to the importance of crash tests, vehicles with no results as of publication date cannot be given an overall rating.

The Previa does not change much for 1995, though the popular supercharged version of the standard engine is now available on base DX models as well as up-level LE models. Dual air bags are standard, and ABS is optional on all models. The Previa is offered in front- or four-wheel drive. All seat seven people. Automatic overdrive is standard except on the front-drive DX. The standard engine, a 2.4-liter 138-hp 4-cylinder, is barely enough to move the Previa's 4000 pounds, even with just a driver. The supercharged version is much more adept, and you won't lose any fuel economy. Handling and ride are about the best you can get in a minivan, especially if you buy an All-Trac version. The interior is comfortable and cargo space is even greater than the Chrysler "Grand" models, but remember the engine's limited power as you load up.

The Ratings

	POOR	GOOD
COMPARATIVE RATING*		
CRASH TEST		
SAFETY FEATURES		
FUEL ECONOMY		
PM COST		
REPAIR COST		
WARRANTY		
COMPLAINTS		
INSURANCE COST		

Safety

CRASH TEST	Moderate
ROLLOVER	High
AIR BAG	Dual
ANTI-LOCK BRAKES	4-wheel (optional)
BELT ADJUSTORS	Standard
BUILT-IN CHILD SEAT	None
OCCUPANT INJURY	Average

General Information

FUEL ECONOMY	17/22	POOR
DRIVING RANGE	376	AVERAGE
PARKING INDEX	Average	
THEFT RATING	Average (4WD=Good)	
CORPORATE TWINS		
WHERE MADE	Japan	
YEAR OF PRODUCTION	Fifth	

Specifications

LENGTH (in.)	187.0	AVERAGE
HEAD/LEG ROOM (in.)	39.4/40.1	CRAMPED
CARGO SPACE (cu. ft.)	152	VERY LARGE
PAYLOAD	1700	LOW
TOW RATING (lbs.)	3500	LOW
SEATING	7	
WHEEL SIZE (in.)	15	

Specifications may vary.

Prices

Model	Retail	Mkup
Previa DX	22,715	17%
Previa DX w/ABS	23,815	17%
Previa LE	30,615	18%
Previa LE w/ABS	31,565	18%

Competition

	POOR	GOOD	Pg.
Toyota Previa			155
Chevy Astro			99
Dodge Caravan			108
Ford Aerostar			112
Pontiac Trans Sport			149

* Due to the importance of crash tests, vehicles with no results as of publication date cannot be given an overall rating.

The T100 Pickup is the first Japanese truck to compete with larger domestic pickups like the Dodge Ram, Ford F-series, and Chevrolet C/K. Engine options aren't quite as broad as with the domestics, but a driver air bag is standard. Four-wheel ABS is only available on the DX V6.

The standard 2.7-liter 4-cylinder engine is just for light duty. The all-new 3.4-liter V6, though stronger than the base engine, doesn't match the power of V8s in most large U.S. pickups. The T100 only comes as a base 4-cylinder, base V6 or DX V6, and the option list is short, so you'll either find what you're looking for or you won't. You can pick from automatic overdrive or 5-speed manual, and 2- or 4-wheel drive. Ride, comfort, inside room, and handling present no surprises. Like most Toyotas, the Pickup has nicely laid-out dashboard and controls.

The Ratings

	POOR		GOOD
COMPARATIVE RATING*			
CRASH TEST			
SAFETY FEATURES			
FUEL ECONOMY			
PM COST			
REPAIR COST			
WARRANTY			
COMPLAINTS			
INSURANCE COST			

Safety

CRASH TEST	Very Good
ROLLOVER	Moderate
AIR BAG	Driver
ANTI-LOCK BRAKES	4-wheel (optional)
BELT ADJUSTORS	Standard
BUILT-IN CHILD SEAT	None
OCCUPANT INJURY	

General Information

FUEL ECONOMY	17/19	POOR
DRIVING RANGE	432	LONG
PARKING INDEX	Hard	
THEFT RATING		
CORPORATE TWINS		
WHERE MADE	Japan	
YEAR OF PRODUCTION	Third	

Specifications

LENGTH (in.)	209.1	VERY LONG
HEAD/LEG ROOM (in.)	39.6/42.4	ROOMY
CARGO SPACE (cu. ft.)		
PAYLOAD	1650	LOW
TOW RATING (lbs.)	5000	AVERAGE
SEATING	3	
WHEEL SIZE (in.)	15	

Specifications may vary.

Prices

Model	Retail	Mkup
T100 Standard 4x2	13,915	11%
T100 Standard V6 4x2	14,895	15%
T100 SR5 V6 4x2	17,795	16%
T100 Deluxe V6 4x4	19,575	16%
T100 SR5 V6 4x4	21,395	17%

Competition

	POOR	GOOD	Pg.
Toyota T100			156
Chevy C/K			101
Dodge Ram			110
Ford F-Series			116
GMC Sierra			120

* Due to the importance of crash tests, vehicles with no results as of publication date cannot be given an overall rating.

Index

Complaint Forms

One of the most valuable, but often unused, services of the government is the Auto Safety Hotline. By calling the Hotline to report safety problems, your particular concern or problem will become part of the National Highway Transportation Safety Administration's (NHTSA) complaint database. This complaint database is extraordinarily important to government decision makers who often take action based on this information. In addition, it provides consumer groups, like the Center for Auto Safety, with the evidence they need to force the government to act. Unless government engineers or safety advocates have evidence of a wide-scale problems, little can be done to get the manufacturers to correct the defect.

Few government services have the potential to do as much for the consumer as this complaint database, so we encourage you to voice your concerns to the government. To make it easy as possible, the following is an actual copy of the Vehicle Owner's Questionnaire that you would receive if you were to call the Hotline with a complaint. By saving you the step of ordering it, we hope you will take advantage of this program— take the time to fill out the questionnaire and send it in.

You can either make a copy of these two pages or remove the page itself. When you've completed the questionnaire, simply fold it so that the postage paid address appears on the outside, seal it on all sides, and drop it in a mailbox. For an additional copy, call 800-424-9393 (or 202-366-0123 in Washington, DC).

The questionnaire asks for information that the agency's technical staff will need to evaluate the problem. This information also gives the government an indication of which vehicles are causing consumers the most problems. After you fill out and return the questionnaire, a few things will happen. A copy will go to NHTSA's safety defect investigators. Then, a copy will be sent to the manufacturer of the vehicle, with a request for help in resolving the problem. You will also be notified that your questionnaire has been received.

You can also use this questionnaire to report defects in tires and child safety seats. In fact, we strongly encourage you to report problems with child safety seats. Now that they are required by law in all fifty states, we have noticed that numerous design and safety problems have surfaced. If the government knows about these problems, they will be more likely to take action so that modifications are made in these life-saving devices.

Form Approved: O.M.B. No. 2127-0008

AUTO SAFETY HOTLINE
VEHICLE OWNER'S QUESTIONNAIRE

U.S. Department of Transportation

National Highway Traffic Safety Administration

NATIONWIDE 1-800-424-9393
DC METRO AREA 202-366-0123

FOR AGENCY USE ONLY

DATE RECEIVED

od-or _____ _____
rt-dt _____ _____
od-rt _____ _____
up-ltr _____ _____

REFERENCE NO.

OWNER INFORMATION (TYPE OR PRINT)

NAME and ADDRESS

DAY TIME TELEPHONE NO. (AREA CODE)

Do you authorize NHTSA to provide a copy of this report to the manufacturer of your vehicle? YES ☐ NO ☐
In the absence of an authorization, NHTSA *WILL NOT* provide your name or address to the vehicle manufacturer.

SIGNATURE OF OWNER

DATE

VEHICLE INFORMATION

VEHICLE IDENTIFICATION NO.*	VEHICLE MAKE	VEHICLE MODEL	MODEL YEAR

*LOCATED AT BOTTOM OF WINDSHIELD ON DRIVER'S SIDE

CURRENT ODOMETER READING	DATE PURCHASED _____ ☐ NEW ☐ USED	DEALER'S NAME, CITY & STATE	ENGINE SIZE (CID/CC/L) _____ NO. CYLINDERS___

☐ TURBO
☐ DIESEL
☐ GAS
☐ FUEL INJECTN

TRANSMISSION TYPE
☐ MANUAL
☐ AUTOMATIC

ANTILOCK BRAKES
☐ YES
☐ NO

RESTRAINT SYSTEM
☐ DRIVERSIDE AIRBAG ☐ MOTORBELT
☐ PASSENGERSIDE AIRBAG
☐ 3-POINT BELT ☐ 2-POINT BELT

CRUISE CONTROL
☐ YES
☐ NO

DRIVETRAIN
☐ FRONT
☐ REAR
☐ 4-WHEEL

BODY STYLE
STAWAG _____ HATCH BK _____
4 DR _____ VAN _____
2 DR _____ PK UP TRK _____
OTHER _____

FAILED COMPONENT(S)/PART(S) INFORMATION (REPORT TIRE INFORMATION ON BACK)

COMPONENT	PART NAME(S)	LOCATION	FAILED PART(S)
		☐ LEFT ☐ FRONT ☐ RIGHT ☐ REAR	☐ ORIGINAL ☐ REPLACEMENT

NO. OF FAILURES

DATE(S) OF FAILURE(S) _____

MILEAGE AT FAILURE(S) _____

VEHICLE SPEED AT FAILURE(S)

MANUFACTURER CONTACTED
☐ YES ☐ NO

NHTSA PREVIOUSLY CONTACTED
☐ YES ☐ NO

APPLICABLE ACCIDENT INFORMATION

ACCIDENT	FIRE	NUMBER PERSONS INJURED	NUMBER OF FATALITIES	PROPERTY DAMAGE EST$	POLICE REPORTED
☐ YES ☐ NO	☐ YES ☐ NO			_____	☐ YES ☐ NO

NARRATIVE DESCRIPTION OF FAILURE(S), ACCIDENT(S), INJURY(IES)

CONTINUE ON BACK IF NEEDED

HS-Form 350 (Rev. 5-92)

INFORMATION ON TIRE FAILURE(S) (IF APPLICABLE)

TIRE IDENTIFICATION NO.*

D	O	T									MANUFACTURER/TIRE NAME	SIZE

* The identification number consists of 7 to 10 letters and numerals following the letters DOT. It is usually located near the rim flange on the side opposite the whitewall or on either side of a blackwall tire.

NARRATIVE DESCRIPTION (CONTINUED)

629.223
TRU

Truck, van and
4 X 4

DATE DUE

OCT. 22			

☆ U.S. G.P.O.: 1992 -- 623-897 / 6008

U.S. Department
of Transportation

**National Highway
Traffic Safety
Administration**

400 Seventh St., S.W.
Washington, D.C. 20590

Official Business
Penalty for Private Use $300

BUSINESS REPLY MAIL
FIRST CLASS PERMIT NO. 73173 WASHINGTON, D.C.

POSTAGE WILL BE PAID BY NATL HWY TRAFFIC SAFETY ADMIN.

U.S. Department of Transportation
National Highway Traffic Safety Administration
Auto Safety Hotline, NEF–11 HL
400 7th Street, SW
Washington, DC 20590

NO POSTAGE
NECESSARY
IF MAILED
IN THE
UNITED STATE